DIALECTICAL RHETORIC

DIALECTICAL RHETORIC

BRUCE McCOMISKEY

UTAH STATE UNIVERSITY PRESS
Logan

© 2015 by the University Press of Colorado

Published by Utah State University Press
An imprint of University Press of Colorado
5589 Arapahoe Avenue, Suite 206C
Boulder, Colorado 80303

   The University Press of Colorado is a proud member of
The Association of American University Presses.

The University Press of Colorado is a cooperative publishing enterprise supported, in part, by Adams State University, Colorado State University, Fort Lewis College, Metropolitan State University of Denver, Regis University, University of Colorado, University of Northern Colorado, Utah State University, and Western State Colorado University.

∞ The paper used in this publication meets the minimum requirements of the American National Standard for Information Sciences—Permanence of Paper for Printed Library Materials. ANSI Z39.48–1992

ISBN: 978-0-87421-981-4 (pbk.)
ISBN: 978-0-87421-982-1 (ebook)

Library of Congress Cataloging-in-Publication Data
McComiskey, Bruce, 1963–
  Dialectical rhetoric / Bruce McComiskey.
    pages cm
  Includes bibliographical references.
  ISBN 978-0-87421-981-4 (pbk.) — ISBN 978-0-87421-982-1 (ebook)
1. Persuasion (Rhetoric) 2. Rhetoric—Study and teaching—History. 3. Rhetoric—Data processing. I. Title.
  P301.5.P47M323 2015
  808—dc23
                                    2014024122

24 23 22 21 20 19 18 17 16 15   10 9 8 7 6 5 4 3 2 1

For Doug and Robin

CONTENTS

PREFACE

Dialectic and rhetoric have traveled, sometimes separately and sometimes together. They have traveled in the bright light of day where other disciplines and arts could commune with them, and they have traveled in the thick darkness of night where no other disciplines or arts could feel or see them. At times they have been exiled from each other's presence in opposite hemispheres, one in daylight and the other in darkness, and they have been forced to switch places, back and forth, occasionally greeting each other on the way, but usually not, being cloaked, gagged, and blindfolded, ushered quickly to new destinations.

Dialectic's journey has been long and difficult with little sense of overall direction or purpose. Dialectic has been used to remove error, explore twofold arguments, define and divide (and sometimes synthesize) a subject, and explain the progression of history toward its end. Dialectic has emphasized probability, reasoned opinion, certainty, Spirit, and materiality. Dialectic has been housed in the opulent mansion of philosophy, the purposeful hunting lodge of rhetoric, the brick efficiency unit of logic, and the shady brothel of sophistry. Dialectic has taken the conceptual shape of an organic body in creative conversation, a pantry of topical invention, a straight and narrow staircase of logical rules, and a battlefield of academic disputation (with students dodging argumentative rocks, arrows, bullets, or bombs, depending on their historical moment). Dialectic has been the thesis, antithesis, and synthesis of ideas, of reality, and of human work at the interface between ideas and reality. From the bird's eye view of history, dialectic's journey has been incoherent.

Rhetoric's journey has also been long and difficult. Rhetoric has been used to invent, discover, or mask reasoned opinion and truth. Rhetoric has directed audiences to adopt ethical values, to accept viable plans, and to judge the quality of actions. Rhetoric has been used to solidify common will in times of strife and to encourage conflict in times of social stagnation. Rhetoric has been the expression of thought, the description of reality, the representation of ideology, and the construction of social psychology. Rhetoric has been a method for generating philosophical truths, for representing truths clearly, and for dressing truths beautifully (with words or voice or expression or gesture). Rhetoric has been an amusement for children and a preoccupation (sometimes obsession) for politicians and preachers. Rhetoric has been a means to social progress and its obstruction, a source of power and the threat of its dissolution, a path to glory and to shame. Rhetoric has been sometimes revered, sometimes valued, sometimes ignored, and sometimes vilified. From the bird's eye view of history, rhetoric's journey has been incoherent.

Whether it is an effect of postmodernism generally, as a disintegration of disciplinary boundaries; or whether it is an effect of the growing disinterest of other disciplines as specialization encourages a kind of sloughing of expendable subjects and methods; or whether it is an effect of rhetoric and composition simply arguing its way back into the academic *agora*—regardless of *why*, the fact is that both dialectic and rhetoric have been released from servitude (though they do still experience occasional bullying), and they are presently wandering around searching for a home. They are tired and battered from their journeys, and they want to settle down, if only for a while, since they have never lived in one place for long. Perhaps they should find one home, live together again as counterparts, or more, but they are not sure how the one feels about the other. They have been forced, in the past, to ignore each other or, worse, to show outward disrespect; yet they have always secretly regretted these actions.

Lately rhetoric has been gaining strength in the safe houses of communication studies and rhetoric and composition. Rhetoric has even gained enough strength to venture out into departments of philosophy and history and sociology, where some have embraced it and others have viewed it as a threat, unsure of its motive. Rhetoric is old and sometimes speaks its mind; some want to hear its reasoned opinions, but others would rather not.

Dialectic is also old and wise, yet it has been left to wander around the outskirts of rhetoric and composition and communication studies, unsure of its reputation, guilty of past wrongs, as is rhetoric, yet also conscious of its power and potential. Rhetoric sometimes speaks of dialectic because it is there, though after their difficult journeys, rhetoric has forgotten dialectic's full scope. Despite their differences, rhetoric is interested in dialectic, wants to get to know it again. Occasionally, rhetoric will shout a polite hello, but the voice of dialectic is weak from travel, and only sometimes does rhetoric hear the feint echo of a returned hello. Whether rhetoric perceives it or not, dialectic always responds.

This book represents a metaphorical embrace. It explores what might emerge if rhetoric invites dialectic into its safe house for a discussion in which the two put aside their differences and agree to work together, according to their original plan, which others interrupted and then lied about. Initially, the two appear slightly defensive: rhetoric thinks dialectic will determine set procedures for their discussion, and dialectic thinks rhetoric will do all the talking. Eventually, they realize these presumptions are unfounded, acquired from their long-time associations with other disciplines and arts that did not have their best interests at heart. Wounds quickly heal, hurt feelings subside, and dialectic and rhetoric agree to explore what might result from their renewed interaction, not only as counterparts (though they both have fond memories of Aristotle), but as collaborators, as partners: "Rhetoric is the collaborative partner of dialectic," they say in unison as they embrace once again, "and the result of our collaboration will be dialectical rhetoric."

DIALECTICAL RHETORIC

Introduction

Historically, dialectic has taken two general forms in relation to rhetoric, both sometimes existing side by side. First, dialectic has been the
topical development of opposed arguments on controversial issues and
the judgment of their relative strengths and weaknesses. This form of
dialectic was the counterpart of rhetorics in which verbal battles over
competing probabilities in public institutions (primarily politics and
law) revealed distinct winners and losers. Second, dialectic has been the
logical development of linear propositions leading to necessary conclusions, usually in scientific and academic contexts. This form of dialectic
was the counterpart of rhetorics in which philosophical, metaphysical,
and scientific truths were conveyed with as little cognitive interference
from language as possible.[1] These oppositional and linear dialectics and
rhetorics are useful in many communication contexts, yet they can also
(like any creative art) lead to certain abuses.

I argue that rhetoric and composition is on the brink of developing a third relationship between dialectic and rhetoric, one in which
dialectics and rhetorics mediate and negotiate the different arguments
and orientations engaged in any rhetorical situation. This process of
mediation and its negotiated results form a hybrid art called *dialectical rhetoric*. Here dialectic and rhetoric join forces equally in a single
mediative practice.

Rhetoric is a dimensional art, and the nature of rhetoric's dimensionality is based on the number and functions of orientations
engaged in any rhetorical act. In *Permanence and Change*, Kenneth
Burke (1954) describes orientations as socialized terministic screens
through which we experience the objects and events in the world
around us. *Orientation* is a general term that encompasses the meanings of more specialized terms like *perspective, attitude, world view*, and
ideology. I borrow the notion of dimensionality from Herbert Marcuse,
who argues that societies have dimensional qualities. Although I discuss orientations and the dimensions of rhetoric more thoroughly in
chapter 3, a preliminary sense of rhetoric's dimensionality will help
contextualize the argument of this book.

DOI: 10.7330/9780874219821.c000

In *One-Dimensional Man*, Marcuse (1964) describes modern techno-logical society as one dimensional, operating under the unifying power of a dominant ideology that denies or co-opts contradictions in both material and social realms, thus reducing the possibility for critical discourse. Two-dimensional societies recognize that all material and social realms are inherently contradictory and that two primary ideologies compete for common attention. Dialectical tension "permeates the two-dimensional universe of discourse" in which the "two dimensions are antagonistic to each other" and "dialectical concepts develop the real contradictions" (97). Marcuse's own preferred treatment of language and ideology in society is itself two dimensional, that is, critical and oppositional. He believes that one-dimensional societies co-opt critical discourse and reduce the possibility for social progress and democracy.

It is possible to extend Marcuse's framework into yet another dimension (not mentioned by Marcuse), a third dimension in which dialectical concepts and contradictions (or, more generally, *differences*) are mediated and negotiated, though not always resolved, constructing alternative orientations upon which new social relationships can be built. This third dimension of society emerged, according to Mark C. Taylor, between the late 1960s and the late 1980s (Taylor 2001, 14) after Marcuse wrote *One-Dimensional Man*, and this third dimension of society is marked by a proliferation of complex differences (not necessarily oppositions) conveyed through digital, networked technologies (138).

Marcuse's notion of social dimensionality (and my extension of it into a third dimension) is also useful as a heuristic for describing dimensionality in rhetoric. However, in my own adaptation of Marcuse's concept, I set aside his obvious two-dimensional bias and value each rhetorical dimension equally, though for different reasons. Diane Davis (2010) argues that one important prior condition for an art of rhetoric is "affectability, persuadability, responsivity," and affectability is a "prerequisite for belonging" (2). Each dimension of rhetoric requires a different sense of belonging and affectability. One-dimensional and two-dimensional rhetorics, with orientations based on rationality or opposition, protect their imagined sovereignty by suppressing affectability once belonging is secured. Three-dimensional dialectical rhetorics encourage, and may even require, a much fuller sense of affectability from writers and audiences, an affectability that is never suppressed but is always open and ongoing.

One-dimensional rhetorics articulate the values and promote the interests of a single (rational) orientation with little or no consideration of different, therefore irrational, orientations. Argumentative challenges to one-dimensional claims do not originate from different orientations (which would be irrational) but are simply negations of the original claims; these negations become the source of rebuttals that reinforce the strength of the rational orientation. With only one legitimate orientation (rationality) considered in any rhetorical situation, one-dimensional rhetorics are never dialectical. If one-dimensional rhetorics acknowledge a separate art of dialectic, it is itself one dimensional, driven by linear logic and rational thought. In one-dimensional rhetorics, once an argument is determined to be irrational, the audience affected by the argument becomes irrational as well. To belong among rational people means to be affected by rational arguments and to be unaffected by irrational arguments. The primary function of one-dimensional rhetorics is social unification and coherence by means of logical argumentation.

Two-dimensional rhetorics articulate the values and promote the interests of a single orientation in direct relationship to one or more opposed orientations, with each orientation engaged in a power struggle against the other(s). The primary function of two-dimensional rhetorics is to reinforce the values of one orientation by critiquing the nature of power imposed by other orientations and dismantling the institutional structures (economic, political, social, cultural) that legitimate such power. Two-dimensional rhetorics are usually dialectical, though only in a simplistic way, because every argument in every rhetorical situation is shaped in opposition to competing orientations; thus, every argument in two-dimensional rhetorics is in some way influenced by another (or an "Other"), though this influence is only negative in effect. When two-dimensional rhetorics acknowledge a counterpart art of dialectic, it is usually itself two-dimensional and functions oppositionally as the exploration of two irreconcilable sides of a controversial issue in order to understand an opponent's case and to avoid contradictions in one's own. Once arguments are determined to be oppositional, they become implicated in a larger structure of hegemonic practices that oppress individuals, and the audiences affected by these oppositional arguments are misguided (duped) at best and traitorous (implicated) at worst. To belong to a community that is defined oppositionally means to be affected by arguments originating within that community and to be unaffected by arguments originating within opposed communities. Although many two-dimensional rhetorics often include a sense of dialectic as a counterpart art, these two-dimensional rhetorics are not themselves dialectical in a positive or powerful enough way to be considered a single hybrid art.

In both one-dimensional and two-dimensional rhetorics, all other orientations are inferior (cognitively irrational, politically oppressive) to the orientation that gives rise to the rhetorical performance in question. When alternative orientations are viewed as inferior, there is no clear rhetorical path to affectability in any complete sense. Dialectic thus assumes no role in one-dimensional rhetorics (unless it is a misnomer for logic) and only a minor role in two-dimensional rhetorics, relegated often to the invention of oppositional arguments.

Three-dimensional rhetorics mediate among the values and interests of *different* (neither irrational nor opposed) orientations competing for public attention, thus creating new orientations in the process. Three-dimensional rhetorics, then, are *always* dialectical because the processes of mediation and negotiation require all orientations in any rhetorical situation to be flexible and malleable, and they require all speakers and writers in these same situations to be affectable. Davis's notion of affectability is particularly relevant to three-dimensional dialectical rhetorics because these rhetorics assume different orientations relatively (or at least potentially) equal in status, and there can be no mediation or negotiation among orientations if participants in rhetorical situations are unwilling to be affected by arguments originating from different orientations. The primary function of three-dimensional dialectical rhetorics is to mediate and negotiate the engagement of orientations in productive relationships that transcend the limiting constraints of unifying or oppositional discourses. These processes of mediation and negotiation make dialectic so integral to the whole process of communication that it is no longer distinguishable from rhetorical performances themselves, resulting in a hybrid art, dialectical rhetoric.

Historically, rhetorics have been one dimensional or two dimensional. Three-dimensional dialectical rhetorics have emerged only recently in the history of rhetoric and composition. Thus, the hybrid art, dialectical rhetoric, which requires a mediative attitude and a willingness to be fully affected, is also a relatively recent development in the discipline. The emergence of three-dimensional dialectical rhetorics is related to the evolution of digital communication technologies, which foster the dialectical engagement of different orientations and enable mediative communication through new rhetorical strategies based on linking. In fact, in "Hypertext as Collage-Writing," George P. Landow (1999) argues that "by permitting one to make connections between texts and text and images so easily, the electronic link encourages one to think in terms of connections" (159). With the advent of Web 2.0, these connections have become more social in their structure and purpose. Nevertheless, like Burke's notion of identification, these connections, these links, also imply division. Landow writes, "Those linkable items not only must have some qualities that make the writer want to connect them, they also must exist in separation, apart, divided. . . . This double effect of linking appears in the way it inevitably produces juxtaposition, concatenation, and assemblage" (159). Linking and dividing are critical functions of three-dimensional dialectical rhetorics, and they are especially enabled in digital communication technologies and emphasized in the social media platforms of Web 2.0.

As I was writing this book, I kept in mind three primary goals: first, to historicize dialectic, rhetoric, and their relationship together, highlighting points of convergence and departure; second, to mediate and negotiate the differences between dialectic and rhetoric, integrating them into a hybrid three-dimensional art called *dialectical rhetoric*; and third, to operationalize three-dimensional dialectical rhetoric by reconnecting it methodologically to its classical function as a topical art.

In chapter 1, "Historical Trajectories of Dialectic and Rhetoric," I describe the history of dialectic and rhetoric and their relationship together, emphasizing points of intersection and divergence. Historical awareness is critical because it gives a sense of how theories have been used for different purposes and how they have been adapted to different social and material situations. Such awareness also serves a heuristic function for modern uses of classic(al) ideas. During the classical period, in both Greece and Rome, two-dimensional dialectics and rhetorics were generally used in tandem as pragmatic counterparts. The Protagorean *Dissoi Logoi*, for example, describes two sources of arguments for every issue, nature and culture. Nature and culture are inherently opposed to each other, and the arguments derived from them are irreconcilable. In *The Gorgias*, Callicles accuses Socrates of playing silly games with this nature/culture distinction by refuting arguments based on nature with oppositional arguments based on culture, and vice versa. Socrates does not deny the accusation. Aristotle's dialectic shifts away from the earlier obsession with the nature/culture opposition and takes a more technical approach to argumentative opposition, thus turning a previously haphazard practice into a powerful topical art. For Aristotle, dialectic uses topics to invent and develop two-dimensional argumentative oppositions and to judge which side is the strongest. Rhetoric is the counterpart of dialectic because orators cannot make a persuasive case for one side of an issue unless they understand the case against them and can avoid internal contradictions in their own arguments. Since ancient Roman rhetorics emphasized legal debate in which one side accuses and another defends, many Roman rhetoricians continued the commitment to two-dimensional rhetorics that began in Greece. Cicero's sense of dialectic is characteristically Aristotelian, and the doctrine of stasis (finding the issue at hand), which was practiced by many Roman rhetoricians, also attests to the use of two-dimensional dialectics as preparation for two-dimensional rhetorics.

From the Middle Ages to the Renaissance, dialectic and rhetoric enjoyed pride of place as two of the seven liberal arts, a curricular structure that guided (but did not determine) education for many centuries. During this time, dialectic shifted from the classical sense of the conversational development of opposed arguments to a more systematized sense of formal debate, which of course remained two dimensional. Although dialectic retained its two-dimensional qualities throughout the Middle Ages in some places and some works, it was also during this time that dialectic began to acquire one-dimensional qualities, thus losing most of its dialectical qualities (all except for the name) and becoming logic. Boethius, for example, rejected the two-dimensional sense of dialectic as the exploration of opposed arguments, describing dialectic instead as the one-dimensional development of abstract linear arguments, and rhetoric as the one-dimensional development of concrete linear arguments. For Boethius, only one argument is true, and any method (dialectic or rhetoric) that develops false arguments, even in the service of invention, is itself false. Martianus Capella (1977), whose book *The Marriage of Philology and Mercury* helped structure liberal education for nearly a millennium, considered both dialectic and rhetoric to be one-dimensional arts of linear logic and true argumentation. As the Renaissance approached, Scholastic logicians continued the tradition of viewing dialectic as one dimensional and linear, while the Italian humanists returned to Aristotle's two-dimensional sense of dialectic as the development of opposed arguments and their relative evaluation. Toward the end of the Renaissance, Peter Ramus (2010), rejecting the humanist recovery of ancient dialectic and rhetoric, shifted invention and judgment into one-dimensional logic (which he, too, called *dialectic*) and relegated rhetoric to style.

Both dialectic and rhetoric suffered unfortunate fates from the Enlightenment to the nineteenth century. The Enlightenment's emphasis on empirical, scientific inquiry left little room for creative arts like dialectic and rhetoric. During this time, dialectic fell out of favor as absurdly impractical academic debate, though it retained some influence as the production of linear logical proofs, and rhetoric also acquired a new commitment to the one-dimensional articulation of scientific truths. For important scholars such as John Locke, however, both dialectic and rhetoric were merely arts of deception. During the eighteenth century, dialectic was recovered from its Enlightenment disparagement by philosophers who were interested in explaining the progress of human history (though they ignored rhetoric), and rhetoric was recovered by teachers and theologians who were interested in rhetoric's role in epistemology, delivery, and style (though they ignored dialectic). During the nineteenth century, influential educator Richard Whately grounded much of his students' training in language on a foundation of one-dimensional logic, which by this time had lost all of its dialectical content, though his rhetoric (to be studied after logic) was characteristically Aristotelian and thus two dimensional. Despite their constantly shifting meanings and values from the classical period through the nineteenth century, dialectic and rhetoric nevertheless remained, for the most part at least, important subjects of advanced academic studies.

Chapter 2, "Dialectic in (and out of) Rhetoric and Composition," examines the emergence of rhetoric and composition within English studies during the late nineteenth century and its vexed relationship with dialectic from that time through the present. Unfortunately, during the late nineteenth century, when first-year composition emerged as a required course at universities across the country, the textbooks used in these classes were either abridged versions of longer belletristic and elocutionary rhetorical treatises or original handbooks emphasizing grammar, five-paragraph themes, and modal structures. Most of these texts considered communication (both speaking and writing) to be one dimensional, and they did not consider dialectic at all. As English composition courses began to emphasize written over oral communication, teachers committed to speech education began to split from English departments and form their own departments of speech communication. Without speech communication's emphasis on rhetorical theory and history, composition studies evolved into an absurdly formalist practice. Throughout the first half of the twentieth century, although rhetoric never completely disappeared from composition studies, the teaching of writing was indeed grounded more in grammar, modes (especially exposition), and five-paragraph themes than it was in dialectic or rhetoric.

During the 1960s, the New Rhetoric movement challenged composition's obsession with formalist (usually one-dimensional) methods, recovering a stronger commitment to two-dimensional rhetorics. However, as Anne E. Berthoff (1982) points out, this (then) new movement did not recover rhetoric's traditional counterpart dialectic.

By the 1970s and 1980s, though, Berthoff and others had begun to reconnect two-dimensional dialectic to its counterpart rhetoric, viewing dialectic sometimes as a kind of dialogic interaction, other times as a means to expand a writer's perspectives, and still other times as a metaphor for the progress of human history. Berthoff remains the composition scholar most committed to harnessing the complementary power of dialectic and rhetoric in the writing class. However, as Andrew Low (1997) points out, Berthoff's internal-dialogic sense of dialectic lost its potential for influence in the field when the fast-approaching social turn devalued anything internal as individual and thus naïve. The most forceful proponents of what came to be known as social-epistemic rhetoric (such as James A. Berlin and Alan W. France) recovered dialectic (again) for composition studies. But they did not recover Berthoff's dialogic dialectic, nor did they recover the dialectic that was the counterpart of classical rhetoric. Instead, proponents of social-epistemic rhetoric, throughout the 1980s and early 1990s, recovered the nineteenth-century philosophical sense of dialectic, especially Karl Marx's materialist version of it.

The 1990s witnessed a shift in dialectic's relationship to rhetoric in composition studies. First, the term *dialectic* generally dropped out of consistent use in scholarship on rhetoric and writing; then, by the late 1990s and into the new millennium, there emerged three critiques of dialectic. The first critique, represented most fully in Victor J. Vitanza's (1997) *Negation, Subjectivity, and the History of Rhetoric*, argues that histories of rhetoric have constructed (or followed) a Hegelian grand narrative of dialectical negation that eliminates the sub/versive middle position ("threes") marked by desire, not opposition. Second, John Muckelbauer's (2009) *The Future of Invention* critiques dialectic from a broadly postmodern view. In place of the negation and loss caused by reliance on Hegelian dialectic, Muckelbauer offers instead affirmative invention marked by repetition and what he calls "singular rhythms." The third critique of dialectic emerges from the application of complexity theory in composition studies, especially by Byron Hawk (2007) in *A Counter-History of Composition*. Complexity itself moves beyond opposition and negation toward an integration of chaos and system, where action implies a response to an environment but actors are not always aware of the full range of ecological forces at work. I end this chapter with the observation that these three critiques of dialectic are, in fact, only critiques of one particular form of dialectic, the thesis-antithesis-synthesis model in which negation is requisite for progress. This nineteenth-century philosophical model of dialectic, however, is not the counterpart of rhetoric. Other models of dialectic have little to do with the negative movement of Hegelian and Marxist dialectics, and my own recovery of dialectic for rhetoric and composition emphasizes its three-dimensional mediative uses. Interestingly, although Vitanza, Muckelbauer, and Hawk all critique philosophical dialectic for its tendency to negate and simplify, their positive articulations of threes, singular rhythms, and complexity actually play strongly into a three-dimensional notion of dialectical rhetoric.

In chapter 3, "The Dimensions of Rhetoric," I explore in greater depth rhetoric's dimensionality, which is determined by the number and functions of orientations engaged in any rhetorical situation. Orientations are socially structured belief systems that guide action in new situations, and each orientation is reinforced by forces of opposition that divide and categorize ideas and arguments. One-dimensional rhetorics serve a unifying function, articulating the values and promoting the interests of a single orientation. Since one-dimensional rhetorics do not consider the values and interests of other (irrational) orientations, they are not dialectical. When proponents of one-dimensional rhetorics invoke dialectic, it usually takes the form of linear logic, which is also not dialectical. Two-dimensional rhetorics often rely on two-dimensional dialectics to understand an opponent's case or avoid internal contradictions. In two-dimensional rhetorics, orientations are always engaged in power struggles, and the function of rhetoric is critical: to support one orientation by dismantling the institutional foundations of power imposed against it by other orientations. The practice of two-dimensional dialectics as a tool for invention and judgment usually precedes the practice of two-dimensional rhetorics, and two-dimensional dialectics and rhetorics are best described as *counterpart arts*. Three-dimensional rhetorics are always inherently dialectical because they mediate the values and interests of competing orientations, seeking not to unify or critique but to negotiate among them, constructing new orientations in the process. Three-dimensional dialectical rhetoric is a single hybrid art in which dialectic and rhetoric are performed simultaneously, not as separate counterpart arts.

Each dimension of rhetoric (unifying, critical, mediative) has its uses and abuses, as does any creative art. The best functional uses of each dialectical/rhetorical dimension are conditioned by the nature of the situations and contexts in which rhetorical acts are performed and orientations are engaged. Thus, the determination of a rhetoric (or an aspect of a rhetoric) as one dimensional, two dimensional, or three dimensional is not itself a value judgment. When the internal structures of social groups lose coherence and their very existence becomes threatened, one-dimensional unifying rhetorics can reestablish core values among group members, strengthening communities and enabling progress. When one social group is threatened by another group (or groups) in some way, perhaps with a loss of power or a loss of rights, two-dimensional oppositional rhetorics can call into question the basis of threatening power structures and create a space for resistance. When social groups enter their ideas into a public arena of competing discourses, each with its own claims to power and knowledge, three-dimensional dialectical rhetorics can enable negotiation among groups and discourses, creating new orientations that ground future communication. Yet all three dimensions of rhetoric, when used by unethical people for unethical purposes, can oppress individuals or groups and co-opt critical discourses in the service of hegemonic power structures.

Chapter 4, "Three-Dimensional Dialectical Rhetorics," more closely examines three-dimensional dialectical rhetorics, not because they are better than one-dimensional and two-dimensional rhetorics, but because they have received less attention in rhetoric and composition scholarship. I begin this chapter by revisiting three scholars I discuss in chapter 2 as opposing the simple and negative functions of philosophical dialectic: Muckelbauer, Vitanza, and Hawk. These three scholars reject only a very narrow method of dialectic, and not the dialectic that is the counterpart of rhetoric (and certainly not three-dimensional dialectical rhetoric). In particular, I revisit these scholars to demonstrate that their respective antidialectical theories actually support a theory and method of three-dimensional dialectical rhetoric, with the mediation of different orientations as its primary function. My ultimate goal in this chapter is to reconnect three-dimensional dialectical rhetoric with its classical function as a strategic and topical art, an art based on the exploration of argument categories characteristic of three-dimensional rhetoric's central purpose, namely mediation. These three-dimensional topics include deconstruction, dialogue, identification, critique, and juxtaposition.

In order to illustrate each of these topics for three-dimensional dialectical rhetoric, I describe five students' essays that use these topics to develop their arguments. These five essays demonstrate that the first task of three-dimensional dialectical rhetoric is to understand the orientations and forces of opposition performed in any rhetorical situation. For writers, orientations and forces of opposition are generative contexts for the application of specific topical strategies, including deconstruction, dialogue, identification, critique, and juxtaposition. Johndan

Johnson-Eilola (1998) reminds us that composition students in the twenty-first century must learn to connect with different people and different texts, not just produce monological, one-dimensional discourse, and these students' essays represent the three-dimensional effort to connect orientations through dialectical rhetoric. As audiences, our task is to understand not only the orientations and forces of opposition as they are presented in each rhetorical performance (print or digital) but also to participate in the production of three-dimensional mediation. Dialectical rhetoric is a creative process, whether we are writing, reading, speaking, or navigating a series of related websites.

In chapter 5, "Three-Dimensional Dialectical Rhetorics in Digital Contexts," I conclude my argument by examining the role of three-dimensional dialectical rhetorics in the context of digital communication technologies. Digital technologies, especially those associated with Web 2.0, highlight the sense of difference within and among discourses and communities through a variety of interactive communication media, such as web pages, blogs, wikis, hypertext, Facebook, MySpace, Instagram, and Twitter, among many others. These "cool" technologies, as Jeff Rice calls them, enable the development and use of certain rhetorical strategies not imaginable during rhetoric and composition's print-specific past, before the rise of electronic communication (Rice 2007, 21). Digital technologies, most of which are relatively new in the overall communication landscape, condition human communication and social interaction in interesting ways, encouraging a decentering of information, favoring nonlinear structures, and increasing the speed of interaction, all of which can have positive and negative effects. The decentering of information increases access but decreases coherence and continuity. Nonlinear document structures increase flexibility but decrease control of purpose and intent. The high speed of interaction increases efficiency but decreases the need for face-to-face communication. A heightened sense of difference in discourse and a decreased reliance on linear structures, among other things, intensify the need for three-dimensional dialectical rhetorics emphasizing mediation.

Many effects of digital technologies on our communication landscape are not necessarily new (Plato complained that writing decentered information from the living memory to the dead text), but they are certainly intensifying, and digital technologies are a rich context for that intensification. Certain rhetorical strategies (deconstruction, dialogue, identification, critique, and juxtaposition, for example), some of which have been around for a long time, have become critical to success in digital contexts. Since digital technologies have irreversibly changed the general communication landscape, these strategies are now also critical for success in all rhetorical contexts, including traditional media such as the plain print of academic essays.

Note

1. There is another sense of dialectic not mentioned here, the nineteenth-century philosophical dialectic of thesis, antithesis, and synthesis. This dialectic is a later development in the history of ideas and ultimately has little direct relation to rhetoric. I discuss this philosophical trajectory of dialectic more thoroughly in chapter 1.

1

HISTORICAL TRAJECTORIES OF DIALECTIC AND RHETORIC

Throughout their history together, dialectic and rhetoric have been engaged in an uncertain and sometimes difficult relationship.[1] At its best, dialectic has been the counterpart of rhetoric, the fullest development of argumentative knowledge on any given subject; and at its worst, dialectic has been the useless claptrap of academic disputation. At its best, rhetoric has been the counterpart of dialectic, a means to construct new knowledge and convey it to public audiences following dialectical deliberation; and at its worst, rhetoric has been the aesthetic dress of dialectical thought or the clear transmission of dialectical truth. Throughout their relationship, the meanings of dialectic and rhetoric have shifted according to the personal interests of individual authors, the institutionalized pressures of social forces, and the material circumstances of historical contexts.

It is not my goal in this chapter to provide a definitive description of dialectic and its relationship to rhetoric for each individual figure or historical period I discuss. My goal is to describe the historical relationships between dialectic and rhetoric by selecting from certain influential figures the salient aspects of their approaches to dialectic and rhetoric that illuminate the historical evolution of the concepts. In other words, I intend to paint a picture of dialectic, rhetoric, and their relationship through time in broad historical strokes rather than minute textual pixels. I will first examine the birth of dialectic and rhetoric in sophistic practice and their systematization as arts in Plato's (1961a; 1961b) *Gorgias* and *Phaedrus*. I will then trace the evolution of dialectic and rhetoric through various subsequent historical contexts, all of which exert different pressures on the individual characteristics of dialectic and rhetoric and on their relationship together, highlighting conditions of acceptance and rejection and the transformations that have accompanied dialectic and rhetoric throughout their journeys.

DOI: 10.7330/9780874219821.c001

DIALECTIC AND RHETORIC IN THE CLASSICAL PERIOD

Before Plato systematized the difference between dialectic (the mutual pursuit of metaphysical truth and ethical action through conversation) and rhetoric (the individual pursuit of popular opinion and public success through uninterrupted speech), many of the fifth-century BCE Sophists made no distinction between a person's knowledge of right and wrong and the language that person used to convey ethical values and recommend right conduct. In the Protagorean text called the *Dissoi Logoi*, for example, the anonymous author writes, "It is necessary for the man who intends to speak correctly to have a knowledge of whatever things he might discuss and to give the city correct instruction in doing good things and thus prevent it from doing bad ones" (Sprague 1972, sec. 8.6). And in the *Defense on Behalf of Palamedes*, Gorgias (1972a) points out that Odysseus's own crime is speaking without knowledge: "It is clear that you do not have knowledge of the things about which you make accusation. It follows that since you do <not> have knowledge, you have an opinion. Do you then, O most daring of all men, trusting in opinion, a most untrustworthy thing, not knowing the truth, dare to bring a capital charge against a man?" (sec. 11a.24). For many of the Sophists, then, what they called *logôn technê* (a phrase that appears in the *Dissoi Logoi*) was essentially the art of appropriate knowledge and ethical speech. And while what we now know as dialectic may not have been practiced by these Sophists, some of them did base certain aspects of their rhetorical practice on the notion that opposing arguments exist and must be understood.

The fifth-century BCE Sophist Protagoras believed that for every matter there are two opposing arguments (*logoi*), and the *Dissoi Logoi* suggests that the opposed arguments are based in the distinction between nature (*phusis*) and culture (*nomos*). In what I like to call the *garage-sale metaphor*, the author of the *Dissoi Logoi* writes, "I think that if someone should order all men to make a single heap of everything that each of them regards as disgraceful and then again to take from the collection what each of them regards as seemly, not a thing <would> be left, but they would all divide up everything, because not all men are of the same opinion" (Sprague 1972, sec. 2.18). This is the culture argument—that judgments regarding what is seemly and shameful derive from individual and communal values. Later in the *Dissoi Logoi*, the author provides the opposing argument:

> I would be surprised if things which were disgraceful when they were collected should turn out to be seemly and not what they were when they

came. At least if people had brought horses or cows or sheep or men, they would not have taken away anything else. Nor, again, if they had brought gold, would they have taken away brass, nor if they had brought silver, would they have taken away lead. Do they then take away seemly things in exchange for disgraceful ones? Now really, if anyone had brought an ugly <man>, would he take him away handsome? (Sprague 1972, sec. 2.26–28)

This is the nature argument—that a thing either is or is not seemly or shameful, and one's individual or cultural values are irrelevant to such judgments. Although the author of the *Dissoi Logoi* does not suggest any practical rhetorical uses for opposing arguments, any modern reader of the text can see applications to concepts such as invention and audience awareness.

In sophistic *dissoi logoi*, opposing arguments (nature, culture) exist side by side and are not brought together in any particular way. Interestingly, in Plato's early dialogues, before he had fully formalized what we now know as dialectic, Plato's character Socrates practiced a strategy of argumentation based in the Protagorean distinction between nature and culture. In the *Gorgias*, Callicles points out how Socrates caught Polus in a contradiction about the nature of rhetoric:

> For, Socrates, though you claim to pursue the truth, you actually drag us into these tiresome popular fallacies, looking to what is fine and noble, not by nature, but by convention. Now, for the most part, these two, nature and convention, are antagonistic to each other. And so, if a man is ashamed and dares not say what he thinks, he is compelled to contradict himself. And you have discovered this clever trick and do not play fair in your arguments, for if a man speaks on the basis of convention, you slyly question him on the basis of nature, but if he follows nature, you follow convention. (Plato 1961a, sec. 482e–483a)

Although the Socrates of Plato's *Gorgias* does claim to favor a method of discourse (called *dialogue* or *dialectic*) based on short questions and answers, which he contrasts with the rhetorical speechmaking of his companions, few readers of the dialogue take Socrates seriously since he is the only character who consistently violates the requirement. And this art of dialogue practiced by Plato's early Socrates is employed purely in the service of refutation.

The technical sense of Platonic dialectic emerges much more fully in the middle dialogues, such as the *Phaedrus*, in which dialectical discourse, through mutual questioning and answering, removes errors of thought caused by the inaccurate perception of reality and clears the way for a brief but profound glimpse at divine truth.[2] Toward the end of the *Phaedrus*, Plato's character Socrates (so very different from the Socrates of the *Gorgias*) explains that dialectic consists of two primary steps. In the first step, conversants "bring a dispersed plurality under a single form" through definition (Plato 1961b, sec. 265d). In the second step, conversants "divide into forms" the subject under study (sec. 265e). Plato calls those who "have this ability" (to define and divide a subject, such as love) "dialecticians" (sec. 266b), and dialectic is the methodology Plato associates with philosophy. In the *Phaedrus*, then, dialectic becomes the mutual pursuit of divine truth through definition and division, and its structural methodology requires questions and answers (not extended speech) since only conversation represents a "living" discourse that evolves through argument and response. And rhetoric, if it is to be a legitimate (not false) art, must also follow a structure mirroring that of dialectic, with an initial concern for definition and a subsequent concern for division into parts, all by means of conversation, not extended speech, which is incapable of response (sec. 258–79). However, even mirroring the structure of dialectic, rhetoric remains little more than the transmission of dialectical truth and could never be considered a methodology appropriate to the loftier pursuits of philosophy.

Aristotle, one of Plato's most famous students, alters the meaning of dialectic and its relationship to rhetoric in significant ways, especially epistemologically but also (though to a lesser extent) methodologically. Epistemologically, Aristotle shifts Plato's definition of dialectic away from the pursuit of metaphysical truth toward the pursuit of reasoned opinion. In the *Rhetoric*, Aristotle calls rhetoric the counterpart (*antistrophos*) of dialectic, both of which concern matters of probability (Aristotle 1991, sec. 1354a).[3] In the *Topics*, Aristotle reinforces this view, suggesting that dialectic enables people to "reason from reputable opinions about any subject"; and, when used as a counterpart to rhetoric, dialectic also enables people, "when putting forward an argument, [to] avoid saying anything contrary to it" (sec. 100a).[4] When deductions deal with universal truths lacking contradiction, they are demonstrative (neither dialectical nor rhetorical); when deductions deal with reasonable opinions, many of which inevitably contain contradictory probabilities, they are dialectical (Aristotle 1984, sec. 100a); when deductions are truncated into audience-specific enthymemes and supported by probable proofs and examples, they are rhetorical (Aristotle 1991, sec. 1355a). Dialectical deductions begin with questions or problems that pose more than one possible position and spin out the contradictory lines of argument possible within each; rhetorical arguments begin with audience-specific claims or propositions and forward a single, coherent position on an issue.

Methodologically, Aristotle retains Plato's general dialectical structure, definition and division, but operationalizes these two steps through topics or sources of argument.[5] Under definition, Aristotle includes such topics as property, genus, sameness, and predication (Aristotle 1984, sec. 101b–104a). Under division, different kinds of dialectical arguments serve to analyze matters for different purposes. Some of these arguments include inductive, deductive, universal, and particular, and their purpose is, in general, to reveal contradictions in the dialectical problem as a whole (sec. 105a), leading to the possibility of more effective (more coherent and convincing, less contradictory and suspicious) rhetoric. For Aristotle, a rhetorical question, the starting point of rhetorical discourse, is singular (should Athens go to war with Sparta?), requiring the rhetor to pick a side (answer yes or no) and make that argument. A dialectical question, the starting point of dialectical discourse, is double (should Athens go to war with Sparta, *or not?*), requiring the rhetor to consider opposing arguments and judge among them (sec. 105b). While Aristotle shifts Plato's definition of dialectic away from the pursuit of metaphysical truth toward the pursuit of reasoned opinion, he nevertheless retains a clear distinction between the epistemological methods of dialectic and the practical methods of rhetoric. The *telos* of dialectic is knowledge of distinctions, and the *telos* of rhetoric is real effects. Although dialectic and rhetoric are counterparts (*antistrophos*)—that is, both participate in *probability*, though in different ways and to different ends—they are not a unified whole. One may (and should) inform the other, but each remains distinct.

During the early Republican period following the Roman conquest of Athens, especially throughout the second century BCE, many Greek intellectuals continued to teach (and pass on to other teachers) the arts they had learned and practiced, including rhetoric. However, during this transition in cultural context, instruction in dialectic ultimately lost its double (two-dimensional) sense of conversation and opposing arguments, and it acquired instead a more linear structure devoted to the discovery of truth, which was appropriate to philosophy yet not very useful to the rhetorical practice of the senate and the courts. According to George A. Kennedy, one important development in the second-century BCE period of Roman occupation was a renewed antagonism between teachers of rhetoric and teachers of philosophy, with philosophers relying on Plato's *Gorgias* as justification for the priority of their discipline over rhetoric (Kennedy 1980, 89). With its loss of connection to the pragmatic art of rhetoric, early Roman dialectic evolved into the one-dimensional practice of logic and the discovery of truth (and rejection of falsity), all for its own sake. There were, of course, attempts to use this specialized dialectic in the service of rhetoric, but they were ultimately unsatisfying, especially to Rome's most successful orator, Cicero. In *On Oratory and Orators* (or, in Latin, *De Orator*), composed during the first century BCE, Cicero associates the simplified dialectic of philosophers with the Greek rhetorician, Diogenes, who taught dialectic as "the art of reasoning well, and distinguishing truth from falsehood," or, more generally, "logic" (Cicero 1970, 126). Cicero, however, opposes this reductive dialectic, rehabilitating in his own works its earlier two-dimensional sense, its association with opposing arguments and the avoidance of contradiction, and its commitment to constructing reasoned opinion instead of discovering truth and falsity. This is the dialectic that would serve Roman political and legal interests during the late Republican period and also reconnect dialectic with its counterpart, rhetoric.

One of the central themes of Cicero's (1970) *On Oratory and Orators* is the relationship between philosophy and rhetoric, which he believed had been split to the detriment of both disciplines, yet dialectic would have to be reformulated (from its earlier identification with logic and truth) in order for this relationship to be reestablished. According to Richard Leo Enos, "Cicero believed that carefully constructed arguments based on probability ought to serve as a guide for the judgment of human conduct. Such an epistemology posited that while truth was imperceptible it was not nonexistent. Consequently, if dialectic could be adapted from the quest for logical certainty and used to attain probable judgments, then a closer approximation to truth could be advanced. Furthermore, eloquence which could direct and clarify perception would serve to aid the dialectical process in the attainment of this goal" (Enos 1988, 39). In *On Oratory and Orators*, Cicero's Crassus explains that philosophy in general includes the study of physics, reasoning, and ethics (Cicero 1970, 23); and in *De Finibus*, Cicero situates dialectic within the art of reasoning, as a method of rational argument, judgment, and disputation (Hohmann 2002, 44). Certainly Cicero believed that reuniting rhetoric with dialectical reasoning about probabilities and ethical judgment of human character would benefit the practice of oratory in Republican Rome. However, with the shift from Republican to imperial rule in the Roman territories, Cicero's interest in discovering and conveying effective rhetorical knowledge became viewed as a threat to the new power structure.[6]

By the time Quintilian (1980) wrote *The Institutes of Oratory* during the first century CE, imperial Rome had become a politically oppressive culture, and the study and practice of rhetoric suffered. Quintilian was ultimately concerned with merging the pragmatic power of rhetoric with the ethical dimension of philosophy; however, the role of dialectic in this merger remains unclear. Toward the end of book 2, Quintilian writes that dialectic is "really a concise form of oratory" (1:361), which may be a reference to Zeno (the closed fist of logic and the open hand of rhetoric) or a concession to release dialectic back to its former status as a linear (one-dimensional) philosophical method concerned with logic and truth (not reasoned opinion), though Quintilian does believe dialectic can also serve oratory, if only in limited ways (1:361). Since the dialectic of Plato, Aristotle, Cicero, and certain Sophists required the spinning out of contradictory positions, and since contradiction was not allowed in the political power structure of imperial Rome, dialectic shifted, under this historical pressure, from the articulation of contradiction to the articulation of a single (true, or at least accepted) position. This political pressure to consider contradiction to be a form of treason forced those who taught and practiced dialectic to shift its general orientation toward abstract principles of sound reasoning. Quintilian's sense of dialectic, then, represents a nascent (re)linearization in the concept.

DIALECTIC AND RHETORIC FROM THE MIDDLE AGES TO THE RENAISSANCE

During the late classical age, many of Rome's public institutions shifted their legitimating religious foundations from pagan ideologies to Christian ideologies, and this shift represents a primary characteristic of the historical transition into the Middle Ages. It is well known that until his conversion to Christianity late in the fourth century CE, during the dawning years of the Middle Ages, Augustine taught rhetoric at Carthage and Rome. In *The Confessions*, Augustine associates the excesses of his life before conversion with the excesses and problematic ethics of the art he taught, rhetoric; and dialectic would have been considered one form of invention for the art of persuasion. Following his conversion, Augustine describes his desire to be relieved of all duties related to rhetoric and its teaching (Augustine 2008, 116). Augustine's conversion to Christianity placed him in a difficult relationship to both rhetoric and dialectic since their classical purposes, generating and employing probable arguments based on reasoned opinion, were not valued in early Christian communication.[7] While it was the oppressive political context of imperial Rome that caused Quintilian's rhetoric and dialectic to lose some of their epistemic functions, it was the foundational Christian context of the early church that caused Augustine's rhetoric and dialectic to lose some of their epistemic functions.

In *Divine Providence and the Problem of Evil*, Augustine clearly divides grammar, dialectic, and rhetoric (or what would later become known as the *trivium*) according to method and purpose: grammar uses the study of literature to instill cultural values; dialectic uses definition, division, and synthesis to discover knowledge; and rhetoric uses persuasive appeals to arouse emotion (Augustine 1948, 314–16). But in *On Christian Doctrine*, Augustine makes it clear that truth (the source of all ethical argumentation) resides in the holy scriptures, not in the rhetorician's or dialectician's power of invention, which results in false reasoning and sophistry if not grounded in Biblical exegesis. Exegesis, the discovery of divine truth through textual interpretation based on nascent (what we would now call) semiotics, is the only legitimate form of invention in Augustine's early Christian system of communication. Dialectic (or Augustine's neo-Platonic variety of it) can be useful for understanding and resolving interpretive disputes in which one argument must be true and the other false (Augustine 1985, 67–68), but this limited use of dialectic is never described at length by Augustine. Toward the end of his life, Augustine added a fourth book to *On Christian Doctrine*; this final book argues that the truth generated by means of exegesis (and, perhaps, clarified by dialectic) is not able, on its own, to persuade congregations to act according to divine biblical precepts. The classical art of rhetoric can serve both truth and falsity, and Augustine believed it was time for the church to use rhetoric to persuade its congregations to believe the truth and act ethically (Augustine 1985, 118–19).

Although Augustine favored the revival of rhetoric in its classical traditions (leaving behind its association with pagan institutions and repurposing it for a Christian ideology) and saw a role for Platonic dialectic (definition, division, and synthesis) in the resolution of exegetical disputes, these positive sentiments toward rhetoric and dialectic did not have much influence throughout the Middle Ages. Whereas rhetoric and dialectic had generally been viewed as complementary arts throughout the classical traditions, these arts became separate concerns in Boethius's (2009) *De Topiciis Differentiis* and Martianus Capella's (1977) influential description of the seven liberal arts.

Also during the early years of the Middle Ages, Boethius, adapting elements from Aristotle and Cicero to serve his own purposes, developed a conception of dialectic and rhetoric that would become characteristic of the late medieval Scholastics, in which dialectic emerged as one-dimensional abstract logic. In *De Topiciis Differentiis*, Boethius

(2009) explains that philosophy uses demonstration to generate universal truths, dialectic uses abstract topics to convince fellow inquirers of true arguments, and rhetoric uses concrete topics to persuade audiences to hold reasoned opinions. Both philosophy and dialectic deal with abstract truths, though in different capacities: philosophy generates true statements for their own sake and dialectic uses these statements in the service of argumentation (Stump 1983, 31–56). While dialectic employs topics to generate true arguments about abstract problems, rhetoric, on the other hand, employs topics to generate reasoned opinions and probable arguments about concrete problems (Hohmann 2002, 45; Leff 2002, 53); and since each art (dialectic and rhetoric) focused on different levels of existence (abstract versus concrete), each art was viewed as separate, not complementary. Whereas Aristotle's dialectical and rhetorical questions are both concrete and situational, Boethius's guiding questions reflect his shift in dialectic toward one-dimensional abstract reasoning: Boethius's dialectical question would be, should humans engage in war? and his rhetorical question would be, should Athens go to war with Sparta?[8] In neither case is there a two-dimensional sense of contradiction in the issue at hand; both dialectic and rhetoric are linear, one dimensional, but one deals with abstract matters and the other deals with concrete, situational matters. For Boethius, dialectical logic was privileged and rhetoric was only studied by the very young.

A generation after the death of Boethius, Capella published *The Marriage of Philology and Mercury*, an influential textbook that would establish the seven liberal arts as a guiding (but not determining) structure for education through the Renaissance. These seven liberal arts consist of the *trivium* (grammar, dialectic, and rhetoric), which emphasizes facility with language, and the *quadrivium* (geometry, arithmetic, astronomy, and music), which emphasizes facility with number.[9] Among the seven liberal arts, dialectic is the most powerful, according to Capella, since its six integral components are fundamental to all the other arts. These fundamental components of dialectic include speech, interpretation, propositions, sums of propositions, judgment, and criticism, none of which include the two-dimensional qualities of many earlier articulations of dialectic. Capella argues that neither language nor number can be explained without the reasoning characteristic of the most important of the seven liberal arts, dialectic (Capella 1977, 106–54). However, it is important to note, as Walter J. Ong (1974) does, that the seven liberal arts formed only a very general framework for education in the early Middle Ages, with different schools adapting and framing these arts to suit their own goals and clientele (138).

In "The Seven Liberal Arts and Classical Scholarship," David L. Wagner explains that from the early seventh century through the tenth century CE, Europe experienced what might be called the *Dark Ages*, in which economic depression, political fragmentation, social ruralization, and a general lack of foreign trade all combined to diminish the possibilities for intellectual advancement. Although the *trivium* remained generally in place in whatever academic institutions remained viable, the three disciplines that comprised this structure became specialized, with the unified structure of the seven liberal arts generally losing influence (Wagner 1983, 21–22). Grammar became the cornerstone of religious training since Latin was the official language of the church but was no longer a living tongue; and dialectic (following mastery of grammar) became the principal method of secular education (22). With a general loss of connection to classical knowledge, and with many public institutions now being managed by the church or by monarchs, rhetoric shifted from communication in politics and law to the characteristically medieval arts of poetry, letter writing, and preaching (see Murphy 1974). Throughout the early Middle Ages, then, one-dimensional grammar and logic (also called *dialectic*) were arts of reasoning practiced by religious and academic orders to discover true knowledge, while rhetoric was a method of communication practiced by working citizens to create real effects (Mack 1993, 8).

The so-called High Middle Ages, or the first three centuries of the second millennium, witnessed a resurgence of interest in classical learning and a renewed dedication to the seven liberal arts. These classical arts were once again being reintegrated, though one-dimensional logic tended to exert primacy in many contexts (Wagner 1983, 23–24). This resurgence was initiated by Muslim scholars during the Islamic occupation of southern Europe around the turn of the second millennium, especially in Spain and Italy. Many of these Muslim scholars translated ancient texts into Latin, and Ibn Rushd in particular introduced translations of (and commentaries on) Aristotle's works, including the *Rhetoric*, into this emerging intellectual rebirth (Borrowman 2008).[10]

During the early Renaissance period, especially in the fifteenth century, Italian humanism emerged as a critique of late medieval Scholasticism, particularly its use of abstract, symbolic language as a primary methodology for one-dimensional logic. The simplified and symbolic Latin of Scholastic logic did not sit well with the Italian humanists, who were interested in the richness and difficulty of classical Latin, not its logical minimalization; and logic, the humanists argued, had become a purely academic exercise among the Scholastics, completely disconnected from practical argumentation. Early Renaissance humanists, such as Lorenzo Valla, rediscovered classical (particularly Ciceronian) rhetoric as an intellectual pursuit and returned dialectic to its two-dimensional classical function as the counterpart of rhetoric (Capozzi and Roncaglia 2009, 79–83). Italian humanism, however, did not supplant Scholastic logic in universities throughout Europe, or even in Italy; Italian humanism existed simultaneously with the study and application of abstract logic in philosophy (Mack 1993, 14–15), and many humanists, including Valla, wrote about one-dimensional logic in addition to two-dimensional rhetoric and dialectic (74–95).

In *Repastinatio Dialecticae et Philosophiae*, Valla challenged the Scholastic obsession with logic (which they called *dialectic*) at the expense of grammar and especially rhetoric (Mack 1993). According to Peter Mack, "By treating dialectic as the study of argument within natural language, Valla drew the subjects of the *trivium* together, because he emphasized the connections between logic, usage, and organization" (96). Against the Scholastic impulse toward specialization, Valla sought to integrate the arts of the *trivium*; and against the Scholastic development of extremely intricate and numerous logical rules (outside the context of actual application), Valla sought to simplify dialectic and return it to its classical place as the two-dimensional invention of arguments for rhetorical practice. Valla writes, "For dialectic used to be an entirely brief and simple thing, which can be seen from a comparison with rhetoric. For what is dialectic but a kind of confirmation and confutation? These very things are parts of invention, which is one of the five parts of rhetoric" (qtd. in Mack 1993, 110). Valla also includes persuasive, probable arguments (not just certain ones) within the scope of dialectic, focusing much of his attention on informal argumentative strategies, such as examples and enthymemes, which the Scholastics would have considered invalid (Capozzi and Roncaglia 2009, 81).

Although Italian humanism did have an important effect on the increased value of rhetoric in school curricula throughout Europe, the humanistic emphasis on two-dimensional dialectic as a method for inventing reasoned opinions in rhetoric was eventually lost.[11] Mack explains that "in historical terms the impact of *Repastinatio Dialecticae et Philosophiae* was disproportionately small in relation to its bold originality" (Mack 1993, 114). Rhetoric remained important throughout the Renaissance, but without invention and dialectic within its purview, rhetoric became the study of tropes and figures and their application in copious ornamentation.

Writing during the first half of the sixteenth century, Peter Ramus (2010) was dissatisfied with both Scholastic logic and the more pragmatic rhetoric of the early humanist tradition. In particular, Ramus saw the configuration of the *trivium* as inefficient, with both logic and rhetoric teaching invention and arrangement (Howell 1956, 147–48). In Ramus's reforms of liberal arts education, he argued that logic alone is the province of invention and arrangement, and dialectic is a form of logic whose goal is "discoursing *well*" (Ong 1974, 179). Rhetoric alone is the province of style and delivery. Ramus, in other words, rejected Aristotle's claim that there are three forms of invention: one for science, resulting in true claims and certain propositions; another for dialectic, resulting in reasoned opinions on all sides of an issue; and another for rhetoric, resulting in probable arguments on one side of an issue. Not only did Ramus reject the roles of invention and arrangement in rhetoric, moving them over to dialectic, but he also rejected the use of dialectic in generating reasoned opinions. The liberal arts were no place for opinions on contingent matters, according to Ramus. Thus, dialectic functioned to generate true arguments and arrange them effectively, and rhetoric functioned to express them beautifully, using tropes and figures to dress dialectical thought. This division of linguistic labor among the arts of the *trivium*, so different from classical descriptions of dialectic and rhetoric, was tremendously influential, especially in England, where Ramist dialectic (invention and arrangement) and rhetoric (tropes and figures) continued to be taught throughout the remaining years of the sixteenth century and into the seventeenth century (Howell 1956, 247–81). Further, Brian Vickers confirms that Renaissance rhetoric after Ramus became, in many of its most influential manifestations, closely associated with poetry (Vickers 1988, 277–86).

However influential it was, Ramus's (2010) simplified *trivium* was often negotiated rather than accepted without question. Thomas Wilson, for example, writing less than a generation after Ramus's publications, accepted the Ramist view of one-dimensional logic as invention and judgment (or arrangement), but he rejected Ramist simplifications of rhetoric to style and delivery. Wilson's rhetoric is distinctly Ciceronian and includes discussions (though uneven in detail) of all five Roman canons of rhetoric. In 1553, Wilson published *The Rule of Reason Conteinying the Art of Logique*. This book was important in the development of logic, dialectic, and rhetoric in the Renaissance because it furthered the cause of Ramism generally, and because it was the first logic written in English for widespread secular (not just elite theological) education (Kneale and Kneale 1962, 299). According to Wilson, logic is the art of reasoning correctly on any subject, and this subject is usually stated as a guiding question. Unlike Boethius, Wilson does not distinguish between abstract and concrete questions. Wilson does, however, distinguish between "single" questions ("What is Philosophy?") and "double" questions ("Is the study of philosophy praiseworthy, or not?") (Wilson 1972, 12). However, whereas Aristotle categorized "single" questions as rhetorical and "double" questions as dialectical, Wilson, instead, categorizes both kinds of questions as purely logical (12). Once a question has been established, one-dimensional logic proceeds through its two primary phases, invention and judgment. According to Wilson, invention includes seeking and discovering the "matter" and "stuffe" that relate to the development of an argument. As with most treatments of the subject at the time, Wilson's theory of invention was based on a system of categorized topics, a "storehouse of places" (91), each designed to focus attention on a different facet of the subject of inquiry. Once invention has led to a detailed knowledge of the subject at hand, the process of judgment begins. There are four "offices" of judgment in logic: definition, division, argument, and refutation (12). The purposes of the first three offices of logic (definition, division, and argument) are to structure invented thoughts into arguments and to evaluate arguments according to purpose (12–57). The purpose of the fourth office (refutation) is to "unknit false" arguments (12) and to dispute contrary arguments (152).

The function of one-dimensional logic in Wilson's system, then, is much like the function Ramus ascribes to it. Logic is responsible for the invention of arguments, their effective arrangement, and even their expression in plain language. In dialectical argument or disputation, speakers and writers present their own arguments that have gone through the process of invention and judgment, and then they refute their opponent's arguments by identifying in them "false conclusions" and "deceitful reasons" (Wilson 1972, 156), or what we would now call *fallacies.* What is unusual in Wilson's treatment of disputation is his clear association of fallacious reasoning with the counterarguments characteristic of dialectical discourse; here dialectical engagement means not developing knowledge through discourse but instead dealing with the incorrect thinking of opponents (who, presumably, have not engaged in copious invention and correct judgment). In *The Rule of Reason*, Wilson cites Zeno's famous distinction between logic and rhetoric: logic is the closed fist, terse and forceful, and rhetoric is the open hand, eloquent and accommodating. Ramus (2010) himself invokes this distinction. However, while Wilson's treatments of logic, dialectic, and rhetoric in *The Rule of Reason* are generally Ramist (thus one dimensional) in orientation, Wilson's (1994) treatment of rhetoric in *The Art of Rhetoric*

(1553), which Wilson viewed as a "companion piece to *The Rule of Reason*" (Medine 1994, 2–3), is decidedly not Ramist and is oriented primarily toward Ciceronian (thus two-dimensional) rhetoric.[12] Wilson's (1994) *The Art of Rhetoric* was only the third book on the subject published in English, and it was the first to treat all five classical cannons of rhetoric (invention, arrangement, style, memory, and delivery) in relation to three genres of discourse (demonstrative, judicial, and deliberative) (Medine 1994, 8–16). For Wilson, invention in rhetoric is topical, and the main function of dialectic is logical refutation.

Toward the end of the Renaissance, scientific inquiry arose to prominence in many educational institutions, leaving the basis of a humanistic education, the seven liberal arts, struggling into obscurity. Scientific method and one-dimensional logic had become the only respected means to generate new knowledge. In *The Advancement of Learning*, first published in 1605, Francis Bacon argues that logic affects people's understanding and reasoning, and there are four arts of logic: inquiry or invention, judgment, retention or memory, and the transmission of knowledge, including speech and writing (Bacon 2000, 61–91). Logic, then, invents and arranges truths and aids in the memory and transmission of these truths. Thus, Bacon not only shifts invention and arrangement over to logic, as Ramus did, but Bacon also shifts style, memory, and delivery to logic, making all of rhetoric simply a division of the larger functions of reasoning (Palmer 1998). Although Ramus respected dialectic as a branch of logic, Bacon saw little use for dialectic in science, associating it with useless generalization and meaningless disputation. In the *Novum Organum*, Bacon writes, "The unaided intellect takes the same way . . . which it takes when directed by dialectic. For the mind longs to leap up to higher generalities to find rest there; and after a short while scorns experience. But in the end this evil is made worse by dialectic used for the sake of ostentatious disputations (Bacon 2004, 71). And later Bacon writes that dialectic offers only the illusion of relevance to meaningful inquiry in the arts and sciences: "Dialectical invention is not concerned with the basic principles or axioms from which arts are built, but only with those which seem to be in agreement with them" (131).

Although Bacon does not admit a significant role for dialectic in the four arts of logic, he does nevertheless still consider rhetoric to have some worth in the popular conveyance of certain knowledge, though only under the strict watch of reason. In *The Advancement of Learning*, Bacon refers to rhetoric as "a Science excellent, and excellently well labored. . . . Although in true value, it is inferiour to Wisdome. . . . Yet with people it is more mightie" (127). And Bacon defines rhetoric as a complementary art to logic: "The dutie and Office of *Rhetorike* is, to apply Reason to Imagination, for the better moouing of the will" (Bacon 2000, 127); and later he writes, "The end of *Rhetorike*, is to fill the Imagination to second [or affirm] Reason, and not to oppresse it" (128).[13] Like Ramus, Bacon views one-dimensional logic as the source of all knowledge and structure, and he views one-dimensional rhetoric as a method of eloquent transmission to public audiences; however, unlike Ramus, Bacon does not give dialectic any significant role in the production of certainty. Under Bacon's influence in the late Renaissance, and continuing into the early Enlightenment, linear, abstract, one-dimensional logic became the super-method of scientific inquiry, generating all significant knowledge and truth.

DIALECTIC AND RHETORIC FROM THE ENLIGHTENMENT TO THE NINETEENTH CENTURY

Although Bacon wrote during what we would now call the *late Renaissance*, his ideas function as a kind of transition from the Renaissance into the Enlightenment. Shortly following Bacon's influential works came two more publications that ushered in a period of intense interest in scientific method and one-dimensional logical reasoning. In 1637, René Descartes's (1993) *Discourse on Method* consolidated experimental procedures for the discovery of truth in science and natural philosophy. And in 1662, Antoine Arnauld and Pierre Nicole published *Logic or the Art of Thinking* (better known as the *Port-Royal Logic*), which established strict rules of logical reasoning, extending and developing Cartesian principles within the framework of linguistic argumentation. Although John Locke would later disparage logic (and rhetoric, and dialectic), Arnauld and Nicole's (1996) book remained enormously influential.

In the latter half of the seventeenth century, Locke adopted Bacon's interest in scientific understanding and the pursuit of truth, injecting it with a heavy dose of empiricism, yet (unlike Bacon) Locke viewed dialectic, logic, and rhetoric as forces that corrupt knowledge and mislead people.[14] In *An Essay Concerning Human Understanding,* Locke (1975) explains that one of the central problems of communication, which is thus also a central problem of knowledge in general, is that words often do not convey precise meanings. Linguistic imprecision does not cause tremendous problems in civil discourse, where approximate understanding serves practical ends well enough. However, in philosophical uses, language must be precise and accurate. Disputation, or debate over contradictions of opinion (what would be called *dialectic*), suffers from the abuse of language because one interlocutor has one definition of a complex term in mind while the other interlocutor has an entirely different definition in mind (503). The winner in such a dispute would only be the most forceful speaker, not necessarily the most truthful speaker. Logic, according to Locke, has become so abstract in its symbolic language it can represent little more than the most simplistic ideas, and when ideas combine or become more specific, abstract logic fails to represent their complexity (Locke 1975, 493–94). Like Bacon, Locke views rhetoric as an art of figurative speech and allusion; however, while Bacon saw potentially positive uses for rhetoric as a branch of logic, Locke sees only manipulation and abuse. According to Locke, the rhetorical arts are the "Arts of Deceiving" and a "great fault" because they "insinuate wrong *Ideas*" and "mislead the Judgment" (508). Only accurate perception and the ethical combination of ideas contribute to the generation of new truths and certainty.

In general, Enlightenment ideologies such as Locke's had a powerful influence, even over disciplines such as law, which historically had an inherent affinity with the kind of confrontational reasoning characteristic of two-dimensional dialectic. Hans Hohmann (2002) points out that several seventeenth-century scholars of law, such as Hugo Grotius and Samuel Pufendorf, "replace the rhetorical quest for conflicting arguments that can serve opposing advocates with a secure method for finding the uniquely correct interpretation of legal norms" (47). Dialectic, once one of the central methodologies of legal studies, had lost favor along with rhetoric, and the influence of Enlightenment epistemological linearity would continue into the eighteenth and nineteenth centuries. Hohmann points out that "in the course of the eighteenth and nineteenth centuries, the links of legal argumentation with both rhetoric and dialectic are in theory ever more pushed into the background in favor of a focus on hermeneutics that ever renews the ever unfulfilled promise of replacing the clash of opposing legal arguments in controversial discussions with solitary scientific determinations of legal meanings" (Hohmann 2002, 47–48). Thus, throughout the eighteenth (and even into the nineteenth) century, in law as in other disciplines, "dialectic is made to deny its dialogic and probabilistic origins in favor of a monological conception of logic emphasizing certainty" (48).

Locke's denigration of rhetoric, dialectic, and logic was characteristic of seventeenth- and eighteenth-century empiricism, founded in scientific, not linguistic, discovery; however, during the late eighteenth century, two separate disciplinary trajectories emerged, each influencing dialectic and rhetoric and their relationship in very different ways. In the "philosophical" trajectory, one figure in particular, Immanuel Kant, rejected classical dialectic because it was a method of argumentation that makes illusion appear real, and he offered in its place transcendental dialectic, or the discovery and critique of illusory reasoning. Later philosophers, such as Georg Wilhelm Friedrich Hegel and Karl Marx would revise this notion of transcendental dialectic, removing it even further from the practical interests of language. Dialectic as a discipline had been recovered without the help of its counterpart, rhetoric. In the "rhetorical" trajectory, certain influential figures, such as Thomas Sheridan, George Campbell, and Hugh Blair, recovered rhetoric as a crucial art of communication. Yet in these three very different treatments of rhetoric, dialectic is nowhere to be seen, or is downright denigrated, and later influential rhetoricians, such as Richard Whately, tended to follow suit. Rhetoric as a discipline had been recovered without the help of its counterpart, dialectic. Dialectic and rhetoric would not become true counterparts again until the twentieth century, and even then the reestablished relationship was, for the most part, unsatisfying.

The Philosophical Trajectory of Dialectic and Rhetoric

In the "philosophical" trajectory of dialectic and rhetoric, dialectic was recovered from its Enlightenment disparagement and reinstated as a central methodology in philosophy and epistemology; rhetoric, on the other hand, was at best neglected or at worst denigrated. During the late eighteenth century, Kant disparaged the classical models of both dialectic and rhetoric as arts of illusion and thus completely contrary to the values of philosophical inquiry. In *Critique of Pure Reason*, Kant (1965) criticizes classical dialectic as false logic: "However various were the significations in which the ancients used 'dialectic' as the title for a science or art, we can safely conclude from their actual employment of it that with them it was never anything else than the *logic of illusion*. It was a sophistical art of giving to ignorance, and indeed to intentional sophistries, the appearance of truth, by the device of imitating the methodical thoroughness which logic prescribes, and of using its 'topic' to conceal the emptiness of its pretentions" (99). And in *Critique of Judgment*, Kant (1987) distinguishes between eloquence and oratory (persuasive rhetoric). Eloquence is the art of stylistic expression, and, as such, it is one of the two beautiful arts (poetry is the other). Rhetoric, however, is the art of persuasion, and, as such, it is a manipulative art. The use of rhetoric is unethical since it borrows stylistic strategies from poetry not for purposes of beautification but for purposes of conquest. Kant writes, "Oratory, . . . insofar as this is taken to mean the art of persuasion (*ars oratoria*), i.e., of deceiving by means of a beautiful illusion, rather than mere excellence of speech (eloquence and style), is a dialectic that borrows from poetry only as much as the speaker needs in order to win over people's minds for his own advantage before they judge for themselves, and so make their judgment unfree. Hence it cannot be recommended either for the bar or for the pulpit" (197). As a persuasive art, then, rhetoric functions only to deceive and to deprive.[15] While Kant recovers dialectic from its classical abuses for his own purposes, he makes no such effort to recover rhetoric.

One strategy Kant uses to recover dialectic for transcendental philosophy is to disconnect dialectic from its classical description and return it to its function in pure logic. Kant writes, "The title 'dialectic' has therefore come to be otherwise employed, and has been assigned to logic, as a *critique of dialectical illusion*" (Kant 1965, 99). Although it is unclear how dialectic had "come to be" thus "otherwise employed," or by whom, it is very clear that Kant's new (transcendental) dialectic is the critique, not the production, of illusion, and it is this "sense in which [dialectic] is to be understood" in *Critique of Pure Reason*.

According to Kant, dialectical illusions occur when logic is misused. In *Critique of Pure Reason*, Kant (1965) explains that there are two sources of knowledge, and both sources together are the province of general logic. The first source of knowledge derives from the sensibility, where objects and sensory data are processed through a priori forms (space, time) and become mental impressions. The study of objects and sense data is empirical (a posteriori) and thus not transcendental.[16] The study of forms and impressions is transcendental because they are a priori, functions of mind present before the perception of objects and sensory data. Specifically, the study of a priori forms and impressions is called *transcendental aesthetics*. The second source of knowledge derives from the understanding, where thoughts in relation to a priori categories (quantity, quality, relation, and modality) lead to concepts. The science directed toward understanding pure thought (a priori categories and concepts) is called *analytic*. Both sources of knowledge (intuitions and thoughts) are necessary; neither alone results in true knowledge, and neither is more important than the other: "Thoughts without content are empty, intuitions without concepts are blind" (93). General logic, according to Kant, is the science of all knowledge, or the relationship between impressions *and* thoughts; analytic, on the other hand, is the science of logic applied only to the second source of knowledge (thoughts, categories, concepts).

According to Kant (1965, 99), analytic is "merely a canon of judgment," a means to determine the truth or falsity of knowledge claims by examining their relationships to intuitions and concepts; analytic is not a means to generate new knowledge claims (this is the province of the various sciences). When analytic is employed (i.e., "misapplied") not as a "*canon* of judgment" (99) but as an "*organon* for the actual production of at least the semblance of objective assertions," then it is called *dialectic* (99). Dialectic, or the logic of illusion, uses logical rules without any connection to intuitions or the objects that generate them, resulting in new and creative (because not grounded) claims that have the formal appearance of truth but may not actually be true in relation to objects and intuitions. Dialectical illusions, then, take on the appearance of analytical proofs, but they lack the verifying function that comes with logic. According to Kant, *transcendental* dialectic critiques (i.e., does *not* produce, but dismantles) dialectical illusions: transcendental dialectic "will expose the false, illusory character of those groundless pretensions, and in place of the high claims to discover and to extend knowledge merely by means of transcendental principles [i.e., as an organon], it will substitute what is no more than a critical treatment of the pure understanding, for the guarding of it against sophistical illusion" (101). Kant adapted dialectic in the service of transcendental philosophy as a means to detect and correct dialectical illusions. While this adaptation retained dialectic's traditional attention to argumentative discourse, it also limited the scope of dialectic to the critique of false claims.

Less than a century after Kant, Hegel would adapt Kantian dialectics for a very different purpose. For Hegel, dialectic would no longer function as a means to critique false knowledge claims (or even produce illusions, for that matter); it would now function to account for the progress of history and consciousness in a purely idealized dialectic of Being (thesis), Nothingness (antithesis), and Becoming (synthesis), in which the final synthesis would form the starting point (the new thesis) of further dialectical progression. Hegel discusses this idealized notion of dialectic in several places, including *Philosophy of History, Phenomenology of Spirit,* and *Logic* I will limit my discussion here to Hegel's *Logic* since there he elaborates his notion of dialectic in direct response to Kant (a move he does not make in any significant way in the other works). Hegel credits Kant with the modern resuscitation of dialectic (Hegel 1975, 117), but he believes Kant's application of the term is far too limited in scope. One of Hegel's central objections to Kant's critical idealism is its static formalism, or its lack of dynamic progression, and Kant's transcendental dialectic serves only to remove dialectical illusions (false knowledge claims that have the formal appearance of truths) from transcendent categories. But Hegel's interest in the progression of human consciousness through history leads him to a new sense of dialectic, one that becomes, for Hegel, the central method for philosophical inquiry and an inherent function of both object and subject. While Kant's notion of truth rests on correspondence between intuitions and thoughts, Hegel's notion of truth rests on a two-dimensional dialectical progression toward synthesis, a "totality of thought" (20).

Hegel identified Heraclitus as the origin of philosophy because Heraclitus recognized, first, that the infinite is in perpetual process (always changing, never conceptually coherent or consistent, as Kant wrongly assumed it was), and second, that the infinite is contradictory (Kant presumed that contradiction was an indication of illusion). According to Hegel, the process of the infinite is driven by the constant engagement of contradictory ideas, represented abstractly as thesis, antithesis (or contradiction), and synthesis, with the resulting synthesis becoming the next thesis in the eternal process. Hegel sees dialectic in everything: thought is dialectical (Hegel 1975, 15), history is dialectical (18–19), science is dialectical (116), nature is dialectical (118). Hegel writes, "Wherever there is movement, wherever there is life, wherever anything is carried into effect in the actual world, there Dialectic is at work" (116); in fact, "Everything that surrounds us may be viewed as an instance of Dialectic" (118). Dialectical methodology in philosophical inquiry, according to Hegel, requires the understanding, first of Being (the thesis), of essence, of what is presumed at any given time to be universal (though it is not). Once Being is understood in this finite sense, it begins to show signs of something more, beyond the limiting scope of definition and concept; it begins to show signs of contradiction and negation (the antithesis) in which "these finite characterizations or formulae supersede themselves, and pass into their opposites" (115). Synthesis, then, resolves contradictions and oppositions (such as Being/Nothingness) into new, more universal unities (such as Becoming). These new unities exist at a higher threshold of abstraction in which formerly opposed entities lose their sense of opposition; yet, until a single great synthesis is finally achieved, the fate of these new unities is always to become a thesis in the continuing dialectical progression of human consciousness. While Kant, as Hegel admits, resuscitates dialectic for modern philosophy, he does so in a limited way, assuming dialectic is merely the art of negative argumentation or the refutation of false claims. Hegel, instead, turns dialectic into a philosophical methodology, removing dialectic from the combative realm of argumentation (thus also removing it from logic) and inserting it into the synthesizing realm of historical progression toward truth and unity.[17]

Soon after Hegel's death in 1831, certain German scholars called the *Young Hegelians* (distinguishing themselves from the more conservative Old Hegelians) began reworking some of the ideas Hegel had elaborated, not the least of which was the notion of dialectic. In "Towards a Critique of Hegel's Philosophy," Ludwig Feuerbach (a founding member of the Young Hegelian movement) criticizes the Being-Nothingness-Becoming dialectic, described by Hegel in the *Logic*, as overly idealist and thus impotent. Ultimately rejecting Hegel's idealist version of philosophical dialectic as a "rational mysticism" (Feuerbach 1983b, 121), Feuerbach urges philosophers to unite their efforts with the objective natural sciences, thus "ground[ing] themselves in *nature*" (Feuerbach 1983a, 170–71). Feuerbach, an objective realist, prefers to examine "nature" as a source of truth: "The deepest secrets are to be found in the simplest natural things, but, pining away for the Beyond, the speculative fantast treads them under his feet. The only source of salvation lies in a return to nature" (Feuerbach 1983b, 127). Marx, also a Young Hegelian in his youth, partially accepted Hegel's critique of Kant, partially accepted Feuerbach's critique of Hegel, and launched his own attack on Feuerbach, arguing that he talks "too much about nature and too little about politics" (qtd. in Jakubowski 1976, 14).

Like Feuerbach, Marx and his colleague Friedrich Engels retained a keen interest in dialectical methodology, especially its two-dimensional sense of progression and contradiction, but they argued that it is not Spirit that drives the dialectic, as Hegel argued, nor is it nature, as Feuerbach argued. Rather, according to Marx and Engels (1976), the mode of production drives the dialectical interaction of material base and institutional superstructure, and each economic formation throughout history has contained the seeds of contradiction that have seen it ultimately fail and evolve dialectically into newer forms. This two-dimensional sense of dialectic would ultimately have a tremendous influence in the future of philosophy and economics, but it would have very little impact on the study and practice of rhetoric, and Marx and Engels themselves ignore the subject of rhetoric altogether. In the entire corpus of writing produced by Marx and Engels (literally tens of thousands of pages), there is little direct theoretical treatment of *language* and no discussion of *rhetoric*.[18] This omission of language and rhetoric from the writings of Marx and Engels is astonishing, at least to modern rhetoricians, given that Marx and Engels's political project was to predict and plan social revolution, two processes that simply cannot proceed without a critical sense of communication. The problem is that Marx and Engels most often viewed language as the expression of consciousness (or ideology) with no direct connection to material existence: "We do not set out," Marx and Engels write in *The German Ideology*, "from what [people] *say*, imagine, conceive, nor from [people] as *narrated*, thought of, imagined, conceived, in order to arrive at [people] in the flesh" (Marx and Engels 1976, 47). Beginning with language and its uses would be an idealist impulse, contrary to Marx and Engels's materialist values.

Rather than claiming language for their own purposes, Marx and Engels view language as having only a marginal role in historical struggles. The following passage from *The German Ideology* illustrates this view: "One of the most difficult tasks confronting philosophers is to descend from the world of thought to the actual world. *Language* is the immediate actuality of thought. . . . The problem of descending from the world of thoughts to the actual world is turned into the problem of descending from language to life" (Marx and Engels 1976, 446). For Marx and Engels, language is merely the expression of consciousness; yet it is not in consciousness but in material existence that meaningful revolutionary action must take place: "For the practical materialist, . . . it is a question of revolutionizing the existing world, of practically coming to grips with and changing the things found in existence" (38); and Marx writes, "The philosophers have only *interpreted* the world in various ways; the point, however, is to *change* it" (Marx 1976, 8). Here language is associated with interpretation, and material action is associated with change. For Marx and Engels, then, theorizing about language and its uses (i.e., rhetoric) amounts to playing with consciousness and not changing the world.

This philosophical trajectory of dialectic and rhetoric, then, resulted in the resuscitation of dialectic as a central methodology in philosophical inquiry, but in this process dialectic lost any connection it once had to rhetoric. Kant disparages rhetoric and elevates transcendental dialectic to the function of critiquing dialectical illusions. Hegel is largely ambivalent toward rhetoric, but recruits dialectic for his philosophical account of human progress. Marx and Engels associate language with ideology and thus view the arts of language as mystifications of real material conditions, yet, like Hegel, they recover dialectic for the philosophical project of explaining human progress. Throughout this philosophical trajectory, dialectic was recovered for various purposes without the simultaneous recovery of dialectic's historical counterpart, rhetoric.

The Rhetorical Trajectory of Dialectic and Rhetoric

The eighteenth century witnessed the development of three different approaches to the practice and teaching of rhetoric, and these three approaches constitute the rhetorical trajectory of dialectic and rhetoric at that time. First, the elocutionary approach, most fully represented in the various works of Sheridan, was concerned largely with delivery and correctness, including grammar, pronunciation, and intonation. Second, the epistemological approach, most fully represented in Campbell's *The Philosophy of Rhetoric*, retained and promoted certain interests of the Enlightenment, particularly its division of the human mind into faculties, including the understanding, the will, the imagination, and the passions, with rhetoric functioning differently in the attempt to influence each faculty. Third, the belletristic approach, most fully represented in Blair's (1970) three-volume *Lectures on Rhetoric and Belles Lettres*, offered "taste" as the guiding principle to the composition of beautiful writing and the discrimination of stylistic merits in literary discourse. In all three of these approaches, dialectic disappeared from rhetoric entirely, and only Campbell viewed logic as prior to rhetoric in function and importance.

The elocutionary movement in rhetoric arose during the eighteenth century in response to what was perceived as both dryness and incorrectness in the oratory of the time, and some elocutionists, such as Sheridan, associated that dryness with an overemphasis on logic and demonstration. Sheridan (1991; 1984a) wrote several works, all focusing on different aspects of the elocutionary movement, including *Lectures on the Art of Reading* (1775), which emphasizes correct pronunciation of letters, syllables, and words, and *A Complete Dictionary of the English Language* (1780), in which almost every word is limited to a single definition and is represented phonetically, thus regularizing both pronunciation and meaning. Sheridan's (1984b) best-known work, however, is the *Course of Lectures on Elocution*, published in 1762. In his introduction to the seven collected lectures, Sheridan critiques Locke for his reductive treatment of language. Specifically, according to Sheridan, Locke places far too much importance on human understanding, thus ignoring the passions and fancy, which govern our social lives.[19] Sheridan argues that Locke's approach to (especially written) language accounts for only half its role in the conduct of human affairs; written words and their definitions address only the understanding. The passions and the fancy, which Sheridan considers more critical to productive social engagement than the understanding, "have a language of their own, utterly independent of words" (Sheridan 1984b, x). Using dry written words to convince the

understanding is fine, but using the auditory senses associated with elocution to propagate good sense and suppress hurtful emotions is a "real
benefit" (xi–xii). In fact, most of humanity's attempts at social reform
since the classical age have failed, in Sheridan's view, since these reforms
have been articulated and promoted in writing, an instrument wholly
unsuited to the task since writing addresses only the understanding and
not the passions or fancy, and thus also not the will. For Sheridan, then,
elocution is not simply a matter of excellent delivery; it is prerequisite to
the very progress of human society.

Sheridan defines elocution as "the just and graceful management
of the voice, countenance, and gesture in speaking" (Sheridan 1984b,
19), whether one is engaged in oratory or reading aloud in public.[20]
And, later, Sheridan explains that delivery, the most fundamental skill
in the practice of elocution, includes "a distinct articulation of words,
pronounced in proper tones, suitably varied to the sense, and the
emotions of the mind; with due observation of accent; of emphasis, in
its several gradations; of rests or pauses of the voice, in proper places
and well measured degrees of time; and the whole accompanied with
expressive looks, and significant gestures" (10). And, since delivery is
so crucial a skill in elocution, most of the remaining lectures address
these individual aspects of delivery.[21] What is most interesting about
Sheridan is that he does not simply ignore reason and logic (though
he does ignore dialectic), as so many others had done in the history of
rhetoric; instead, Sheridan criticizes the obsession with reasoning and
the understanding, arguing that the dry language of empirical science
has gotten us nowhere. Elocution, or effective oral delivery, is the salvation of humanity. For Sheridan, logic and dialectic have no place in
the elocutionary movement.

During the late eighteenth century, Campbell also recovered the
study of rhetoric from its Enlightenment disparagement, yet, unlike
Sheridan, he retained, in the end, a certain devotion to empiricism in
the study of human nature. In 1776, Campbell published *The Philosophy
of Rhetoric*, which bases its rhetorical practice (in part, at least) on
Lock's Enlightenment psychology. Here Campbell (1963) argues that
the function of rhetoric is to adapt discourse to its purpose, addressing the audience's understanding, imagination, passion, and will (key
terms from Locke's [1975] *An Essay Concerning Human Understanding*),
and to persuade audiences toward right conduct and moral reasoning
regarding uncertain matters that require deliberation and judgment.
In the opening passage of *The Philosophy of Rhetoric*, Campbell writes,
"In speaking there is always some end proposed, or some effect which

the speaker intends to produce in the hearer. The word *eloquence* in its greatest latitude denotes, 'That art or talent by which the discourse is adapted to its end.' All the ends of speaking are reducible to four; every speech being intended to enlighten the understanding, to please the imagination, to move the passions, or to influence the will" (Campbell 1963, 1). Although Campbell was interested in recovering rhetoric from Locke's denigration of the art, he did not, in the process, abandon Enlightenment epistemological assumptions; he merged them with a new philosophy of rhetoric that could serve the ideological interests of the Enlightenment and also the practical interests of working clergy.[22]

According to Campbell, rhetoric emerges from the intersection of two "parent arts," logic and grammar (Campbell 1963, 35). Although related to logic and grammar, rhetoric is in no way an equal partner in the relationship: "If then it is the business of logic to evince the truth, to convince an auditory [audience], which is the province of eloquence, is but a particular application of the logician's art" (34). The soul of a discourse is its reasoning and thought, which are governed by the art of logic, and the function of logic is to make universal truth apparent "for the sake of information" (33). Logic develops true thought and precedes expression, which begins with the art of grammar. Grammar is concerned with purity of syntax, or "the composition of many words into one sentence" (35), whose purpose is the clear and correct representation of truth in language. Rhetoric is concerned with style, or "the composition of many sentences into one discourse" (35), whose purpose is to infuse the clear and correct representation of truth with "beauty and strength" (35). Of these three arts (logic, grammar, and rhetoric), rhetoric is sequentially last: "Where grammar ends eloquence begins" (35). Thus, logic generates truth, grammar states it clearly and correctly, and rhetoric makes it beautiful.

Interestingly, Campbell associates dialectic with Scholastic "syllogizing" (Campbell 1963, 61), and Campbell cites "Mr. Locke" as the inspiration for his own opinion that dialectic "serves more to display the ingenuity of the inventor, and to exercise the address and fluency of the learner, than to assist the diligent inquirer in his researches after truth" (62). This "scholastic art of disputation" (70) is useless in the moral and natural sciences and is rejected in the mathematical sciences. According to Campbell, the art of dialectic, which at one time conferred glory on the scholar as a successful joust conferred glory on a knight, "is now almost forgotten" (62). And Campbell sees no good reason to resuscitate this dead discipline "as eloquence seems to have been very little benefitted by it, and philosophy still less" (62). In fact, dialectic encourages two common faults (Campbell calls them "evils"), including the constant impulse to challenge even the most self-evident truths and the tendency to whip up clouds of words that prevent us from "discerning that we are moving in a circle all the time" (62). In the opening passage of his treatment of dialectic, Campbell explains that he only addresses the subject because it "might appear strange" to be silent on the matter; it is clear, however, that Campbell sees little use for dialectic in logic, grammar, or rhetoric, and he even identifies some dangers in its application.

Soon after Campbell's *The Philosophy of Rhetoric* was released, Blair published *Lectures on Rhetoric and Belles Lettres* (1783), a three-volume tour de force of the belletristic movement, connecting rhetoric to the production of beautiful compositions and the appreciation of literary texts. In the introduction to *Lectures on Rhetoric and Belles Lettres* (i.e., Lecture I), Blair explains the twofold purpose of his text, to provide guidelines for the production of compositions that exhibit stylistic acuteness and to provide methods for the discrimination of merits among the best authors. Both production and discrimination are governed by taste (Blair 1970, 1:10–11, 19). While Campbell felt at least some responsibility to mention dialectic, even if only to criticize it, Blair feels no such obligation; and while Campbell made rhetoric the child of logic and grammar, Blair accords to rhetoric a much more powerful role in thought itself. In most accounts of the relationship between rhetoric and logic (or dialectic), including Campbell's, logic is methodologically prior to rhetoric, but Blair does not entirely agree. Although he was an influential figure in the development of belletristic rhetoric, which is usually concerned more with style than with thought, Blair also believed rhetoric had the power to sharpen and refine knowledge. It is true that any great rhetorician must be acquainted with all of the liberal arts "to lay in a rich store of ideas relating to those subjects of which the occasions of life may call them to discourse or to write" (1:5). Yet it is also true that the "study of eloquence and composition" merits intellectual attention because "it is intimately connected with the improvement of our intellectual powers" (1:8).

When we write, Blair explains, we are not simply recording thoughts from our minds; we are "cultivating reason itself" (Blair 1970, 1:8). In "Lecture I," Blair writes, "True rhetoric and sound logic are very nearly allied. The study of arranging and expressing our thoughts with propriety, teaches us to think, as well as to speak, accurately" (1:8). And later, in "Lecture XII: Structure of Sentences," Blair justifies his lengthy discussion of a rather tedious subject with another appeal to the interconnection of rhetoric and logic: "Thought and Language act and re-act upon each other mutually. Logic and Rhetoric have here, as in many other cases, a strict connection; and he that is learning to arrange his Sentences with accuracy and order, is learning, at the same time, to think with accuracy and order" (1:312). Yet while Campbell and his predecessors had relatively clear ideas about what constitutes logic (and, in some cases, dialectic), Blair does not. Rhetoric is epistemic, it seems, but only in relation to a vague methodology called "logic" and to a vague collection of disciplines called the "liberal arts." While Blair's first lecture outlines a theory and practice of rhetoric that relies on knowledge but also strengthens understanding and hones reasoning, the rest of the lectures (save the last two sentences of "Lecture XII," quoted above) address topics one would expect from an elocutionist, including taste, beauty, sublimity, correctness, style, kinds of public speaking, parts of discourse, delivery, and different kinds of writing (historical, philosophical, poetic, and dramatic).

Dialectic and Rhetoric in the Nineteenth Century

Perhaps frustrated by the disconnection of logic and rhetoric (as in the elocutionary and belletristic movements) or the empirical bent that logic had acquired in relation to rhetoric (as in the epistemological approach), Whately made a concerted effort early in the nineteenth century to rehabilitate Aristotelian logic in the service of reasoning and argumentation in his 1826 *Elements of Logic* (see McKerrow 1987). Further, while Whately integrated some of the concerns of the three movements of eighteenth-century rhetoric in his 1828 *Elements of Rhetoric*, he primarily turned to Aristotle for inspiration. Whately wrote both treatises as textbooks, and both texts were used extensively in schools throughout Europe and the United States.

Whately's (2008) *Elements of Logic* recovered one-dimensional logical reasoning from Locke's critique, suggesting that one cause for the fall of logic had been its overblown claim to be everything to all people: "On the utility of Logic many writers have said much in which I cannot coincide, and which has tended to bring the study into unmerited disrepute. By representing Logic as furnishing the sole instrument for the discovery of truth in all subjects, and as teaching the use of the intellectual faculties in general, they raised expectations which could not be realized, and which naturally led to a re-action. The whole system, whose unfounded pretensions had been thus blazoned forth, has come to be commonly regarded as utterly futile and empty" (6). Whately believes one-dimensional logic is an important way to demonstrate the truth or falsity of propositional claims, but it is certainly not a means to discover truth or arrange arguments. This is the province of the various arts and sciences, including, of course, rhetoric. Logic, according to Whately, focuses on three primary operations of the mind: apprehension, judgment, and reasoning. Whately writes, "An act of *apprehension* expressed in language, is called a *term*; an act of *judgment*, a *proposition*; an act of *reasoning*, an *argument* (which, when regularly expressed, is a syllogism)" (69). While many have described only the final operation of the mind as the sole province of logic, Whately believes logic addresses all three equally. However, it is also true that the syllogism, which is part of reasoning alone, is the fundamental structure of logic generally.

In *Elements of Rhetoric*, Whately (1963) draws heavily from Aristotle to develop his theory of persuasion based on probability, audience, and (like Campbell) moral reasoning. In the preface, Whately argues that logic (there is no mention of dialectic) is important, though not absolutely necessary, for the study and practice of rhetoric: "Several passages will be found in the following pages which presuppose some acquaintance with Logic; but the greatest part, will, I trust, be intelligible to those who have not this knowledge. At the same time, it is implied by what I have said of that Science, and indeed by the very circumstance of my having written on it, that I cannot but consider him as undertaking a task of unnecessary difficulty, who endeavours, without studying Logic, to become a thoroughly good argumentative writer" (xli). Interestingly, whereas Ramus (2010) considered invention and arrangement to be the sole province of logic since it is inefficient for more than one art to claim those functions, Whately turns the tables on this formulation (though he never mentions Ramus). For Whately, it is "the business of Logic . . . to *judge* of arguments, not to *invent* them" (40). Logic, then, is the formal means to judge arguments, but rhetoric is the art of discovering and arranging arguments. Whately writes, "The finding of suitable arguments to prove a given point, and the skillful arrangement of them, may be considered as the immediate and proper province of Rhetoric, and of that alone" (39); later, Whately writes, "The art of inventing and arranging Arguments is . . . the only province that Rhetoric can claim entirely and exclusively" (40). This restructuring of logic and rhetoric was a radical move for the time, and it was also a clear return to the classical view that rhetoric is epistemic.

Whately divides the art of rhetoric into appeals to the understanding producing conviction (or what we would now call *argumentation*) and appeals to the will producing persuasion. Part 1 of *Elements of Rhetoric*,

on argumentation, concerns the invention and arrangement of propositions and arguments. A proposition is a claim we offer as true, though it
may be considered by others to be in doubt; an argument is the evidence
we provide in support of a proposition. Arguments are divided according to their form (regular, irregular), subject matter (necessary, probable), intention (direct, indirect), and "the relation of the subject-matter
of the premises to that of the conclusion" (sign, induction) (Whately
1963, 45). Many of the kinds of arguments discussed by Whately are
immediately recognizable as *topoi* from Aristotle's *Rhetoric*. While many
consider persuasion alone to be the sole province of rhetoric, Whately
argues that persuasion, or the influencing to the will to action (the subject of part 2 of *Elements of Rhetoric*), is not possible without conviction
first; so, for Whately, the entire art of persuasion rests, first, on successful
argumentation and, thus, on conviction (175–76). While argumentation
relies on propositions and arguments to secure conviction, persuasion
relies on appeals to the passions to secure the will to act, yet only moral
motives are acceptable (177–79).[23]

In the philosophical trajectory of dialectic and rhetoric, while Kant,
Hegel, and Marx and Engels were interested in dialectic, rhetoric had
fallen out of the picture, especially in Marx and Engels's writings since
they associated language with ideology. And in the rhetorical trajectory of dialectic and rhetoric, while Campbell, Blair, and Whately (but
not Sheridan) were interested in reasoning and/or logic, dialectic (in
Sheridan, too) had fallen completely out of the vocabulary of the verbal
arts that had once made up the classical *trivium*. Nevertheless, despite
rhetoric's disconnection from its classical counterpart dialectic, and due
to the powerful influence of Wilson, Campbell, Blair, and Whately, rhetoric had returned during the eighteenth and nineteenth centuries to a
prominent place in the school curriculum since most universities at the
time were in the business of preparing civic leaders for communication-
intensive careers. Whately's (1963) *Elements of Rhetoric* and abridged versions of Blair's (1970) *Lectures on Rhetoric*, in particular, were used in the
first-year communication classes that emerged in English departments
shortly before the turn of the century.

Although dialectic and rhetoric have both faded in and out of favor
and in and out of relation, the fact is that both have been consistent subjects of liberal education throughout much of Western history. In early
English departments, however, it was only rhetoric (not dialectic) that
was recovered in the service of composition studies; dialectic would have
to wait until the 1970s to be reunited with its counterpart, rhetoric. In

the next chapter, I pick up where this chapter leaves off, in the late nineteenth century; there I describe dialectic's relationship to the emerging discipline of rhetoric and composition. Finally, I rebut certain challenges to dialectic from recent movements in rhetoric and composition studies, namely sub/versive historiography, affirmative invention, and complexity theory.

Notes

1. Frans H. van Eemeren and Peter Houtlosser agree, stating that "the perceptions and descriptions of the two perspectives [dialectical and rhetorical] vary considerably over time. The same applies even more strongly to their mutual relationship and the way in which the one perspective may be subordinated to, combined with, or even integrated in, the other" (van Eemeren and Houtlosser 2002, 3).

2. David M. Timmerman (1993) argues that Plato systematized informal sophistic *dialegesthai* into what we now know as dialectic, coining the term *dialektikē* in the process.

3. In his edition of Aristotle's *Rhetoric*, George A. Kennedy leaves *antistrophos* untranslated. Kennedy explains in a footnote that "counterpart" is the most common translation, but he also offers a few other options (Aristotle 1991, 28–29).

4. For a detailed discussion of rhetoric and dialectic as counterparts in Aristotle, see Jacques Brunschwig (1996), L. D. Green (1990), Hamner H. Hill and Michael Kagan (1995), and Brad McAdon (2001). Emile Janssens (1968) discusses the transitions in the meaning of dialectic from its oral form in Homer (*dialegesthai*) to its philosophical form in Plato and Aristotle (*dialektikē*).

5. Sara Rubinelli (2006) outlines several different functions of topics in Aristotle and Cicero.

6. So frustrated was Cicero at the political and civil oppression of imperial Rome that he wrote a series of speeches against Antony (one of the triumvirate Emperors) and in favor of a return to Republican government in Rome. In 43 BCE, Plutarch (1932) explains, Cicero was executed for his anti-imperialist views and for airing them so publicly. For modern commentary on these events, see Elizabeth Rawson (1975, 278–98).

7. For a discussion of Augustine's relationship to both rhetoric and Christianity, see Kathy Eden (1990).

8. Recall that Aristotle's rhetorical question is should Athens go to war with Sparta? and his dialectical question is should Athens go to war with Sparta, *or not?*

9. See Beth S. Bennett (1991) for a discussion of Capella's rhetoric in relation to late Roman satire.

10. For a more detailed discussion of the Islamic influence on the rediscovery of classical knowledge during the Middle Ages, see F. E. Peters (1968) and Richard E. Rubenstein (2003). Also, Tuomo Aho and Mikko Yrjönsuuri (2009) and Eleonore Stump (1983; 1989) discuss the evolution of one-dimensional logic and dialectic during this time, though they emphasize European influences.

11. Ernesto Grassi (2001) engages in a modern recovery of Renaissance humanism in relation to the first principles (or *archai*) of philosophy and logic.

12. Lois Agnew (1998) discusses Wilson's conception of rhetorical style in relation to Ciceronian ethos.

13. For a more detailed treatment of Bacon's theory and practice of rhetoric, see Vickers (1996) and John C. Briggs (1989).

14. David L. Vancil (1979) explains that Locke's (and Hume's) rejection of dialectic, rhetoric, and logic had a strong influence on the denigration of topical invention generally. This influence would hold firm until at least the nineteenth century.

15. For a more detailed discussion of Kant's critique of rhetoric, see Don Paul Abbott (2007) and Robert J. Dostal (1980).

16. In *Critique of Pure Reason*, Kant largely rejects empiricism, especially what he calls Locke's "*physiology* of human understanding" (Kant 1965, 8), in favor of understanding "reason in general in respect of all knowledge after which it may strive *independently of all experience*" (9).

17. In "Hegelian Rhetoric," Thora Ilin Bayer (2009) points out that Hegel himself ignores the subject of rhetoric throughout his works. Nevertheless, it is evident that Hegel studied rhetoric in his youth, and he clearly uses identifiable rhetorical strategies, especially in the *Phenomenology*.

18. In 1841, Marx received a PhD in classical Greek philosophy from Berlin University, and, interestingly, we know from an 1837 letter to his father that Marx (then only nineteen years old) had both read and translated parts of Aristotle's *Rhetoric* (Marx 1979). But nowhere (in the letter or in anything else Marx subsequently wrote) is there any further discussion of this text or of rhetoric in general.

19. Another criticism Sheridan launches against Locke concerns Locke's obsession with constant definition and attention to diction. Instead of focusing on diction and definition after language has developed in ambiguous ways, as Locke proposed, Sheridan argues that schools should teach children from birth "the specific meaning of all the words they use" (Sheridan 1984b, viii). If teachers did their jobs properly, words would not develop ambiguous meanings and Locke's appeal to definition would be needless. Since Locke's discussion of the problem of language remains only theoretical and does not address practical education, Sheridan argues that Locke's "noble Essay on the Human Understanding, has hitherto proved of little benefit to the world" (ix).

20. Oratory and reading aloud are actually closely aligned arts in Sheridan's works. See M. Wade Mahon (2001) for a more detailed discussion.

21. "Lecture II: addresses articulation and pronunciation, "Lecture III" addresses accent, "Lecture IV" addresses emphasis, "Lecture V" addresses pauses and stops, "Lecture VI" addresses tone, and "Lecture VII" addresses gesture.

22. In *George Campbell*, Arthur E. Walzer (2003) discusses Campbell's rhetoric in relationship to the Enlightenment and to Campbell's own religious views.

23. Part 3 of the *Elements of Rhetoric* treats style in a rather perfunctory way, valuing perspicuity, energy, and elegance over all other virtues; and part 4 treats elocution in a way that appears closely aligned with Sheridan's treatment of the subject (and, in fact, Whately mentions Sheridan's lectures on reading aloud). These final two sections, relatively brief and unoriginal, appear to be mere nods in the direction of rhetorical traditions that had become popular during the eighteenth century.

2

DIALECTIC IN (AND OUT OF) RHETORIC AND COMPOSITION

What we now know as the discipline of English emerged during the late nineteenth century in the fertile ground of German-style research universities that were rapidly being established throughout the United States with money and land granted through the Morrill Act of 1862. At these new state universities, the existing discipline of rhetoric and oratory merged with new academic interests in literary studies, philology, and written composition, forming the first modern departments of English. During this transitional period in the late nineteenth century, two shifts in particular occurred that caused teachers of rhetoric and oratory to question English as their disciplinary home. First, increasing enrollments at traditional colleges and a new population of underprepared students at land-grant colleges caused some educators to recognize a literacy crisis, creating the need to establish a first-year course that would teach students the basic speaking and writing skills necessary for success in college.[1] Second, a shift from spoken rhetoric to written composition in these classes caused the workload of their instructors to increase exponentially since class sizes were often not limited and themes were written at least weekly and sometimes daily.[2] Once the most prized teaching assignments in nineteenth-century universities, capstone courses in rhetoric and oratory, by the turn of the century, had become entry-level, remedial classes in written composition.[3]

After the turn of the century, speech educators found little support for upper-level courses in rhetoric and oratory since their subject had been relegated to the first year and reduced to remediation, and since this required first-year course now emphasized writing, not speech. Secession from English was nothing new (philology had already begun that process), and the secession of speech from English would give rhetoric and oratory the chance to be revitalized as a serious academic discipline with a significant research agenda. The formation of the National Association of Academic Teachers of Public Speaking in 1914, and the subsequent gradual secession of speech communication from English,

DOI: 10.7330/9780874219821.c002

enabled new departments of speech to develop their own first-year general-education course in communication, their own undergraduate majors in journalism and mass media (among other related subjects), and their own graduate degrees. The first PhD program in mass communication studies was established at the University of Iowa in 1943 by Wilbur Schramm, who, interestingly, had his own PhD in English literature (Rogers 1994, 1). Soon other PhD programs would follow, training a core of committed scholars and teachers to develop further courses and programs in communication studies and to advance the disciplinary status of speech communication through scholarly publication.

This eventual secession of speech from English created a number of academic problems that would hurt composition studies as a discipline. Newly formed departments of speech communication retained not only specialized responsibility for teaching oral communication but also specialized responsibility for academic research on the rhetorical tradition and its relation to dialectic, developing a neo-Aristotelian model in which dialectic was the methodology associated with argumentation and rhetoric was the methodology associated with persuasion. During the years between its inaugural issue in 1914 and 1940, the *Quarterly Journal of Speech* published numerous articles on the classical tradition of rhetorical theory (especially about Plato, Aristotle, Cicero, and Quintilian, among other figures), many more relating rhetoric to other academic themes (including psychology, logic, information theory, and business), and several articles connecting dialectic (usually in conjunction with its counterpart rhetoric) to specific methods of argumentation, including legal cross-examination, academic debate, formal logic, and informal discussion. The inaugural issue of *Speech Monographs*, published in 1934, includes an article on the controversy between classical rhetoric and dialectic. Articles about the rhetorical tradition and its connection to dialectic have always filled the pages of journals published in communication studies.

Although there is evidence from the earliest issues of *College Composition and Communication* that interest in the rhetorical tradition had not entirely vanished from composition studies after 1914, it is true that those who published on composition and its pedagogical applications tended to ignore dialectic and rhetoric in favor of grammar, modes, and five-paragraph themes.[4] John C. Brereton explains that, during this transitional period following the gradual secession of speech from English, composition studies lost its "saturation in a rhetorical tradition of some two thousand years" and replaced it with a "streamlined curriculum" that "emphasized error correction and the five modes of discourse" (Brereton 1995, 17). In the report of a survey conducted from 1927 to 1928, Warner Taylor (1929) explains that composition in the nineteenth century was grounded in rhetorical instruction, using traditional textbooks by George Campbell, Hugh Blair, and Richard Whately. (Recall, however, that Campbell, Blair, and Whately all had impoverished understandings of dialectic and its relationship to rhetoric.) Nevertheless, by the 1920s, these traditional rhetorics had been replaced by new "rhetorics" (in name only) emphasizing grammar and volumes of model essays to be imitated. While in communication studies, argumentation (and dialectic, which was considered a branch of argumentation) was a main focus in speech education, Taylor points out that in composition, as of 1928, argumentation was being taught less frequently than it was even at the end of World War I. From the secession of speech beginning in 1914 until the revitalization of composition as a serious academic discipline in the 1960s and 1970s, the teaching of writing centered around grammar, modes, and five-paragraph themes, and the dominance of these subjects was perpetuated by a booming textbook industry driven by a market audience of graduate students and adjuncts trained in literature.

While speech communication was establishing scholarly journals and PhD programs throughout the first half of the twentieth century, no such development in composition studies emerged until the late 1960s and early 1970s, with the exception of *College Composition and Communication*, which published its first issue in 1950. Two journals that published scholarship on the rhetorical tradition by rhetoric and composition specialists had roots in the late 1960s but developed interdisciplinary followings in the 1970s. *Philosophy and Rhetoric* published its first issue in 1968, and although the first issue of the *Rhetoric Society Newsletter* was also published in 1968, this issue contained only the constitution of the Rhetoric Society of America (RSA), which called for the distinctly interdisciplinary theory and practice of rhetoric. The first issue to contain any content about rhetorical theory or practice did not appear until 1972. In 1976, the *Rhetoric Society Newsletter* became a full-fledged journal and the RSA board changed the name to the *Rhetoric Society Quarterly*. Relatively short articles on composition theory and practice were published in *Freshman English News* (*FEN*) from its first issue in 1972 through 1991, when *FEN* became the full-fledged journal we now know as *Composition Studies*.[5] With increasing interest in scholarship on rhetoric and composition came an opportunity to establish PhD programs in the discipline, and this process began in the 1970s (Connors 1991, 55; Lauer 2004, 110).[6]

Before the 1970s, undergraduate composition programs were directed (often reluctantly) by scholars trained in literature or education, and first-year writing courses were taught by graduate students and adjuncts, also trained in literature. Most of the first PhD programs in rhetoric and composition were also administered and taught by scholars trained in literature or education but whose true passion was the emerging field of rhetoric and composition (see Bizzaro 1999). For many of those early scholars, doctorates in literature or education were merely the necessary means to ends associated with their first love, composition studies. These early programs would soon produce new scholars whose graduate training was rhetoric and composition (not literature), lending renewed credibility to quickly emerging rhetoric and composition PhD programs and advanced writing courses. During the early 1980s, many new journals published their first issues (*Journal of Advanced Composition,* 1980; *Pre/Text,* 1980; *Writing Center Journal,* 1980; *The Writing Instructor,* 1981; *Journal of Teaching Writing,* 1982; *Rhetoric Review,* 1982; *Computers and Composition,* 1983; *Rhetorica,* 1983; *Written Communication,* 1984), providing numerous credible venues for the scholarship in rhetoric and composition that was being produced by emerging specialists in the discipline.

During the 1960s and early 1970s, in addition to the establishment of PhD programs and new specialized journals, other developments would continue to change the face of composition studies. As Robert J. Connors explains, "The years between 1963 and 1969 saw an explosion of theoretical work in rhetoric and composition that was almost unprecedented. In these six years, many of the most important works of such New Rhetoricians as Rohman, Pike, Corbett, Christensen, Larson, Hunt, Rogers, and others were published" (Connors 1997, 105). Yet even as early as the 1970s, Ann E. Berthoff pointed out that the New Rhetoricians were more interested in taxonomies of discourses and rigid heuristics than they were in "conceptions of meaning" (Berthoff 1981, 97).[7] Drawing theoretical grounding from psycholinguistics, many of the New Rhetoricians, Berthoff explains, "have no notion of the dialectic of particularizing and generalizing, of exemplifying and classifying, of naming and interpreting" (101), "of sorting and gathering, . . . of language and thought" (105), of "parts and wholes, form and function, order and accidents, beginnings and ends" (105). Berthoff writes, "What is missing in psycholinguistics and in the various new rhetorics that take guidance from cognitive scientists is a philosophical understanding of the making of meaning" (101), which, Berthoff argues throughout her work, is inherently dialectical.

Even those early New Rhetoricians who grounded their theories and methods in classical rhetoric (not psychology or linguistics) reconnected composition to the rhetorical tradition outside of any significant relation to dialectic. In 1965, Edward P. J. Corbett (1965) published the first edition of his landmark *Classical Rhetoric for the Modern Student.* Although this volume was published and often used as a composition textbook, it also served as a guide to the discipline of composition as a whole, a way for writing teachers to emerge out of the deadening formalism that had characterized composition since the secession of speech.[8] The thrust of Corbett's *Classical Rhetoric for the Modern Student* is strictly rhetorical, with dialectic mentioned only once—in Corbett's analysis of Socrates's rhetoric in Plato's *Apology.* Here dialectic refers only to Socratic "question-and-answer style" (227). Even James L. Kinneavy's wide-ranging *A Theory of Discourse,* first published in 1971, promotes an Aristotelian model of rhetoric (and cites Corbett on several occasions) despite its additional incorporation of twentieth-century discourse theories such as semiotics. While Kinneavy (1971) mentions dialectic a few more times than Corbett does, it is clear that the thrust of *A Theory of Discourse* is rhetorical and not dialectical.

While *dialectic* remained a key term in relation to rhetoric in communication studies, throughout the 1960s and early 1970s the rhetorical tradition was being recovered as a subject of academic research in rhetoric and composition without an understanding of dialectic as the counterpart of rhetoric. During the late 1970s and throughout the 1980s, however, rhetoric and composition specialists regained some interest in *dialectic,* invoking the term in three different senses: as dialogic interaction, as the methodical expansion of perspectives, and as the dynamic progression of human history. By the 1990s, this brief interest in dialectic had waned (Low 1997), and from the late 1990s through the first decade of the new millennium, dialectic was the subject of critique from at least three different perspectives, including sub/versive historiography, affirmative invention, and complexity theory.

DIALECTIC IN RHETORIC AND COMPOSITION

In early rhetoric and composition scholarship, the recovery of dialectic lagged well behind the recovery of the rhetorical tradition; and when dialectic was invoked as a key concept, it often took on only a vague meaning. The earliest treatments of *dialectic* specifically in composition studies came during the 1970s, not in discussions of legal argumentation, informal logic, or the philosophy of language (as they did in communication studies), but instead in brief discussions of writing pedagogy. These early uses of the term tended to reduce dialectic from its traditionally rich rhetorical and philosophical meanings to a rather simple sense of interaction or a vague sense of relationship.[9] However, by the late 1970s and early 1980s, the term *dialectic* had begun to appear more frequently in rhetoric and composition scholarship; it had also begun to acquire more specific meanings derived mainly from the work of modern critics who were influenced by classical sources. During this furtive time, three traditions emerged involving the use of dialectic in rhetoric and composition. In the first tradition, dialectic is viewed as dialogic interaction, with Plato and I. A. Richards invoked as inspiration. In the second tradition, dialectic is viewed as the methodical expansion of perspectives, with Aristotle and Burke invoked as inspiration. In the third tradition, dialectic is viewed as a model for the progression of human history in which opposing forces influence each other over time and in specific contexts, with Hegel, Marx, and a variety of modern Marxists invoked as inspiration.

Dialogic Interaction

The dialogic model of dialectic is historically grounded in Plato's conversational (question-answer) method for revealing error in, and removing error from, philosophical propositions. In the *Phaedrus*, Plato describes the method of dialectic as questions and answers leading to a recursive process of definition and partition (Plato 1961b, sec. 259–79). Once dialectical truths are reached, that is, there can be no further partition of the subject and each definition is exact; then, Plato explains in the *Republic*, all interlocutors involved in the conversation will be able to recount the origins of each truth and the process by which it was revealed (Plato 1961c, sec. 532–33). During the twentieth century, this Platonic sense of dialogic dialectic was developed most fully by Richards and Berthoff. Ultimately, Berthoff's dialogic dialectic lost influence in composition because the theoretical inspiration for dialogue in rhetoric and composition shifted from Plato to Mikhail Bakhtin, and the theoretical inspiration for dialectic shifted from Plato to Georg Wilhelm Friedrich Hegel and Karl Marx. In chapter 4, I suggest that there are good reasons to reconnect dialogic discourse to its classical function as a form of dialectic (though I do not return to Plato as a source of inspiration).

Berthoff was the first scholar in rhetoric and composition to use *dialectic* as a key term throughout most of her work (i.e., in more than just one

or two articles). During the late 1970s and early 1980s, Berthoff explored
the uses of dialectic not just as a method of invention for rhetoric but as a
means to more structured and productive thought, which is the foundation of all writing. In both *The Making of Meaning* and *Forming/Thinking/
Writing*, Berthoff takes her definition of dialectic from Richards, who
calls it "the continuing audit of meaning" (qtd. in Berthoff 1982, 47;
1981, 42, 51, 77), or self-reflective thought, metacognition.[10]

In *The Making of Meaning*, Berthoff offers a dialectical vision of writing and composition instruction to counter the (then) current practices
of teaching grammar, linear writing processes, modes, tagmemic heuristics, and even problem solving (specifically the nondialectical transformation of writer-based prose into reader-based prose [Berthoff 1981,
11]). Writing, Berthoff insists, must be "understood as a non-linear, dialectical process in which the writer continually circles back, reviewing
and rewriting" (3), and this nonlinear, dialectical process is inherently
dialogic: "*Dialogue* and *dialectic* are cognate" (75).

Although there are a few times Berthoff understands this dialectical
dialogue as a two-dimensional exchange between writer and audience
(Berthoff 1981, 72), the dialogue is usually presented by Berthoff as
internal (thus one dimensional), as the writer struggling to create and
audit meaning. According to Berthoff, "Some experienced writers can
keep track of what they are saying in that interior dialogue and thus can
audit their meanings in their heads, but students with learning and language difficulties should write it down, continually. In that way they can
learn to recognize the interior dialogue and keep the dialectic going"
(77). For Berthoff, one-dimensional dialectic offers the advantage of
self-conscious knowledge, or metacognition. Dialectic, she writes, "is
characteristic of all critical study of language: interpreting our interpretations, thinking about thinking, arranging our techniques for arranging, knowing our knowledge" (4). In fact, the very act of making meaning itself is inherently dynamic and dialectical, not linear (12, 43), and
dialectic is the heart of method itself, or the relationship between knowing *that*, knowing *why*, and knowing *how* (51).

Berthoff's best-known contribution to a dialectical pedagogy for writing instruction is what she calls the double-entry or dialectical notebook.
Berthoff describes the dialectical notebook as a critical and productive
strategy for making the dialectical character of meaning overt. In *The
Making of Meaning*, Berthoff writes,

> I ask my students (all of them: freshmen, upperclassmen, teachers in grad-
> uate seminars) to furnish themselves with a notebook, spiral-bound at the
> side, small enough to be easily carried around but not so small that writing

is cramped. . . . What makes this notebook different from most, perhaps, is the notion of the double-entry: on the right side, reading notes, direct quotations, observational notes, fragments, lists, images—verbal and visual—are recorded; on the other (facing) side, notes about those notes, summaries, formulations, aphorisms, editorial suggestions, revisions, comment on comment are written. The reason for the double-entry format is that it provides a way for the student to conduct that "continuing audit of meaning" that is at the heart of learning to read and write critically. The facing pages are in dialogue with one another. The double-entry notebook is for all kinds of writing, creative or critical; any assignment you can think up can be adapted so that it can teach dialectic, another name for the continuing audit. (Berthoff 1981, 45)

The audit of meaning that emerges from the dialectical notebook begins the process of forming, or giving complex structure to thought itself (form emerges from chaos). The metacognition found in the dialectical notebook represents a crucial stage in the writing process in which students realize "intention and structure are dialectically related" (Berthoff 1981, 103). In *Forming/Thinking/Writing*, Berthoff asks composition students to apply the dialectical notebook as a method for exploring a series of relationships, including listing and classifying, naming and defining, and generalizing and interpreting. While many of the exercises described throughout *Forming/Thinking/ Writing* appear on the surface to be relatively simplistic, at least by more modern standards, Berthoff's double-entry notebook is complex; however, it was generally not as influential as it should have been in composition through the 1980s.

Ultimately, little happened during the 1980s to advance the work Berthoff had done on the subject of dialectic and the method of the dialectical notebook. In the mid-1980s, Michael Allen (1986) critiqued Berthoff's dialectical notebook as an epistemologically limited method for developing a writer's thoughts. So Allen added the rhetorical constraint of audience, requiring students to bring their dialectical notebooks to class and have their classmates write interpretive observations on the left-hand page. Although I appreciate Allen's application of audience to the dialectical notebook, making it more two dimensional, I am also struck by the fact that Allen missed Berthoff's own mention of this possibility. A year or two later, Kate Ronald (1989) and Hephzibah Roskelly (1988) each explored the dialectic of chaos and form (a theme prevalent throughout Berthoff's own work) in relation to the dialectical notebook, with Ronald illustrating the technique using student writing. Yet these essays are just extensions of Berthoff's work, illustrating or elaborating it.

During the late 1980s, interest in dialogic rhetorics reemerged in composition studies as a component of social-epistemic rhetoric. While Berthoff based her (mostly) individualist theory of dialogic dialectic on Plato and Richards, social-epistemic scholars were basing their social theories of dialogic rhetoric on Bakhtin. For Bakhtin scholars, dialogue was a social-epistemological phenomenon that had no need for individualist dialectics. So Bakhtinian rhetorics, based on a theory of social dialogue, were being developed without any connection of dialogue to dialectic, leaving Berthoff's work to languish in social-epistemic rhetoric's rejection of individualist epistemologies (internal dialogue) and the rhetorical strategies based on them (the dialectical notebook).

Despite Bakhtin's (1981) own claim that rhetoric is a monologic discourse, as opposed to the dialogic discourse of, for example, the novel, Charles I. Schuster (1985) recovered Bakhtin's dialogics for a social theory of rhetoric, particularly relating Bakhtin to new social conceptions of style (but not to dialectic). John Trimbur (1987) wrested the notion of "inner speech" away from individualists like James Moffett (1985), who argued that we should use meditation to liberate our inner speech, by relating the social polyphony inherent in all language to the flow of inner speech (but not to dialectic). John R. Edlund (1988) related Bakhtin's notion of "assimilation" to the social theory of language acquisition (but not to dialectic). The 1990s and early 2000s saw many dozens more scholars relating Bakhtin to the general movement of social-epistemic rhetoric, but none related Bakhtin's dialogics to dialectic in any significant way. Both Frank Farmer (2005) and Kurt Spellmeyer (1993) discussed dialectic briefly in relation to Bakhtin's dialogics, yet this is the dialectic of nineteenth-century philosophy, not the dialectic that is the counterpart of rhetoric. In chapter 4, however, I argue that Bakhtinian dialogics can be a useful strategy in the hybrid art of dialectical rhetoric, and I invoke Farmer again in that context.

The Methodical Expansion of Perspectives

In what is perhaps the most recognizable sentence in all of rhetorical theory, Aristotle begins his *Rhetoric* thus: "Rhetoric is the *antistrophos* of dialectic" (Aristotle 1991, sec. 1354a). Although *antistrophos* is usually translated "counterpart," its exact meaning remains unclear. However, one thing is certain: Aristotle views dialectic as the methodical (syllogistic) spinning out of argumentative possibilities, usually in two-dimensional pro/con or oppositional structures (answering the question, for example, should Athens go to war with Sparta, or not?). Once fully elaborated, arguments may then be evaluated for logical strength and internal coherence by the speaker, who arrives eventually at the most reasonable and advantageous opinion possible. However, with an audience of only one or two, even the best dialectical deductions will have no practical effect if the opinions generated through syllogistic reasoning are not brought to a larger audience by means of rhetoric. Whereas dialectic's function is to explore multiple sides of a controversial issue, rhetoric's function is to take up the strongest position and make a convincing case. The worst mistakes one can make in rhetoric—defending a weak proposition without understanding its structural fissures, or weaving a complicated argument without recognizing contradictions inherent in its claims—stem from a lack of dialectical argumentation. During the 1970s and 1980s, certain composition specialists began to recover this Aristotelian sense of dialectic through Burke, whose work was heavily influence by Aristotelian rhetorical traditions. These composition specialists used Aristotelian and Burkean dialectic as a means to expand a writer's perspectives prior to the composition of rhetorical discourse.[11]

In "Burke for the Composition Classroom," Philip M. Keith (1977) adapts Burke's dialectical methods as models for writing exercises. Keith's "dialectical exercises" teach composition students to "develop an argument and avoid the simplifications that the methods of the standard handbooks force on them in the name of clarity and control" (348). These Burkean dialectical strategies encourage students to explore etymology, question their commitment to a thesis, complicate what appears simple, expand the circumference of ideas through opposition and synthesis, and translate ideas from abstract to concrete and concrete to abstract (349–51). For Keith, dialectic is not most productively viewed as a structuring principle or pattern but is instead "an inventional procedure for discovering subjects" (348). The traditional (i.e., composition-textbook) drive for clarity and control requires students to reign in their thought processes, limiting the potential for creativity; dialectical invention encourages students to expand and explore ideas, discovering new insights before choosing an argumentative approach to a topic or deciding on a thesis. Two years later, in "Burkean Invention, from Pentad to Dialectic," Keith repeats some of the same exercises from his earlier essay but adds a longer discussion of the pentad as a "dialectical device" (Keith 1979, 140) for expanding a writer's perspective.

In "Conflict in Collaboration: A Burkean Perspective," Bill Karis (1989) argues that Burkean dialectic, as the expansion of perspectives, can function as an antidote to the epistemologically limiting function of the ideology of consensus in collaboration. Karis writes, "While . . . calls for compromise and collaboration . . . have become commonplace in discussions of collaborative writing, . . . the *predisposition* to finding manageable solutions or the 'truth' on some middle ground before fully exploring the problem through dialectic can become a restrictive element in the collaborative process" (113). According to Karis, Burkean dialectic allows for a kind of mediative argumentation, but it also allows for the articulation of competing (irreconcilable) arguments, one of which might ultimately be best. Karis writes, "A predetermined commitment to compromise . . . at the beginning of a collaborative project restricts and constrains the dialectical process which might permit the group members to discover or create the best possible solution. It presupposes that the correct or best solution is always located in the middle and thereby excludes other potential solutions" (115). Although Burke suggests that identification is certainly a goal in all rhetorical encounters, Karis warns that "neglecting the dialectical, which happens too often by way of appeals for cooperation, may cause participants in collaborative situations to move too quickly toward identification" (117).

In "A Case for Kenneth Burke's Dialectic and Rhetoric," Timothy W. Crusius (1986) digs much deeper into Burke's classical understanding of the relationship between dialectic and rhetoric, arguing that "Burke preserves Aristotle's position that the two verbal arts are 'counterparts' of each other" (23). Whereas Keith and Karis treat Burkean dialectic (including pentadic analysis) as invention for rhetoric, Crusius points out that Burke never viewed the relationship this way: "The Pentad is not a contribution to rhetorical invention, toward finding something to say to realize one's purpose. Rather Burke dealt with it exclusively as a contribution to dialectic, a way to question assertions about motive" (23), thereby expanding one's understanding of any given situation. Thus, for Burke, dialectical argumentation, articulated in his *A Grammar of Motives*, is the "exploration of verbal forms" (Crusius 1986, 24), and rhetorical identification, articulated in his *The Rhetoric of Motives*, is the "overcoming of estrangement" (24). Dialectic and rhetoric, then, are separate but complementary arts, neither necessarily preceding the other in any linear process of communication.

Keith, Karis, and Crusius all treat dialectic as a methodical way to expand a writer's argumentative perspective on complex issues. For Crusius, dialectical exploration (whether Aristotelian or Burkean) is an end in itself, though nevertheless useful to rhetoric; but for Keith and Karis, dialectical argumentation is invention for rhetoric. In all of these cases, the emphasis of dialectic is on *argumentation*, a term with a vexed history in rhetoric and composition, and Keith's, Crusius's, and Karis's calls for the incorporation of argumentative dialectic into composition pedagogy generally fell on deaf ears. There are at least two reasons for rhetoric and composition's relative lack of interest in Aristotelian and Burkean argumentative dialectic, including argument's status as one of the modes and rhetoric's hegemony as a discourse category.

Argument was one of the four modes of discourse, which were being actively rejected throughout the 1970s and 1980s, so argument's primary methodology, dialectic, was also generally ignored. The modes of discourse made their way into composition pedagogy during the nineteenth century through textbooks written by Alexander Bain and John Genung, among others, with description, narration, exposition, argument, and persuasion usually among the classifications (Connors 2003b, 3–4; Kitzhaber 1990, 119–20). As Connors points out, the unified structure of the four modes of discourse eventually saw pockets of resistance. During the 1930s, single-mode textbooks became popular, and courses focusing exclusively on narration, exposition, or argument soon emerged. In the 1940s, WWII initiated an obsession in academia with science and technology; thus, in response, rhetoric and composition emphasized expository writing and all of its subgenres, including "definition, analysis, partition, interpretation, reportage, evaluation by standards, comparison, contrast, classification, process analysis, device analysis, cause-and-effect, induction, deduction, examples, and illustration" (Connors 2003b, 7). Description and narration shifted their location to the new discipline of creative writing, and argument shifted its location to speech communication (7). By the 1960s, with the rise of the New Rhetorics, the modes fell out of favor, at least in theory if not in practice, and this rejection of the modes generally included argument and its principal methodology, dialectic. However, Sharon Crowley points out that argument was never a very good mode since it required an attention to audience and the use of "non-empirical forms of evidence" (Crowley 1990, 110), and composition specialists soon saw good reasons to resurrect argument as a discourse category.

Yet in order to recover argument for rhetoric and composition, while leaving behind its modal status, the classical distinction between dialectic as argument and rhetoric as persuasion had to be dissolved into the assumption that all intentional discourse is rhetorical and persuasive, including argument. This assumption eliminated the distinguishing foundation of dialectic as a form of argumentation, and when argument was recovered in composition studies, it was recovered as a form of rhetoric, which has no need for dialectic. In fact, so strong has been the rejection of argument's modal status that even very recent efforts to recover argument as a legitimate genre for composition studies identify argument clearly with rhetoric. For example, John Ramage, Michael Callaway, Jennifer Clary-Lemon, and Zachary Waggoner explain that their 2009 book *Argument in Composition* "is heavily influenced by Burke's approach to rhetoric" (Ramage et al. 2009, xi). Their chapter on the history of argumentation is generally symptomatic, especially in their treatment of Aristotle's influence.

Aristotle's discussion of argumentation and its principal method, dialectic, occurs in the *Topics*; Aristotle's discussion of catharsis and its principal method, poetry, occurs in the *Poetics*; and Aristotle's discussion of persuasion and its principal method, rhetoric, occurs in the *Rhetoric*. But the only works cited and discussed by Ramage et al. in their treatment of Aristotle's theory of argumentation are the *Poetics* and the *Rhetoric*. This choice of representative texts (i.e., omitting Aristotle's book on argumentation) is inexplicable unless one realizes that in composition studies, argument dissociates its identity as a mode by aligning its identity with rhetoric.[12] Echoing Burke in their discussion of Aristotle, Ramage et al. explain that Aristotle "makes a clear and convincing case for the importance of establishing a common ground with one's audience by attending to their beliefs and assumptions" (Ramage et al. 2009, 58). For Aristotle, dialectic is the spinning out of argumentative possibilities using full syllogisms without considerations of audience; audience is a function of rhetoric and the artful contraction of syllogisms into enthymemes so constructed that the audience fills in the missing premises. Audience, for Aristotle, is a concern of rhetoric, not argument. Further on, Ramage et al. suggest that Aristotle "certainly recognizes a place for emotions in argument" (58). This claim is true of Aristotle's view of rhetoric, with *pathos* as one proof with which enthymemes can be constructed; however, this claim simply cannot be made regarding Aristotle's view of argument since the subject of emotion is never raised in the *Topics*. Finally, Ramage et al. suggest that Aristotle "seems to imagine a limited number of venues and occasions where arguments take place (the legislature, the courtroom, the ceremonial occasion)" (59). However, they argue, "argument today is a good deal more diffuse" (59). Again, Aristotle limits only rhetoric (and thus persuasion) to these three occasions; there is no such limitation of dialectic (and thus argumentation) to these three occasions in the *Topics* because dialectical argumentation is not governed by the context of any particular situation.[13]

In rhetoric and composition, if argument is a mode and all discourse is persuasive, then argumentation (in the classical sense at least) and its principal method, dialectic, would have little place in the modern writing class. In the process of dissociating modal status from argumentation, modern scholars of argumentation in rhetoric and composition have also dissociated argument's principal classical methodology, dialectic. Thus, even contemporary scholarship on argument in rhetoric and composition tends to ignore argument's classical connection to dialectic in favor of associating it with the methods of rhetoric.

A Model for the Progression of Human History

In her 1991 essay "Marxist Ideas in Composition Studies," Patricia Bizzell (1991) pointed out that members of the composition studies community (unlike members of the general American academic culture) tended to find affinities with Marxist ideas. The reason Bizzell gives is that "we rhetoricians like to see ourselves as social reformers, if not revolutionaries" (53), drawing often from European and Third World Marxists like Bakhtin, Paulo Freire, and Lev Vygotsky (53). The problem, Bizzell indicates, is not that we are afraid to be associated with Marxists; it is that in our appropriations of Marxist thought for composition studies, we tend to "denature the Marxism, . . . to assimilate the Marxist thinker into a more apolitical discourse" (53). Bizzell proposes that composition studies should begin to develop more politicized rhetorics and pedagogies using Marxist ideas like ideology, hegemony, contradiction, and resistance as foundations. However, one Marxist idea left out of Bizzell's plea is dialectic, or the method of historical materialism, which makes all of these other Marxist ideas coherent and meaningful. Ideology and hegemony make sense in the context of the dialectical engagement of base and superstructure; contradiction and resistance make sense in the context of the dialectical transformations of oppression and revolution. Interestingly, prior to the publication of Bizzell's essay, at least three scholars in composition studies had invoked dialectic as a methodology deriving specifically from Marx and Marxism.

In 1978, Louise Yelin (1978) published "Deciphering the Academic Heiroglyph: Marxist Literary Theory and the Practice of Basic Writing." Yelin began her academic career teaching basic writing at Hostos Community College in New York City, the hub of open-admissions trends, and she described her first encounter with Mina Shaughnessy's *Errors and Expectations* as liberating. However, as she tried, with mixed results, to implement some of Shaughnessy's pedagogical strategies in her own classroom, Yelin became frustrated. Shaughnessy's *Errors and Expectations*, Yelin concludes, is "the most recent instance of a tradition of enlightened liberalism which began with John Stuart Mill"; in fact, all of basic writing "is an educational project whose underlying ideology is this kind of liberalism" (Yelin 1978, 15). Enlightened liberalism is not itself bad since it "offers the teacher of Basic Writing a valuable respect for the individualism and a concomitant optimism about what can be accomplished in Basic Writing" (15). However, what liberalism does not offer in the context of basic writing theory and pedagogy is a way to "explain the factors which militate against the success of programs such as open admissions" and the basic writing programs that grow from them. In contrast to liberalism, Yelin explains, "a Marxist analysis suggests that we can better understand the limitations of Basic Writing—as well as its strengths—if we examine it as part of a web of cultural, political, and economic structures and institutions" (15). Yelin derives inspiration for her Marxist analysis from Marx himself but also from Antonio Gramsci and Raymond Williams.

When Marxism is imported without two-dimensional dialectic, the emphasis is on concepts like those listed by Bizzell (ideology, hegemony, contradiction, and resistance); however, when we place those ideas in the context of two-dimensional dialectic, they become elements of the dynamic process of human activity, "products of human social history" (Yelin 1978, 18). Yelin explains that, unlike Shaughnessy's liberal humanism, Williams's Marxism "emphasizes the dialectical nature of the relationship between our students' alternative or emergent cultures and the established cultural institutions in which we meet them" (19). Further, Williams's dialectical materialism acknowledges the interplay between language as a social system of signs and each individual's capacity to use the system in unique ways, depending on social context. For Yelin, then, Williams's dialectic encourages both instruction in the linguistic system of dominant institutions (avoiding comma splices) and a "consciousness of languages in their social and political contexts" (23), dealing with "questions of correctness and error without presenting them arbitrarily, but rather, by placing them in an historical context" (23).

Turning from correctness to more rhetorical constructs, Yelin explains how Williams's two-dimensional dialectic would play out in the revision of a standard basic writing assignment, the description of a person:

> The Marxist view of the individual, that the self can be understood only in relation to its social and historical setting, suggests that a fully articulated description of a person comprehends the web of relationships in which the individual is located. In presenting the assignment, then, we can discuss this network or series of networks—family, racial or ethnic group, class—and the relationships between them. In addition, we can consider

the relationship of writer, subject, audience as a way of making explicit the connection between a particular act of writing and the institutional context in which it occurs; as a way, that is, of subjecting to scrutiny the social conditions which determine the processes and products of composition. (Yelin 1978, 24–25)

And these processes of composition, Yelin is careful to point out, are "not individual, but dialectical, in the sense that individuals use and shape a collective language" (Yelin 1978, 25). The practice of basic writing, then, according to Yelin, is situated in the dialectical intersection between students and institutions: "Basic Writing is, in effect, the terrain in which the relationship between 'emergent' [student cultures] and 'dominant' [university, corporate cultures] is realized" (29). Using this methodological sense of dialectic in both the structure and practice of writing pedagogy, students better understand the larger historical and social contexts in which their own educations are embedded. This is the value of two-dimensional dialectical Marxism for basic writing, of course, and for all of composition studies.

Even during the 1980s, after Berthoff had become more interested in social dialectics resulting in critical consciousness, drawing extensively from Paulo Freire, her work still "downplay[ed] the projects of large-scale political change that always accompany Freire's practice" (Bizzell 1991, 53). While Bizzell called on composition specialists to put Freire "back into a Marxist context," Judith Goleman had already begun the process of putting Berthoff into a Marxist context, connecting her dialectic of metacognition to the social aspects of historical materialism, using Marx, Fredric Jameson, and Louis Althusser as inspiration. In "Reading, Writing, and the Dialectic since Marx," Goleman explains that Marxist dialectic is "a means by which to analyze the dominant social and historical forces producing structures of meaning" (Goleman 1988, 110–11), and she describes a writing course in which her students used Berthoff's dialectical notebook to explore culture from a historical-materialist perspective. It is here that we most clearly see the shift in dialectic's source and object. The source (or, from a more rhetorical perspective, the exigency) of dialectic shifts from Berthoff's chaotic thought in search of form to Goleman's ideological contradictions in need of historical-materialist critique. The object of dialectic shifts from Berthoff's metacognition and the making of meaning to Goleman's conscious awareness of social oppression and critical exposure of ideological mystifications. Though Goleman's essay was not an impetus in composition's social turn, it certainly did exemplify a more general shift in the use of the term *dialectic* (i.e., from a sense of one-dimensional dialectic as the methodical audit of meaning toward the two-dimensional sense of dialectic as the progression of human history).

Although James A. Berlin's use of the term *dialectic* as productive inter-action is relatively generic in his taxonomies of writing pedagogies, his use of the term becomes much more specifically Marxist in discussions of rhetorical historiography. In "Revisionary History: The Dialectical Method," Berlin argues that new historiographies of rhetoric must avoid the ruse of objectivity characteristic of prior histories of rhetoric, and "contemporary Marxism" offers the most productive model for such an effort. According to Berlin, "The Marxian problematic has always addressed the question of power," which leads historiography away from inventing coherent narratives of heroes and events and toward uncover-ing rhetoric as the object of historical conflict and the source of hege-monic oppression. Setting aside objectivity and the drive for coherence requires first that "the historian must be aware of her own ideological position" (Berlin 1987a, 56). Only then can the dialectical historian acknowledge "that the account offered is a product of the interaction of the interpretive frameworks brought to the concrete historical events and the events themselves" (56). Such a perspective shows us that rheto-ric mediates the dialectic between "the material and social conditions of society," on the one hand, and "the political and cultural," on the other hand, making rhetoric "the core of a society's educational activi-ties" (52). The dominant rhetoric of any given time in history serves the economic, political, and social interests of the ruling class, and learning to speak and write in sanctioned institutions places students in a subor-dinate role, accepting dominant ideologies as though they were natural. However, as Berlin points out, "there are always competing rhetorics at any historical moment because there are always competing ideologies" (55). Thus, the best histories of rhetoric tell two-dimensional dialectical stories of ideological competition and material domination, not coher-ent one-dimensional narratives of the winners and their triumphs. The dialectic Berlin invokes here is clearly a Marxist one that views the prog-ress of human history (and the situation of rhetoric within that history) as one of conflict and revolution, of opposition and change.

Although rhetoric alone was being revived for composition studies during the 1960s and early 1970s, a number of scholars in composition began by the late 1970s to recover rhetoric's counterpart, dialectic, as well. For some, dialectic was inherently dialogic, and they adapted this Platonic dialectic to the writing class through pedagogical techniques like the dialectical notebook. Others considered dialectic to be an Aristotelian means to expand a student's perspectives before writing, converting Burke's pentad into invention heuristics that help students avoid knee-jerk arguments that are weak and easily refuted. Still others considered dialectic to be the Hegelian or Marxist progression of human history, applying dialectic's historical and critical stance both to the discipline of rhetoric and composition generally and also to writing assignments in the composition classroom. As I explain in the next section, however, dialectic's fortunes in rhetoric and composition were short lived.

DIALECTIC OUT OF RHETORIC AND COMPOSITION

By the early 1990s, rhetoric and composition scholars seemed to have lost interest in *dialectic* altogether, with only a few scholars using the term loosely. Anne DiPardo (1990) and John D. O'Banion (1992) both used dialectic as a way to articulate the relationship between narration and exposition. Kathleen E. Welch used dialectic to mean "productive clash" (Welch 1993, 133), and she applied this sense of conflict to three pedagogical techniques for teaching writing (the "writing workshop," "critics' sheets," and the "teacher/student dialogue on paper") (134). K. A. Raign (1994) related Platonic dialectic and stasis theory in an (uncomfortable, anachronistic) alliance, teaching composition students new critical-thinking skills. In 1997, Andrew Low recognized the obvious "decline of the dialectical tradition" (Low 1997, 373) late in the twentieth century, offering his own alternative based on Piercean pragmatics, but he spent less than two pages describing it. The most interesting development in dialectic since the late 1990s in rhetoric and composition has not been a resurgence of interest in it, as communication studies has experienced, but a series of direct challenges to dialectic.[14]

Understanding the variety of challenges to dialectic requires understanding exactly which dialectic is being challenged. I argue that the three primary challenges to dialectic in recent scholarship on rhetoric and composition (sub/versive historiography, affirmative invention, and complexity theory) critique only a narrow conception of dialectic, one whose origins lie in eighteenth- and nineteenth-century philosophy, not the dialectics whose origins lie in their relationship to the rhetorical tradition. In classical theories of language, especially as they were systematized by Aristotle (and developed in Rome and maintained throughout the Middle Ages), dialectic involved spinning out possible sets of arguments (structured as syllogisms) related to controversial issues and then judging among them; rhetoric involved taking one of those sets (or sides or positions or orientations) and making a case, truncating dialectical syllogisms into rhetorical enthymemes and adding ethical and emotional appeals to make the case persuasive. This distinction between dialectic-argumentation and rhetoric-persuasion is strongly maintained in the discourse of communication studies; however, as I have already pointed out, this distinction is often lost in the discourse of rhetoric and composition. Arguments among rhetoric and composition scholars against dialectic are not usually arguments against the dialectical method of argumentation and judgment (i.e., the counterpart of rhetoric). Rather, these arguments against dialectic tend to challenge Hegelian and Marxist notions of opposition, negation, and synthesis (i.e., philosophical dialectic as the generating principle and utopian end of human progress), and these critiques most often originate in postmodern and poststructuralist theory.

Hegel's idealist dialectic viewed the progression of history as the interplay among Being (thesis), Nothingness (antithesis), and Becoming (synthesis), all driven by a transcendental force called Spirit. The progress of history, then, is a process of birth and death (or creation and negation) resulting in change, and all of the change Hegel envisioned was teleological, oriented toward the ultimate achievement of Spirit, a unified (ideal) goal or end (*telos*). Marx (and, later, Engels, too) also believed that history progresses through the dialectical engagement of opposing forces, with the negation of false consciousness leading to communal integration and social cooperation. For Marx, the opposing forces are the material base and the ideological superstructure, which are not driven by Spirit but by the mode of production. While Hegel's idealist dialectic ends in a unity of thought, Marx's (and Engels's) historical-materialist dialectic ends in the total communion of work and property (i.e., in Communism).

Postmodern theorists tend to reject modernism's obsession with negation, with dualism, and with the teleological progression toward epistemological unity and social emancipation, all of which are symptoms of modernist philosophical dialectics. As early as the 1980s, Linda Hutcheon observed that what postmodern theory needed was "a way of talking about our culture which is neither 'unificatory' or 'contradictionist' in a Marxist dialectical sense" (Hutcheon 1988, 21), adding that the "visible paradoxes of the postmodern do not mask any hidden unity which analysis can reveal" (21). At the end of *The Postmodern Condition*, Jean-Francois Lyotard describes paralogy as a rejection of the dialectical idealism of Hegel and the historical-materialist dialect of Marx (and Engels): "We no longer have recourse to the grand narratives—we can resort neither to the dialectic of Spirit nor even to the [dialectical] emancipation of humanity as a validation for postmodern scientific discourse" (Lyotard 1989, 60). Invention, particularly in scientific discourse, Lyotard tells us, is no longer a function of teleological grand narratives driven by dialectical progression (invention and negation leading to unity); postmodern invention is, instead, a function of "the little narrative (*petit récit*)" (60), each vying for attention in the agora of public discourse. Rather than an ultimate synthesis or communion, Lyotard explains that "it is now dissention that must be emphasized" (61), the inevitable and perpetual language game itself, with no sense of progress toward a grand end. Jean Baudrillard's work also critiques Marxist dialectics, assuming instead the complete implosion of historical materialism. In *Simulacra and Simulations*, Baudrillard posits "the reabsorption of every dialectic of communication in a total circularity of the model" (Baudrillard 1995, 83) since the very tensions that drove traditional dialectics (base/superstructure, subject/object, production/consumption, reality/ideology, truth/falsity, signifier/signified) had already exploded into a profusion of meaning. Gilles Deleuze, in a discussion of his early interest in the history of philosophy, muses, "What I most detested was Hegelianism and dialectics" (Deleuze 1994, 6); and in *Difference and Repetition*, Deleuze explains that this opinion derived from dialectic's reliance on "the negative" (157).

While Low identifies the rise of dialogics in rhetoric and composition as a cause of the decline of dialectic, one could also very easily say that the rise of poststructuralism and postmodernism in rhetoric and composition caused a decline of interest in dialectic generally because of *philosophical* dialectic's association with modernist methodologies and politics. However, it is interesting to note that the very theorists who reject dialectic as modernist and negative also offer many contributions to a reconstituted dialectic in relation to rhetoric. Thus, the authors of the three challenges to dialectic, discussed in the next few pages, will reappear in chapter 4 as proponents of ideas leading toward three-dimensional dialectical rhetorics.

The Challenge from Sub/Versive Historiography

In *Negation, Subjectivity, and the History of Rhetoric*, Victor J. Vitanza (1997) argues that histories of rhetoric have constructed (or followed) a modernist, Hegelian grand narrative of determinate negation that eliminates the middle. Drawing from an eclectic collection of poststructuralist theorists, Vitanza critiques two-dimensional, philosophical dialectic as a force that constructs identities by way of an opposition and synthesis that negates. Vitanza favors, instead, rhisomatic schitzoanalysis (*à la* Deleuze and Guattari 1987), among other methods, as a way to empha- size multiplicity and difference. Recalling a question once asked by Berlin ("Victor, what is it that you want?"), Vitanza responds, "Desire in language and everything else. Desire in *logos*, but also in *ethos* and *pathos*. And I want this desire reflected in histories of rhetorics" (3). Such a desire would not be based on repulsion, opposition, or negation, but instead on attraction and radical multiplicity, a desire that is "both affirmative and also disruptive" (3). This "free-flowing desire," Vitanza writes, "would be against the very principle of *identity* itself," if identity is constructed through negation, and would "reintroduce the excluded middle" (4), the "repressed, suppressed, oppressed" (6). Through desire (attraction, not negation), Vitanza would reclaim the multiplicity and vastness of rhetoric's history, "especially its parts that do not allow for systematization, for completeness, without exclusion, without purg- ing" (4). For "systematization *is* the result of exclusion. Wherever there is system (totality, unity), there is the trace of the excluded" (4). This desire for the excluded is, Vitanza explains, sub/versive.

Systems (identities, narratives, dialectics) exist and persist by negating contradiction. But Vitanza offers an alternative practice: "Just link. Just link. Just link" (Vitanza 1997, 5). Vitanza's linking (not negating) histo- ries of rhetoric "would become a series of flows, energies, movements, capacities, a series of parts and segments capable of becoming linked together in ways other than those which congeal them by standard aca- demic operating procedures" (5). Linking counters negation; linking is denegation, and its purpose is to "denegate the negative" (13). Through historical (historiographical) linking, Vitanza hopes to "denegate the principles of identity, contradiction, and excluded middle" (7), link- ing them back to (inserting them back into) histories of rhetoric (13). Dialectical procedure, or negative dialectic, "disenables . . . because it excludes" (12); Vitanza writes, "I want to purge all binary machines and replace them with desiring machines" (22). Binaries negate and synthe- size, but desires integrate and multiply.

Vitanza considers three general approaches to the history of rhetoric. First, structuralist histories construct traditional oppositions (master/ slave, man/woman, and so on) as the driving force of their narratives. Second, negative deconstructionist histories reverse the value system of traditional oppositions (slave/master, woman/man, and so on) but leave the logic of opposition in place, basing their narratives on these reformulated binary structures. Third, nonpositive affirmative or den- egating histories always reach out to the excluded third, the excessive, the sublime. For Vitanza, both structuralist and negative deconstructionist histories operate according to a two-dimensional dialectical logic of opposition/synthesis, and therefore negation. However, nonpositive (sub/versive) affirmation operates according to a "non-dialectical" logic of trinary excess and inclusion (denegation), linking always to what has been excluded (the third) by structuralism and negative deconstruction. I argue that Vitanza's nonpositive, affirmative approach to writing histories of rhetoric is three dimensional, and while Vitanza calls this approach "non-dialectical," I believe linking, inclusion, and denegation can be crucial strategies in three-dimensional dialectical rhetoric.

Vitanza calls this practice of invoking the third (of including the excessive, the sublime) the "third sophistic" or "affirmative deconstruction." Here "affirmative" means "any attempt to denegate or desublimate the negative"; "The History of Rhetoric must be denegated" (Vitanza 1997, 58), must "include what, heretofore, has been excluded or purged" (67). Stating his purpose, Vitanza explains, "I will attempt to turn binary machines into desiring machines, to turn one's and two's into three's" (58).

A third sophistic in the writing of rhetorical history requires a new emphasis on the "excess" that always "escapes dialectic" (Vitanza 1997, 68). Vitanza explains that "whereas *negation*—which is the principle of definition or rhetorical invention—is a strategy that de*term*ines what something is by way of *excluding* . . . *excess*, or nonpositive affirmation, on the other hand, is a tactic that denegates negations by way of *reincluding*" (63). The third sophistic is a search for excess negated by two-dimensional dialectical histories of rhetoric; it is "an incredulity toward covering-law models or grand (causal) narratives of history (writing), such as an Hegelian or Marxist dialectical view of history as leading to ethical and political emancipation" (238). According to Vitanza, "If the strategy of *ex*cluding the third is a strategy of negative dialectic, the strategy of *in*cluding the third is a strategy of denegating (libidinalizing) the negative" (269). Whereas negative dialectic works within a logic of opposition and contradiction (and synthesis and negation), a third sophistic works within a logic of inclusion and difference (Vitanza 1997, 276). From opposition and negation (i.e., dialectic) to inclusion and difference (i.e., nondialectical, nonpositive affirmation)—this is the movement from traditional (structuralist) and revisionary (negative deconstructionist) to sub/versive (affirmative deconstructionist) histories of rhetoric.

Throughout *Negation, Subjectivity, and the History of Rhetoric,* Vitanza (1997) argues against two-dimensional dialectic, which he says negates opposition and eliminates the middle ground. This logic of opposition and negation poses political problems since identities (subjectivities) become defined more by what they are not than by what they might desire to be. Three-dimensional desire to link leads to affirmative invention, a sub/versive third sophistic that includes difference and multiplicity in histories of rhetoric. In chapter 4, I argue that Vitanza's third sophistic desire for "some more" *links* dialectic and rhetoric into a third art, dialectical rhetoric.

The Challenge from Affirmative Invention

In *The Future of Invention: Rhetoric, Postmodernism, and the Problem of Change,* John Muckelbauer (2009) takes up some of the same critiques of modernist two-dimensional dialectics that we see throughout Vitanza's work. For Muckelbauer, traditional approaches to rhetoric, even those that on the surface appear to be irreconcilably opposed, "actually share a common, 'foundational' commitment to a dialectical image of change and to the movement of negation that engineers it" (x); thus, Muckelbauer explains, "the negative movement of dialectical change is the generative engine for whatever 'difference' or 'novelty' results" (4). Interestingly, Muckelbauer attributes a kind of immorality to dialectical negation, calling it dangerous and destructive (an ethical shame). Muckelbauer declares that dialectical invention and dialectical rhetoric inevitably carry with them "ethical and political dangers" (8, 9, 10, 12), and he warns against the "dangerous and destructive" force of dialectic's negative movement (30, 36). Given all of these dangerous and destructive consequences of dialectic, Muckelbauer declares that "it seems reasonable to think that the dialectic must be overcome" (10).

Muckelbauer illustrates "the dialectical movement of negation" through three "styles of engagement" (Muckelbauer 2009, 6): advocacy, critique, and synthesis. First, advocacy "emphasizes a traditionally privileged concept and negates its traditionally underprivileged counterpart" (6). Second, critique "flips the dialectical coin and privileges the underdog . . . by recognizing that the system of imbalances reproduced by the conservative position has resulted in countless injustices and outright atrocities" (7). Muckelbauer explains that both advocacy and critique advance according to a two-dimensional dialectical logic of negation. Muckelbauer's third style of engagement is synthesis, which "attempts to overcome the oppositional movement itself by synthesizing these opposing poles" (8). Muckelbauer explains that synthesis "attempts to develop a sense of change that is not inherently dependent on the monotonous and dangerous movement of negation and refusal. As a result, it looks to the space *between* the poles, *between* opposing positions" (8–9). "And yet," Muckelbauer continues, "in the very effort to render this in-between, the existence of poles are [*sic*] still presumed" (9). Advocacy, critique, and synthesis are all deeply implicated in the modernist two-dimensional dialectics that, according to Muckelbauer, restrict invention (dangerously, destructively) to a process of negation.

Throughout *The Future of Invention*, Muckelbauer offers a postmodern challenge to "the entire 'Hegelian framework' of dialectical negation" and its manifestations in rhetorical theory and practice (as advocacy, critique, and synthesis): "This postmodern challenge is a response to dualism and to binary opposition" (Muckelbauer 2009, 5). Muckelbauer explains that "binary oppositions are not a problem just because they are binaries, but because they are active and mobile embodiments of particular power dynamics that act through negation. *What is at issue in binary oppositions is not the abstract existence of opposite terms, but the pragmatic movement of negation through which such oppositions are generated and maintained*" (5). The goal Muckelbauer sets for himself in *The Future of Invention* is "inventing a style of engagement that is irreducible to the dialectical movement of negation" (5), a style he finds represented in affirmative (not negative) change conceived and invented through singular (not dialectical) rhythms.

Muckelbauer proposes that "there is a simpler kind of affirmative repetition that circulates within the dialectic's recognizably complex repetition, and "this affirmative repetition" is "composed of 'singular rhythms'" (12). Muckelbauer explains:

> These singular rhythms indicate an unidentifiable and unrecognizable dimension of repetition that circulates within the identifiable and recognizable movement of dialectical negation. So if the negative movement of dialectical change cannot be overcome and can only be repeated, this does not mean that all repetition is the same or that all repetition necessarily reproduces the same. Instead, it only means that everything hinges on *how* one repeats (rather than *if* one repeats). In other words, in any particular encounter, everything depends on one's orientation within repetition: an orientation toward negation itself or an orientation toward the singular rhythms within negation. (Muckelbauer 2009, 12–13)

According to Muckelbauer, singular rhythms "are immanent to all appropriative, dialectical movement. And further, even as these rhythms remain trapped within a dialectical movement, indeed, *precisely because they remain trapped*, they manage to go elsewhere" (Muckelbauer 2009, 33). That "elsewhere" is a process of "affirmative repetition, or the repetition of intensive, singular rhythms" (33), which are "extracted and secreted through [dialectic's] repetition" (42).

Ultimately, Muckelbauer relates affirmative invention and singular rhythms to experimentation and exploration in writing. Muckelbauer writes, "An affirmative inclination is inseparable from an experimentation, an attempt to explore, for instance, what a particular concept can become capable of by connecting it elsewhere" (Muckelbauer 2009, 43); "An affirmative inclination encounters writing as an experimental pathway, a relay on an intensive, inventional circuit" (43). Thus, an inventive writing pedagogy of singular rhythms leans toward "provoking immanent experimentation" (44). And experimentation requires uncertainty and confusion as starting points leading to invention and singular rhythms. Muckelbauer writes, "Experimenting with what a concept *can do* requires a kind of uncertainty about *what the concept is*. So each inquiry begins in a certain confusion in its attempt to extract singular rhythms" (48).

Experimentation and inventiveness are critical to writing, of course, but Muckelbauer's critique of all other approaches to writing as dialectical, thus dangerous and destructive, concerned only with negation, ignores the fact that rhetoric, at times, *needs* to be negative, oppositional, and, yes, maybe even dangerous if those who find it dangerous do not have our own best interests at heart. I wonder, for example, how far the civil rights movement would have gotten experimenting with singular rhythms and not negating (dangerously, destructively) the hegemonic racist discourses of the time. Without what Muckelbauer calls "dialectical critique" (the direct negation of the rhetoric produced by oppressors committing injustices and atrocities), many social revolutions would have no means to advance except to construct for themselves an affirmative safe house of singular rhythms. Sometimes effective rhetoric requires a critical stance against an oppressive "Other," and this critical stance, while inherently dialectical, is by no means ethically or politically dangerous.

While the rhetorical pursuit of singular rhythms limits rhetoricians unnecessarily to exploratory discourse, I do believe exploratory discourse can serve important rhetorical functions. Indeed, if rhetoric is always and everywhere dialectical (in the Hegelian sense that Muckelbauer gives the concept), then rhetoric is limited to critical and responsorial functions, which inhibit growth and change. New communication technologies provide a fertile context in which affirmative invention and singular rhythms produce new rhetorical strategies that acknowledge multiplicity without negating oppositions.

Thus, although Muckelbauer spends much time critiquing Hegelian dialectic as it relates to rhetoric and composition, I am convinced that his theory of affirmative invention and singular rhythms supports the fusion of rhetoric and dialectic (not philosophical dialectic, but the dialectic that is the counterpart of rhetoric) into a three-dimensional hybrid art, dialectical rhetoric.

The Challenge from Complexity Theory

While Vitanza and Muckelbauer situate their rejections of two-dimensional dialectic in poststructuralist and postmodern theory, Byron Hawk situates his rejection of two-dimensional dialectic in complexity theory, especially Mark C. Taylor's articulation of it, which is, in part at least, a critical response to poststructuralism and postmodernism, especially as they are articulated in the works of Michel Foucault, Jacques Derrida, and Jean Baudrillard. In *Hiding*, Taylor writes, "To think what poststructuralism leaves unthought is to think a nontotalizing structure that nonetheless acts as a whole. Such a structure would be neither a universal grid organizing opposites nor a dialectical system synthesizing opposites but a seamy web. . . . These webs and networks are characterized by a distinctive logic that distinguishes them from classical structures and dialectical systems" (qtd. in Taylor 2001, 11). In a *JAC* interview conducted by Thomas Rickert and David Blakesley, Taylor explains, "We no longer live in the either-or world of walls but now live in the both-and world of webs" (Rickert and Blakesley 2004, 818). And in *The Moment of Complexity*, Taylor makes an interesting distinction between "binary opposition," in which the relationship between terms is incommensurable, and "dialectical differentiation," in which the relationship between terms is mutually constituting (Taylor 2001, 94). Despite their emphasis on mutually constituting difference rather than incommensurable opposition, dialectical systems are nevertheless closed (93) and driven by a principle of negativity (62); they are simple rather than complex, unable to account for "chance, accident, or contingency" (93). For Taylor, then, even though dialectic emphasizes difference over opposition, it still privileges methodological negation and is simple in structure, unable to deal with the moment of complexity.

Because it is limited to dualist structures that emphasize negation, two-dimensional dialectic is not complex, and, as Hawk explains in "Toward a Rhetoric of Network (Media) Culture," the "simplicity" of dualist, dialectical structures "is always abstracted from complex realities" (Hawk 2004, 831). Complexity theory extends dialectic's dualist, negative structuring metaphor, not into a third sophistic search for excess or a postmodern search for affirmative invention and singular rhythms, but instead into complex webs or networks of relationships among productive, complex adaptive systems, not all of which can be known by any single actor (or rhetor) at any given time. "Situations," Hawk writes, "are more complex than dialectics accounts for" (834); thus, he concludes, "if rhetoric and composition is to move forward and adapt to the coming networked cultures, it can no longer settle, much less strive for, the production of overly simple systems to account for the complexity of writing" (846). According to Hawk, dialectic is one of those simple systems.

In *A Counter-History of Composition*, Hawk specifically critiques Berlin's dialectical approach to composition pedagogies and rhetorical invention as overly simple, unable to grasp the full complexity of digital technology and networked culture (Hawk 2007, 8). Although Hawk often critiques dialectic in general as simplistic, he takes particular issue with Berlin's increasingly Hegelian interpretations of Coleridge's vitalist dialectic (of subject and object, of polarities in the world in relation to polarities in the mind) as overly "mind-centered" (50, 73). In his earliest works, Berlin dissociates Coleridge's complex dialectic of polarities from other (more simplistic) Romantic and expressivist dialectics, based, for example, on Plato. However, by the mid-1980s, Berlin's attitude toward dialectic was beginning to change, altering, too, his view of Coleridge: "Berlin is interested in the way Coleridge's method is continually generative of the subject through interpretation. But the more open-ended, organic aspects of Coleridge's dialectical model fall away in favor of a synthetic, Hegelian reading as Berlin begins to apply this dialectical model to history and his emerging political and pedagogical interests" (73). One work in particular appears to have hastened the Hegelian influence on Berlin's (1987a) own dialectical method and his views of dialectic in general: "Revisionary History: The Dialectical Method."[15]

Hawk argues that "Revisionary History" is a turning point in Berlin's own understanding of dialectic since it emphasizes the subject as the center of dialectical method, the subject as interpreter of history through language (Hawk 2007, 73–74); this emphasis on the subject, Hawk explains, "begins moving Berlin's approach toward a more Hegelian dialectic" (74). Berlin's Hegelian, subject-centered dialectic "falls back on the personal, individual consciousness of the mediator, even though it is tempered by language and history" since "everything the historiographer attempts to mediate is reduced to that historiographer's framework" (74). Despite his overt rejection of subjective epistemologies in favor of social epistemologies, Berlin's own method of "dialectics is always self-dialectics" (74). In his early works, Berlin tends to see value in different dialectics, such as Coleridge's vitalist version, for their specialized functions in particular historical contexts. However, what Hawk perceives as the emerging Hegelian dialectic in Berlin's later work forces Berlin into a critique-and-synthesis movement that seeks an ultimate good, social-epistemic rhetoric, which is produced in the dialectical engagement of writer, audience, and reality. This ultimate Hegelian commitment, in Berlin's later works, shuts down dialectical development and blinds him to the specific historical validity of other, more complex epistemologies and methodologies (76). As Taylor (2001) points out in *The Moment of Complexity*, "closed systems" like dialectic—like *Berlin's* dialectic, Hawk would add—"inevitably run down and cannot be revived" (Hawk 2007, 114).

Ultimately, Hawk argues that "a new paradigm built around complexity [or, more specifically, complex vitalism] could produce a post-dialectical understanding of contemporary pedagogies of invention for the emerging scene produced by digital technology" (Hawk 2007, 7). Hawk finds a model for postdialectical methodology in Coleridge's own vitalist view of the interaction of polarities, in which each element (subject and object, self and world, nature and mind, and so on) is held intact and maintained by the imagination in a generative relationship (99–100). It is this open relationship that generates knowledge, not a closed, teleological, dialectical drive to synthesize through negation. What Berlin's own dialectical method causes him to miss is complexity itself:

> He misses not only complex vitalism's post-dialectical approach to complex interrelationships [because his own Hegelian dialectic blinds him to it] but also the notion of bodily experience and knowledge as being the local moment out of which more complex understanding is connected and initiated. By emphasizing the subject's conscious, rational choice, Berlin loses the complexity of the local, of the way the body is connected to its social, cultural, historical, and technological environments. But because Berlin rests on dialectics as the sole means to understand transaction among the elements of the communication triangle, he cannot theorize an epistemology that is more complex than a dialectic among static points on the triangle. (Hawk 2007, 113)

Hawk's postdialectical method, open not closed, generative not teleological, enables new considerations of "how conscious knowledge emerges from complex embodied situatedness, . . . positing a continuum between mind and body rather than a split" (Hawk 2007, 114). "For a post-dialectical method," Hawk explains, "the point is not to

determine an origin or even a meaning but to map points of intervention, insertion, or connection" (201). Complexity itself, in fact, is post-
dialectical: it is "a focus on systems, dynamic change, complexity in both
physics and life sciences, an emphasis on situatedness, and an acceptance of the unconscious or tacit elements of lived experience" (224).
Dialectic, Hawk concludes, simplifies experience and blinds us to the
richness of complex vitalist methods.

Like Vitanza and Muckelbauer, Hawk critiques Hegelian dialectics
in rhetoric and composition, not the dialectic that is the counterpart
of rhetoric. When we rethink the relationship between dialectic and
rhetoric, reformulating them into a three-dimensional hybrid art, then
Hawk's rhetorical articulation of complexity theory does not contradict
the methods of dialectical rhetoric since dialectical rhetoric does not
create simplified, oppositional structures. Three-dimensional dialectical
rhetoric, like Hawk's notion of complex vitalism, is open (not closed),
generative (not teleological), connective (not divisive), and mediative
(not determinist). In fact, Sarah Kember and Joanna Zylinska argue
that affirmative vitalism is weakest when it rejects mediative dialectics
(Kember and Zylinska 2012, 180–85). Thus, Hawk's understanding of
complexity theory in the context of networked technologies creates a
fertile context for a complex theory and practice of dialectical rhetoric.

The critiques of dialectic offered by Vitanza, Muckelbauer, and
Hawk have been misplaced, directed toward the negative movement
of nineteenth-century philosophical dialectic, not the dialectic that
became what we now know as *argumentation*, although (unlike Vitanza,
Muckelbauer, and Hawk) I also find value in negation. And even some
postmodern theorists do not believe that the rejection of dialectic is
entirely productive. For example, Steven Best and Douglas Kellner
assert that "much postmodern theory rejects dialectics in principle. . . .
Yet by rejecting dialectics, postmodern theory tends to be more frag-
mentary and empiricist, failing to articulate significant mediations, or
connections, between various social phenomena" (Best and Kellner
1991, 223–24). Further, Mark C. Taylor, whom Hawk uses as inspiration
for his rejection of dialectic, would ultimately attenuate his own stance
on dialectic: "While there is undeniably a creative dimension to all cognitive processes, it is too simple to insist that the ostensibly objective
world is actually a psycho-social construction. We need a more nuanced
and, indeed, dialectical understanding of the interplay between subjectivity and objectivity" (Rickert and Blakesley 2004, 817). My hope, however, is not to defend philosophical (idealist or materialist) dialectic but
to recover the dialectic that is the counterpart of rhetoric for writing

instruction. It is irrelevant whether the decline of interest in dialectic among twentieth-century specialists in rhetoric and composition was caused by the secession of communication studies from English or the rapid rise of interest in dialogics or the misplaced critique of philosophical dialectic. It was probably all of these anyway. The fact is that dialectic has an important place in the communication arts, especially writing, and we can better understand the relationship between dialectic and rhetoric and composition by understanding the dimensional qualities of societies and of rhetorics. These are the subjects of the next chapter.

Notes

1. John C. Brereton points out that Harvard was the first major college to create a required first-year composition course (Brereton 1995, 11–13), which it did in 1885, and most American colleges followed Harvard's example.

2. These topics run throughout Robert J. Connors's (1997; 2003a) work, but they are particularly the focus of the essay "Overwork/Underpay" in *Selected Essays of Robert Connors* and the chapter "Licensure, Disciplinary Identity, and Workload in Composition-Rhetoric" in *Composition-Rhetoric: Backgrounds, Theory, and Pedagogy*.

3. There is a great deal more to the historical development of English as a discipline than I can recount in these pages. For a full description of this development, see my introduction to *English Studies: An Introduction to the Discipline(s)* (McComiskey 2005).

4. Most histories of composition locate its formation as a discipline with the recovery of rhetoric as a grounding subject in the 1960s (Connors 1997; Connors, Ede, and Lunsford 1984; Fleming 2009; and Nelms and Goggin 1993). However, there is ample evidence that the rhetorical tradition remained important to at least a few of those in English who were committed to teaching first-year writing and administering the (usually) required sequence. For example, despite disciplinary division (resulting from formal secession), teachers of speech and teachers of writing merged forces once again in 1950, forming the Conference on College Composition and Communication (CCCCs) under the auspices of the National Council of Teachers of English. Surely this merger did not occur in a vacuum, fully formed out of nothing. During the very first CCCCs in Chicago, spring 1950, Kenneth Burke delivered one of the two main addresses (Gerber 1950, 12). Burke's *A Grammar of Motives* had been published five years earlier and his *A Rhetoric of Motives* would come out later that year. Both works foreground *dialectic* and *rhetoric* as key terms for his general theory of dramatism. Also, Richard Weaver is listed as a participant in workshop 5A, "Grammar in the Freshman Composition Course," of the 1950 CCCCs (Burke 1952, 21). Weaver apparently did not support teaching grammar in the first-year course, suggesting that at his own school, the University of Chicago, a committee was addressing the issue by writing a textbook on language and linguistics (21). Three years later, Weaver would publish *The Ethics of Rhetoric*, which argues that both dialectic and rhetoric are critical aspects of the theory and practice of communication (Weaver 1953, 27).

    Further, in a 1955 issue of the still relatively new journal *College Composition and Communication* (*CCC*), three courses are described that were intended to train graduate students and adjuncts for teaching first-year composition. Two of these courses foregrounded rhetorical theory and history as the foundation of effective writing instruction. In this issue of *CCC*, Albert R. Kitzhaber describes a course he began teaching in 1950 at the University of Kansas, the "Rhetorical Background of Written English," as beginning with a general orientation. But by the second course meeting, Kitzhaber would "lecture on the rhetorical tradition—a rapid survey touching on those aspects of classical theory that have most relevance to the teaching of composition" (Kitzhaber 1955, 196). Subsequent class periods focused on British and American rhetorical traditions, some of which Kitzhaber countered as simplistic and formulaic (197). During the semester, students were required to read all of either Aristotle's *Rhetoric* or Cicero's *De Oratore* (Kitzhaber 1955, 196). While Kitzhaber appears to assume that his audience clearly understands the importance of the rhetorical tradition to the teaching of writing, Joseph Schwartz of Marquette University makes a more intentional argument for including rhetorical theory and history in his description of English 280, "Seminar in the Teaching of College Composition." According to Schwartz, any course on teaching college composition must emphasize linguistics and rhetoric, but mostly rhetoric (200). However, Schwartz continues,

> The beginning teacher is woefully weak in this area. The fundamental principles of rhetoric apply no matter how composition or grammar is taught. No one would dream of teaching Shakespeare without having read the plays; merely reading the critics would be of little help. Yet instructors regularly teach composition after having read only the weakened variations of rhetorical principles in modern textbooks. The instructor who has read Aristotle, Cicero, and Quintilian is difficult to find. Yet without an understanding of the basic principles of rhetoric, the most that an instructor can do is mark errors in spelling and punctuation. Invention, disposition, and style are still the fundamental tools of the writer. (Schwartz 1955, 203)

Burke, Weaver, Kitzhaber, and Schwartz all attest to the fact that rhetoric (and, at least in the case of Burke and Weaver, dialectic) never entirely vanished from composition studies after the secession of speech from English. Composition was viewed as a pedagogical subject, focused on a single, required, general-education course, so the disciplinary home of the rhetorical tradition, where research was conducted to advance our understanding of the subject, was generally speech communication, not English. Since there was no formal education in rhetoric and/or dialectic in English departments (except the occasional teacher-training course taught by the director of composition), textbooks determined practice, and they were filled with lessons, exercises, and rules (Connors 1997, 94).

5.   In *Authoring a Discipline: Scholarly Journals and the Post-World War II Emergence of Rhetoric and Composition*, Maureen Daly Goggin (2000) provides an insightful history of rhetoric and composition based on its primary outlets for disciplinary scholarship.

6.   Fred Newton Scott's early composition curriculum and PhD program in rhetoric at the University of Michigan is an obvious exception; however, as Connors points out, Michigan's programs were unique, and they ultimately faded upon Scott's retirement in 1927 (Connors 2003a, 182–84).

7.   *The Making of Meaning* was published in 1981, but it was a collection of papers and addresses mostly from the 1970s. The essay cited here "incorporates passages from papers read at the CCCC in Denver (1978) and Minneapolis (1979)" (Berthoff 1981, 94) and was printed in *The Making of Meaning* a few years later.

8.   In *From Form to Meaning: Freshman Composition and the Long Sixties, 1957–1974*, David Fleming notes that nowhere in the history of first-year composition at the University of Wisconsin, Madison, are these kinds of reforms evident (Fleming 2011, 22–23). The recovery of rhetorical theory and an emphasis on the composing process would not happen at UWM for quite some time. I suspect actual col-

lege curricula lagged decades behind the trends we often locate in scholarship on rhetoric and composition.

9. I am thinking in particular of Sondra Perl's 1975 discussion of the dialectic between language and learning among new students in open-admissions colleges, Malinda Snow's (1977) brief exploration of the writer-audience dialectic, and Theodore L. Huguelet's 1979 argument for the five-paragraph dialectic theme, whose introduction is followed by a concession paragraph that begins with the word "admittedly."

10. In *The Making of Meaning*, Berthoff (1981) cites *How to Read a Page* and *Speculative Instruments* as sources for Richards's definition of dialectic (47). Richards takes this definition from his own translation of Plato's *Republic* into Basic English, where, unfortunately, he mistranslates the Greek word ἀποδέξασθαι (*apodeksasthai*) as "audit" (Richards 1942, 143), when its actual meaning is "receive" or "understand" (the opposite of "render" or "articulate"). Basic English, a list of 850 words in which all meanings could be expressed with a minimum of semantic interference, was developed by C. K. Ogden (1932) and promoted by Richards (1943). Interestingly, the two most accurate translations of ἀποδέξασθαι ("receive" and "understand") do not appear in the list of 850 Basic English words. Then again, neither does "audit." Ultimately, I am more amused than troubled by Richards's mistranslation for three basic reasons: first, his definition of dialectic captures the general *spirit* of Plato's discussion (even if it is based on a mistranslation); second, his definition is compelling for *modern* rhetoric and composition; and, third, Berthoff's use of Richards's definition is likewise compelling, and no less dialectical, despite Richards's error.

11. In 1975, Peter Elbow published a chapter titled "The Value of Dialectic" in his book *Oppositions in Chaucer*, and in 1986 he reprinted that chapter for a different audience in *Embracing Contraries: Explorations in Learning and Teaching*. Although Elbow does not mention Aristotle in "The Value of Dialectic," he does elsewhere in *Embracing Contraries*. And the function of dialectic described here is clearly the expansion of perspectives, to "see and think *more*" (Elbow 1986, 241), "to suggest a new, larger system" (243) of thought.

12. Ramage et al.'s (2009) work is symptomatic of a larger trend, of course. In *Teaching Argument in the Composition Course: Background Readings*, Timothy Barnett (2001) includes a selection from only one classical source that he believes grounds the majority of modern theories of argumentation, Aristotle's *Rhetoric*. Barnett's excerpt from the *Rhetoric* does not even begin with the first sentence that identifies rhetoric as the counterpart of dialectic; it begins with Aristotle's definition of rhetoric as "the faculty of observing in any given case the available means of *persuasion*" (qtd. in Barnett 2001, 5; my emphasis). Although I focus my critique in the next few pages on Ramage et al.'s book, these four scholars are certainly not alone in their misidentification of Aristotle's *Rhetoric* as a treatise on argumentation or their assumption that argument is a form of rhetoric.

13. Even as recently as 2011, A. Abby Knoblauch (2011) recognized that the primary fault of our most popular argument textbooks is their incessant privileging of persuasive discourse over argumentative understanding.

14. Interestingly, in communication studies since the early 1990s, dialectic has again become an intense focus thanks to the development of the pragma-dialectical approach to argumentation (see van Eemeren and Grootendorst 2004). In what Hanns Hohmann calls a "recent trend, . . . the affinities of argumentation in general and legal argumentation in particular with dialectic and rhetoric have been increasingly acknowledged again" (Hohmann 2002, 48). Michael Leff attributes this resurgence of interest in dialectic within communication studies to a parallel resurgence of interest in informal logic (Leff 2002, 58), and Fred J. Kauffeld attributes dialectic's resurgence to twentieth-century advances in the philosophy of

language (Kauffeld 2002, 97). Legal argumentation, informal logic, and the philosophy of language are academic developments that ushered in a renewed interest in dialectical argumentation in communication studies; however, no such renewed interest emerged in rhetoric and composition.

15. It is important to at least acknowledge that Berlin would reject Hawk's characterization of his dialectic as Hegelian (thus idealist and teleological). Berlin describes his own dialectic as Marxist (thus materialist and critical) and postmodernist (thus continually challenging hegemonic grand narratives).

3
THE DIMENSIONS OF RHETORIC

In the introduction, I explained that rhetoric is a dimensional art, and rhetoric's dimensionality is based on the number and functions of orientations engaged in any rhetorical act. In this chapter, I expand my earlier discussion of the three dimensions of rhetoric. Here I return briefly to Herbert Marcuse's (1964) *One-Dimensional Man*, drawing a more detailed picture of rhetoric's dimensions than I provided earlier. Since any theory of dimensionality (whether of societies or of rhetorics) requires a clear sense of both identity and difference, I then turn to Kenneth Burke's (1954; 1961) description of orientations in *Permanence and Change* and *Attitudes Toward History* and Michel Foucault's (1970) description of the forces of opposition that define and divide orientations in *The Order of Things*. Finally, I exemplify each of the three dimensions of rhetoric with reference to modern rhetorical theory and composition studies.

DIMENSIONALITY IN RHETORIC

Marcuse was a critical theorist, not a rhetorician, even though he was clearly more interested in the practical and political effects of language than his more theoretical colleagues during the waning years of the Frankfurt Institute for Social Research (Swift 2010).[1] However, despite his occasionally practical and political interests, Marcuse believed (increasingly throughout his career, and especially in *One-Dimensional Man*) that the instrumental language of modern technological society was closing the universe of discourse, limiting the political power of dialectical criticism by co-opting it into a petrified rhetoric that cannot represent (or, worse, actively conceals) the contradictory realities of social existence. In general, Marcuse associates rhetoric with one-dimensional language and dialectic with two-dimensional language, and he believes dialectic is most powerfully manifest in aesthetic, not practical, discourse.[2] As I indicated in the introduction, it is useful to extend Marcuse's description of one-dimensional and two-dimensional societies

DOI: 10.7330/9780874219821.c003

into a third dimension that acknowledges difference but moves beyond opposition toward mediation.

In one-dimensional societies, unified beliefs and the language that represents them appear rational since they divert attention away from contradiction and make opposition inconvenient. According to Marcuse, one-dimensional beliefs permeate the language of media discourse and "shape the universe of communication in which one-dimensional behavior expresses itself" (Marcuse 1964, 85). The universe of media discourse, managed by powerful people whose interests lie in social unification, provides the language with which all members of society describe their world, even if that language enables only incomplete (possibly disadvantageous) descriptions. This language is specifically anticritical and thus antidialectical. James Arnt Aune describes six strategies that characterize the purposes of one-dimensional rhetorics:

(1) replace thought with operations;

(2) eliminate real political tensions by bureaucratic abridgment;

(3) unite contradictions through paradox;

(4) replace persons with functions, while leaving language highly "personalized";

(5) replace concepts with images; and

(6) permit radical dissent, but co-opt it through strategic framing. (Aune 1994, 83–84)

Through these rhetorical strategies, media discourse creates for society certain habits (of thought, of behavior, of expression) that serve the rhetorical function of unification and become almost mystical in their unconscious application, thus depriving speech and language of their cognitive (dialectical, two-dimensional) functions (Marcuse 1964, 85). Under the pressure of one-dimensional unification and its promotion in media discourse, Marcuse argues, the critical functions of dialectical thought "are losing their authentic linguistic representation," and the "linguistic form" of one-dimensional discourse "militates against a development of meaning" (86). This linguistic form takes shape in "self-validating, analytical propositions" (88) that close off the universe of discourse and insulate it from all resistance (90), and the structure of one-dimensional discourse "leaves no space for distinction, development, differentiation of meaning: it moves and lives only as a whole" (93). This "functionalized, abridged, and unified language" (95) forms the rhetoric of one-dimensional thought, and it is specifically "antidialectical language" (97).

In two-dimensional societies, language is a crucial site for the positive articulation of material contradictions because, as Marcuse explains, "the physical transformation of the world entails the mental transformation of its symbols, images, and ideas" (Marcuse 1964, 66). Thus, no real social change can occur without a complementary change in the language we use to talk about society. Critique, Marcuse's method of challenging ruling-class power, adopts the perspective of the working class and reveals ways in which the contradictions of their lives do not fall comfortably inside the universal coherence promoted (falsely) by ruling-class ideology. Critical theory, then, "aims at the very structure" of one-dimensional society, revealing its "ideological and political character" and elaborating dialectical concepts that go "beyond the fallacious concreteness" of one-dimensional discourse (107). There are two primary relationships that drive the methodology of Marcuse's dialectical critical theory: the relationship of history to the present and the relationship of reality to thought. In one-dimensional society, history becomes a subject to be studied in school and has no direct relevance to present action, and thought alone drives present action since reality is contradictory and does not support idealist concepts. Dialectical critical theory describes the historical development of real material conditions, complete with all of their contradictions, thus problematizing any unified, idealistic description of the world. And dialectical critical theory describes contradictions in the present material context for thought and action, revealing the oppressive politics of abstract thought that denies the existence of half the real world. Two-dimensional rhetorics, then, would invoke material contradictions in historical context as a critical strategy to combat the unifying forces of one-dimensional discourse. J. Robert Cox (1990) explains that such critical rhetorics would recover the historical development of unifying arguments, demonstrating their situated nature; dissociate the unifying strategy from the warrants and claims of one-dimensional arguments; and establish a choice among alternative arguments based on situational demands and ethical considerations. Even Marcuse himself understood the limitations of critical rhetorics. According to Cox, Marcuse acknowledges that critical rhetorics cannot themselves create a new and free society; such a revolution can only emerge from the practical argumentation of free individuals with unencumbered consciousness (i.e., the *result* of critical rhetoric).

While I borrow Marcuse's sense of dimensionality, I want to make it clear that Marcuse would reject the three-dimensional impulse to mediate difference. For Marcuse, discourse is always either affirmative and unifying (one dimensional) or negative and critical (two dimensional) (Anderson and Prelli 2001, 74). Since negative, critical discourse originates from outside of unifying discourse and thus challenges dominant culture, any other form of discourse (including three-dimensional mediation) would be implicated in unethical politics. Marcuse favors always maintaining the tension of opposition in two-dimensional engagement (see especially pages xliv–xlv and 19–34, though really the entire book is about this issue). But Marcuse's two-dimensional critique of one-dimensional society and discourse is very much a product of its historical moment, the two decades that followed World War II. This period was marked by the political centralization of power, the militarization of science and technology, and the ubiquitous presence of media, such as television, controlled by a few powerful institutions. These were the social forces at work between the lines (and sometimes in the very words) of *One-Dimensional Man*, and these forces conditioned Marcuse's devotion to two-dimensional critique. More recently, however, the development of what Jeff Rice (2007) calls "cool technologies" (in *The Rhetoric of Cool*) has given rise to new means to mediate orientations (including social media and technologies for visual representation and manipulation), and new media audiences are increasingly willing to be affected (Davis 2010) by these mediations. Three-dimensional rhetorics are both strategic, targeting certain effects in audiences, and topical, drawing from sources of arguments that have found a comfortable home in new media discourse, including deconstruction, dialogue, identification, critique, and juxtaposition.

ORIENTATIONS AND FORCES OF OPPOSITION

In order to fully understand the dimensional relationships among orientations in any rhetorical act, it is necessary first to explore what exactly is being engaged, namely orientations. I borrow the term *orientation* from Burke's (1954) *Permanence and Change*, where he outlines a theory of perspective based on linguistic socialization and begins to explore the importance of human motives in rhetorical action, a theme that would become an obsession in later works.[3] Burke describes orientation as the socialized way in which we experience objects and events in the world through the screen of language. Objects and events, regardless of their "real" character, are never merely discrete aspects of human experience; they are always connected through a complex series of "linkages" that interweave these objects and events into larger units of meaning (14).[4] Different orientations employ different socialized linkages in order to make sense of what would otherwise appear to be chaotic or random. Citing Burke, Diane Davis explains that "belonging is not fixed ontologically by a shared essence but is instead a function of rhetorical identification, which is itself an effect of shared symbol systems" (Davis 2010, 1). Since linkages and orientations are inherently social, they are also always already rhetorical—formed, maintained, and changed through the strategic use of signification.[5]

Orientations are not only our socialized means to understand the past and the present, but they are also our source of expectancy and thus our source of motivation to act. As Burke points out, "A sign, which is here now, may have got a significance out of the past that makes it a promise of the future. Orientation is thus a bundle of judgments as to how things were, how they are, and how they may be" (Burke 1954, 14). Orientations have cognitive significance, then, since they condition our understanding of objects and events in human experience. But they also have pragmatic significance since, as bundles of judgments, they condition our choices of means through which we interpret and interact with the objects and events of our experience. Burke writes, "In a statement as to how the world is, we have implicit judgments not only as to how the world may become but also as to what means we should employ to make it so" (14). Thus, any rhetorical act, whether concerning past, present, or future matters, deals intimately with orientations, and orientations are formed in the active and social process of judgment, not through passive perception or objective observation.

Orientations condition our own decision-making processes and our views of other people's decision-making processes. According to Burke, "As judged by a different scheme of orientation, from a different point of view, a particular linkage is a deceptive one, making for faulty means-selecting" (Burke 1954, 16) since a "different orientation would entail a different way of linkage" (16). Decision making emerges from the motive to act in a particular context according to the implicit judgments of an orientation, "which involves a vocabulary of ought and ought-not, with attendant vocabulary of praiseworthy and blameworthy" (21); "A terminology of motives . . . is moulded to fit our general orientation as to purposes, instrumentalities, the 'good life,' etc." (29). Over time, bundles of judgments become context specific, allowing for a certain degree of seeming contradiction. The statement *thou shalt not kill*, as one critical aspect of an orientation, may apply only to interactions with neighbors and not to dealings with murderers and terrorists.[6] Thus, in different rhetorical contexts, we ourselves (let alone others) might invoke different orientations, different linkages, for different purposes.

Orientations perceived as stable sources of identity are, as Davis points out, "both retroactively essentialized and grounded in the [false] presumption of a prior essence (Davis 2010, 1). However, orientations are not objective social structures that can be fully known or accurately described outside the context of rhetorical performance; instead, I argue (with Burke and Davis) that orientations are organic and evolving structures that emerge from historically grounded and constantly shifting relationships between general social structures (some of which are represented in powerful institutions) and individual life experiences. Thus, although many orientations imply certain common beliefs among those who claim membership, there is in fact much leeway within orientations for creativity and difference. Since orientations are constantly evolving, and since they are not always coherent sets of easily identifiable beliefs (observable through, say, sociological or psychological research), then the most fruitful place to observe and analyze orientations is in discourse itself, in the ways in which orientations are invoked and represented through rhetorical performance.[7] A rhetorical performance, then, is the purposeful construction of socialized linkages that form orientations through the strategic use of signification; and since *strategic* implies a degree of conscious choice, it becomes paramount that orientations (ours, of course, but also the orientations of others) become, as much as possible, conscious aspects of our rhetorical decisions.

This choice among orientations and their performance in rhetoric is never easy or automatic since not all orientations are equal in all contexts. Burke explains that "an orientation is largely a self-perpetuating system, in which each part tends to corroborate the other parts. Even when one attempts to criticize the structure, one must leave some parts of it intact in order to have a point of reference for [one's] criticism. However, for all the self-perpetuating qualities of an orientation, it contains the germ of its dissolution" (Burke 1954, 169); "The members of a group specifically charged with upholding a given orientation may be said to perform a *priesthood function.* . . . The decay of a priesthood . . . leads to a division between *priests* and *prophets.* The priests devote their efforts to maintaining the vestigial structure; the prophets seek new perspectives whereby this vestigial structure may be criticized and a new one established in its place" (179). Since orientations are dialectically connected to historical phenomena, and since historical phenomena necessarily change with time, there are occasions when once-popular orientations no longer adequately explain present phenomena or the motives of action in present contexts. According to Burke, "If the conditions of living have undergone radical changes since the time when the scheme of duties and virtues was crystallized, the serviceability of the orientation may be impaired. Our duties may not serve their purposes so well as they once did. Thus we may no longer be sure of our own duties, with the result that we may cease to be sure of our motives. We may then be more open to a new theory of motivations than we should be at a time when the ideas of duty were more accurately adjusted to the situation" (Burke 1954, 21). In these cases, so common throughout human history, some hold on to old orientations with fierce nostalgia while others attempt to replace old orientations with new, more relevant, or more appropriate ones.

Yet the very kind of argumentation necessary to discredit even the most outmoded orientations is not easy to achieve since old orientations are usually maintained well past the point of viability or usefulness because of their association with "institutions, customs, [and] ways of livelihood" (Burke 1954, 26). In *Attitudes toward History*, Burke explains that "as a given historical frame nears the point of cracking, strained by the rise of new factors it had not organically taken into account, its adherents employ its genius casuistically to extend it as far as possible" (Burke 1961, 23). Rhetors who reject dominant frames or orientations must construct dialectical contradictions, attempting to show that the present motives and acts engaged in by a community are no longer consistent with the situations in which they are performed. When obsolete orientations limit our ability to understand the world around us, we should engage these orientations in dialectical contact with other more viable orientations, laying bare the forces of opposition that divide them.

Constructing dialectical contradictions requires not only the identification and description of orientations but also the identification and description of the forces of opposition that make us perceive orientations as mutually exclusive. Burke makes it clear, in fact, that there would be no need for identification if there were no divisions (Burke 1969, 22–25).[8] Yet, like orientations, forces of opposition are not objective structures that exist prior to discourse; instead, they evolve organically in the process of interaction. They are performed. In the words of Stephanie L. Kerschbaum, the markers that signify difference in interaction are dynamic, relational, and emergent (Kerschbaum 2012, 618–28). Kerschbaum clarifies the distinction between difference as objective structure and difference as relational process:

> In contrast to understanding difference as a thing or object that can be named or described, I define difference as a relation between two individuals that is predicated upon their separateness from one another, or what Bakhtin refers to as noncoincidence of being. This relation is

signaled by the display and uptake of markers of difference. Difference-as-relation drives communicative efforts because it is part of a continual interplay between identification and differentiation. This interplay reveals the lived experience of difference as highly dynamic. Categories rarely capture that dynamism because categorical coherence lies in the ability to move across contexts. In addition, categories tend to suppress attention to the agency expressed by individual actors as they display and respond to difference. Thus, I want to shift some emphasis away from the categories and move toward understanding how categories take on meaning within interactions. Marking difference is a rhetorical lens—rhetorical because it emphasizes the relationship between speaker/writer and audience as well as the situated nature of all communicative activity—that acknowledges the important role that identity categories play in interaction. At the same time, markers of difference underscore attention to difference as it is performed during the moment-to-moment vicissitudes of communication. (Kerschbaum 2012, 624)

To engage difference in writing is to construct forces that divide orientations, and, as I have said, these differences and divisions are performed in each rhetorical act.

Foucault's work, particularly *The Order of Things*, is helpful here. Most people are comfortable playing in the safe house of coherent orientations. The move to engage orientations dialectically is, as Foucault points out, an unnatural impulse: "We are all familiar with the disconcerting effect of the proximity of extremes, or, quite simply, with the sudden vicinity of things that have no relation to each other" (Foucault 1970, xvi). Yet engaging incoherent orientations is precisely the initial move we must make in order to proceed dialectically, and rhetoric is required in order to make this move. Foucault calls contradiction a "discursive function," and Burke tells us that negation "is a function peculiar to symbol systems" (Burke 1966a, 9). Like Foucault's "extremes" and Burke's "negation," the force of opposition is also a function of language and discourse, and rhetoric is the art with which we might influence its functions.

Forces of opposition divide orientations by means of criteria: an object or event must meet the criteria that undergird the force of opposition before becoming part of an orientation or being forced out into other orientations, if they will have them. Foucault writes,

There is no similitude and no distinction, even for the wholly untrained perception, that is not the result of a precise operation and of the application of a preliminary criterion. A "system of elements"—a definition of the segments by which the resemblances and differences can be shown, the types of variation by which those segments can be affected, and, lastly, the threshold above which there is a difference and below which there is a similitude—is indispensable for the establishment of even the simplest form of order. Order is, at one and the same time, that which is given in things as their inner law, the hidden network that determines the way they confront one another, and also that which has no existence except in the grid created by a glance, an examination, a language; and it is only in the blank spaces of this grid that order manifests itself in depth as though already there, waiting in silence for the moment of its expression. (Foucault 1970, xx)

According to Foucault, the classical episteme was dominated by the search for resemblances, the drive to find commonalities and claim them as our own. But those searches and drives shifted in the modern episteme: "Resemblance, which had for long been the fundamental category of knowledge—both the form and the content of what we know— became dissociated in an analysis based on terms of identity and difference" (Foucault 1970, 54). Foucault continues,

The activity of the mind . . . no longer consist[s] in *drawing things together*, in setting out on a quest for everything that might reveal some sort of kinship, attraction, or secretly shared nature within them, but, on the contrary, in *discriminating*, that is, in establishing their identities, then the inevitability of the connections with all the successive degrees of a series. In this sense, discrimination imposes upon comparison the primary and fundamental investigation of difference: providing oneself by intuition with a distinct representation of things, and apprehending clearly the inevitable connection between one element in a series and that which immediately follows it. (Foucault 1970, 55)

What Foucault calls "identity" is the structuring principle of orientations, and what Foucault calls "difference" is the structuring principle of the forces of opposition: seeking identities forms orientations, and seeking differences forms forces of opposition.

Dialectical rhetoric requires speakers and writers to place different orientations into certain productive modes of engagement. Prior to dialectical engagement, however, different orientations are viewed as mutually exclusive and incompatible. In order for orientations to be viewed in this way, two conditions must be present simultaneously: each orientation must be sovereign and internally coherent, and each orientation must posit or assume a force of opposition (or a complex of interrelated forces of opposition) that separates it from other orientations at fundamental levels. From a rhetorical perspective, what Chaïm Perelman and Lucie Olbrechts-Tyteca call "strategies of association and dissociation" function to construct and reinforce orientations and forces of opposition. We use strategies of association to articulate the values and interests that form and maintain orientations, whether our own or others'.

Perelman and Olbrechts-Tyteca (1969) write, "By processes of association we understand schemes which bring separate elements together
and allow us to establish a unity among them, which aims either at organizing them or at evaluating them, positively or negatively, by means
of one another" (190). We use strategies of dissociation to divide and
disconnect values and interests from orientations, whether our own or
others'. Perelman and Olbrechts-Tyteca continue, "By processes of *dissociation*, we mean techniques of separation which have the purpose of dissociating, separating, disuniting elements which are regarded as forming a whole or at least a unified group within some system of thought"
(190). Since association and dissociation are strategies in a rhetorical
process, it is most productive to view orientations not as immutable
structures but as evolving through relationships with other orientations;
thus, for each development within an orientation, there must be an
equal and corresponding development in the force of opposition.

In order to engage in dialectical rhetoric, there must be something
(or some things) to engage. Dialectical rhetorics engage orientations.
Orientations are defined through processes of association, linkage, and
articulation, and they are also defined through processes of dissociation and differentiation. Although orientations and forces of opposition
generally drive dialectical rhetoric, they are not structures that can be
described in any objective way; instead, orientations and forces of opposition are performed in the act of rhetoric, constructed in the process of
dialectical engagement. In the next three sections, I describe how one-
dimensional, two-dimensional, and three-dimensional rhetorics engage
orientations, with each rhetorical dimension constructing orientations
and forces of opposition differently in the context of rhetorical acts.

ONE-DIMENSIONAL RHETORICS

One-dimensional rhetorics articulate and promote the values and
interests of a single orientation without directly acknowledging alternative orientations, except perhaps as sources of rebuttal. This single
orientation (though *actually* linguistic in substance, social in character,
diverse in membership, and evolving in structure) is *performed* as essential. Essential orientations are rhetorical fictions in which identities and
relationships are performed as though they were real (not linguistic),
ontological (not social), universal (not diverse), and constant (not evolving). Often directed toward purposes of social unification and coherence, one-dimensional rhetorics use rhetorical strategies, such as linear argumentation, propositional logic, and the rational evaluation of

claims, that generally do not recognize contradictions in material existence or social discourse. Within the confines of individual orientations, one-dimensional rhetorics reinforce social coherence and strengthen the bonds that form and maintain communities; reinforcing coherence and strengthening bonds are important functions of one-dimensional rhetorics, especially when communities are in crisis or simply lack cohesiveness.[9] However, these orientations, performed as essential foundations of identity in one-dimensional rhetorics, also have the potential to become petrified, unable to respond to new demands or evolve with emerging contexts.

Many fully developed modern systems of argumentation are one dimensional, based on a single, general (or universal) orientation that might be called *rationality*. One-dimensional rhetorics often use rationality as a metaphor to suppress what Davis (following Burke) calls "originary divisiveness." In the context of one-dimensional rationality, culture and difference are viewed as impediments to effective argumentation. One-dimensional systems of argumentation are not dialectical, nor do they invoke dialectic as a counterpart art, except as linear logic (which is not really dialectical). A characteristic one-dimensional rhetoric (based on rationality, not dialectic) is represented in Stephen Edelston Toulmin's *The Uses of Argument*.

Toulmin's (1958) *The Uses of Argument* has been tremendously influential in rhetoric and composition, and deservedly so.[10] Toulmin sets up *The Uses of Argument* as a critique, from the perspective of "practical reasoning," of "the abstract and formal criteria relied on in mathematical logic and much of twentieth-century epistemology" (viii). For Toulmin, practical reasoning is not based in methods for seeking truth and falsity through abstract logical rules; practical reasoning, instead, "is concerned with the soundness of the claims we make—with the solidity of the grounds we produce to support them, the firmness of the backing we provide for them—or, to change the metaphor, with the sort of *case* we present in defense of our claims" (7). Toulmin explains that this new model of practical reasoning is not based in sciences such as psychology, sociology, or mathematics, but in "jurisprudence" (7). Based on this model of legal practice, "A sound argument, a well-grounded or firmly-backed claim," according to Toulmin, "is one which will stand up to criticism" (8). The foundation upon which an argument might "stand up to criticism" is its *rationality*, the only legitimate orientation upon which to construct an argument. Toulmin's model of argumentation is, thus, one dimensional.

The intent of Toulmin's method is to test the soundness, solidity, firmness, strength—that is, the rationality—of arguments against real or imagined criticism. This criticism, however, does not represent a different or opposed orientation since the only orientation opposed to rationality would be irrationality. The criticisms in Toulmin's model are simply demands for the further production of "grounds (backing, data, facts, evidence, considerations, features) on which the merits of the assertion are to depend" (Toulmin 1958, 11). Criticisms, then, are challenges to the rationality of the argument in question; they are not alternative arguments arising from the values and interests of a different orientation. And it is not the role of the arguer to challenge or negotiate these criticisms; it is the role of the arguer to reinforce and strengthen the arguments in play so they succeed despite being challenged, and the challenger must yield to the force of the argument. According to Toulmin, "A claim need be conceded only if the argument which can be produced in its support proves up to standard" (11–12), and this standard, according to Toulmin, is not specific to the values and interests of communities and orientations but is instead rationality.

Toulmin's model is generally linear since the only engagement (certainly not dialectical) encountered in the process of argumentation is with the "challenges" that must be answered by presenting additional grounds. Toulmin (1958) suggests that there are "phases" through which every argument passes, regardless of the "field" (discipline, community, orientation, etc.) in which an argument is made, making these phases of argumentation "field-invariant," or not dependent in any way on the individual making the case or the context in which the case is made. The first phase in Toulmin's process is to ask a difficult question about a difficult problem and evaluate answers or solutions according to the force of each one's modality. Answers and solutions do not emerge out of social groups or orientations; they emerge from rational minds capable of judging the adequacy of answers or the efficacy of solutions by attributing to each a term representing its argumentative strength, such as "possible" or "probable" or "necessary." Such terms indicating the "force" (or position in the gray area between truth and falsity) of a claim or argument, like the phases themselves, are field invariant, the same regardless of who makes the argument or where it is made (17–19). During the second phase in Toulmin's process, we choose from among the possibilities the answer or solution that has the highest degree of probability for success, which may be unequivocal or in need of qualification (17–22). These decisions regarding which answer or solution to choose, and thus which to argue for and which to reject, are based on rational judgment, not on community membership, social standing, or orientation. They are universal, rational, and, thus, field invariant.

Although the force of a claim (its modal status represented in a term like *possible* or *probable* or *necessary*) is field invariant, the criteria of use for such terms vary from field to field—they are "field-dependent." The force of the modal term *probably* will be the same in the humanities and in the sciences (i.e., it will signify the same degree of qualification); however, Toulmin argues that the criteria of its use in these two fields will be different. Humanists will be more comfortable making and accepting claims based in probability than scientists will. Toulmin suggests, then, that "the force of commending something as 'good' or condemning it as 'bad' remains the same, whatever sort of thing it may be, even though the criteria for judging or assessing the merits of different kinds are very variable" (Toulmin 1958, 33). It is tempting to assume that Toulmin's appeal to field-dependent criteria is an appeal to the effects of communities or orientations on the nature of argumentation, but this is not the case, and Toulmin is careful to prevent this reading: "In considering . . . the different grounds on which something may have to be ruled out in the course of an argument, we found plenty of differences on going from one field to another, but nothing which led us to conclude that any special field of argument was intrinsically non-rational, or that the court of reason was not somehow competent to pronounce upon its problems" (40). According to Toulmin, then, regardless of what field an argument enters, there is one universal criterion that trumps all others and the differences they might imply—reason or rationality.

Any claim not certainly true or certainly false, regardless of its modal force or the criteria governing its use, is probable, and probability is the province of practical reasoning and argumentation. Whereas formal logic lays out truths in a linear and progressive string of certain propositions leading to a true conclusion, practical reasoning and argumentation, on the other hand, lay out arguments in complex arrangements of claims, data, warrants, backing, qualifications, and rebuttals. The claim is the assertion to which we commit ourselves following evaluation (by means of reason and rationality) of the strength or modality of alternative answers and solutions to an initial guiding question. Data are the facts or grounds upon which we base the strength of the claim. Warrants are the reasons that connect the data to the claim. Backing is the evidence (laws, policies, etc.) that legitimates the warrants as relevant and salient. Qualifications are the modal terms that signify the strength of the claim. Rebuttals represent exceptions in which the claim does not apply or is not legitimate.[11] Toulmin's layout of arguments is one dimensional since claims and all of their attendant argumentative functions are directed toward articulating the values and interests of a single orientation (rationality), even in what Toulmin calls the "rebuttal," which is little more than an exception limiting the scope of the claim.

While the intent of Toulmin's critical method is to test the rationality of arguments against criticism, it is instead the intent of practical methods of argumentation *based on* Toulmin's model to *produce* sound, solid, firm, and strong arguments that resist direct challenges. In its practical adaptations (by Timothy W. Crusius and Carolyn E. Channell, Karen J. Lunsford, and William Versterman, among many others), Toulmin's model has become a tool for the invention and effective structuring of argumentative discourse, especially in writing. Once students discover the claim they want to make, they then explore the data, warrants, and backing that might be marshaled in support of their claim, and they consider the qualifications and rebuttals they must acknowledge in order to prevent an audience from easily discrediting the argument as a whole. Toulmin's model, in other words, is easily adapted to the construction of arguments that articulate and promote the values and interests of a single orientation without opposing competing orientations or negotiating different orientations. This productive model generally considers effective arguments to represent the values and beliefs of rational people, and this model is not dialectical.

One-dimensional rhetorics are useful for articulating and promoting the values and interests of a single orientation, especially during times of social incoherence when the synthesis of values and purposes serves ethical and productive ends. Yet, however useful they may be, one-dimensional rhetorics can also reinforce adherence to values that do not serve communities as a whole in productive ways, constructing orientations that, for example, favor only a few, deny the salience of competing orientations, or mask the ideological nature of power.[12] These problematic orientations are especially destructive when they are promoted as rational and any opposing orientation is denigrated as irrational. When one-dimensional rhetorics undermine the social well-being of communities (by promoting exclusionary values, denying competing orientations, or masking sources of power), these destructive rhetorics must become subject to further dialectical discourse, including two-dimensional critique and three-dimensional mediation.

TWO-DIMENSIONAL RHETORICS

Two-dimensional rhetorics articulate and promote the values and interests of a single orientation in direct relationship to opposing orientations, with each orientation engaged in a power struggle against the others. Like the single-orientation characteristic of one-dimensional rhetorics, the opposed orientations of two-dimensional rhetorics are also performed as essential (real and constant), and their essential qualities become emphasized in the process of opposition. Two-dimensional rhetorics use argumentative and persuasive strategies to shore up one orientation against the power imposed by the other(s) and to dismantle the institutional structures (economic, political, social, cultural) that impose power to the detriment of some. Two-dimensional rhetorics are usually dialectical because the purpose of this discourse is to develop and articulate one orientation by critiquing other orientations, and the content and structure of two-dimensional discourse is intimately conditioned by the content and structure of the object of criticism.[13] Since the oppositional orientations that emerge in two-dimensional rhetorics are performed as essential, they too are prone to petrification.

Two contextual circumstances often establish a need for two-dimensional, critical rhetorics. First, when the values and interests that form orientations become stagnant, unable to respond to shifting historical conditions, there often emerge, from within a particular community, progressive subcommunities offering counterorientations in direct opposition to what are perceived as obsolete orientations. This is what Burke calls the "prophet function" (Burke 1954, 179): here the purpose is to critique orientations that no longer adequately account for present motives and to offer alternative orientations in their place. In *Writing the Future*, Gunther Kress writes that "critique is essential in periods of social stability as a means of producing change; by bringing that which is settled into crisis, it is a means of producing a cultural dynamic" (Kress 1995, 5). Since the material and social world around us is constantly evolving, it is necessary for healthy communities to evolve in response; the prophet function challenges stagnant orientations and produces a dynamic in which new, more responsive orientations can emerge.

The second circumstance that establishes a need for two-dimensional rhetorics exists when the values of one culture and its orientations come into competitive contact with other cultures and orientations that have opposing values. In these cases, there often emerge, from without, sources of power directly challenging the sovereignty of at least one orientation. Mary Louise Pratt calls these circumstances "contact zones," or "social spaces where cultures meet, clash, and grapple with each other, often in contexts of highly asymmetrical relations of power, such as colonialism, slavery, or their aftermaths as they are lived out in many parts of the world today" (Pratt 1991, 35). Under such circumstances, two-dimensional, dialectical, critical rhetorics protect the interests of one orientation by calling into question the (oppressive) interests of opposing orientations.

In rhetoric and composition studies, two-dimensional rhetorics became popular during the 1980s and 1990s, the result of a social turn in the field (and in the humanities generally). This social turn witnessed the infusion of a wide variety of critical theories (including feminism, Marxism, critical pedagogy, and cultural studies) into the discourses of rhetoric and composition. Most of the two-dimensional varieties of these social rhetorics presuppose that ideology is false consciousness and that critical discourse unveils the mystifications of ideology, resulting in true consciousness.[14] Early articulations in the social turn used these theories as a basis for a thorough critique of asocial or antisocial (individualist, objectivist) composition theories and pedagogies, such as current-traditional, cognitivist, and expressivist approaches. These early articulations used two-dimensional, dialectical, critical rhetorics in order to create a viable social antithesis to the individualist and objectivist theses that dominated rhetoric and composition during the 1970s.

Social-epistemic rhetoric was one of the most influential two-dimensional, dialectical, critical theories that emerged from the social turn in rhetoric and composition.[15] Berlin's theory of social-epistemic rhetoric emerged dialectically from a two-dimensional, critical rejection of cognitivist and expressivist pedagogies for writing instruction, and this critique was based on each pedagogy's relationship to the keyword *ideology*.[16] Berlin situates rhetoric within ideology: when ideology is situated within rhetoric, rhetoric becomes the objective means to combat ideology; on the other hand, Berlin argues, when rhetoric is situated within ideology, rhetoric is always ideological and can never escape its nature as politicized discourse (Berlin 1988, 477). The central problem with cognitivist rhetoric is that it "refuses the ideological question altogether, claiming for itself the transcendent neutrality of science," and it "encourages discursive practices that are compatible with dominant economic, social, and political formations" (478). Expressivist rhetoric is openly ideological, "opposing itself in no uncertain terms to the scientism of current-traditional rhetoric and the ideology it encourages," but it is constantly "open to appropriation by the very forces it opposes" (478). Social-epistemic rhetoric evolved out of a response to the ideological problems of both cognitivist and expressivist rhetorics: it "is self-consciously aware of its ideological stand [contra cognitivist rhetoric], making the very question of ideology the center of classroom activities, and in so doing providing itself a defense against preemption [contra expressivist rhetoric] and a strategy for self-criticism and self-correction" (478).

After Berlin dialectically opposes the antithesis of social-epistemic rhetoric to its theses cognitivist and expressivist rhetorics, he describes the internal structure and methods of social-epistemic rhetoric as dialectical. In a social-epistemic context, Berlin writes, rhetoric is "a political act involving a dialectical interaction engaging the material, the social, and the individual writer, with language as the agency of mediation" (Berlin 1988, 488). One problem with both cognitivist and expressivist rhetorics is that they are not dialectical; these rhetorics favor the observer (though in different ways) and do not engage the observer in dialectical contact with discourse communities or material conditions. However, Berlin explains, "knowledge is never found in any one of these but can only be posited as the product of the dialectic in which all three come together" (488). While Berlin's notion of linguistic mediation appears to move in the direction of three-dimensional rhetorics, the fact is that Berlin never explains exactly how language mediates among the observer, the discourse community, and the material conditions of existence. Berlin skirts this issue by arguing that language mediates everything because absolutely everything is language. Berlin explains, "This dialectic is grounded in language: the observer, the discourse community, and the material conditions of existence are all verbal constructs" (488). In fact, even the very people who engage in rhetoric are functions of language and are thus implicated in the total dialectic (and not external to it, as observers): "For social epistemic rhetoric, the subject is itself a social construct that emerges through the linguistically-circumscribed interaction of the individual, the community, and the material world" (489). Since language is thoroughly bound up in the dialectical interaction of individual, social, and material processes, which are inherently historical and are in constant flux, Berlin explains, social-epistemic rhetoric "offers an explicit critique of economic, political, and social arrangements" (490). Thus, while social-epistemic rhetoric itself emerged out of a dialectical critique of cognitivist and expressivist rhetorics, its very rhetorical and pedagogical methodologies, too, are two dimensional, dialectical, and critical in orientation.[17]

Riding the wave of the social turn, Alan W. France's *Composition as a Cultural Practice* draws heavily from cultural materialism, feminism, Marxism, and cultural studies in order to critique "dominant" orientations in composition pedagogy from the perspective of social-epistemic rhetoric. In the first few sentences of the opening chapter, "Assigning Places," France writes, "The introductory composition course is crucially implicated in the process of cultural reproduction. Its content is the set of discursive rules that assign students to their proper place in the institutional hierarchies of corporate capitalism. . . . When we teach students to construct an 'authentic self' and to subordinate that self to the rules of a dominant discourse, we are reproducing ideological formations of truth, whether we intend to or not" (France 1994, 1). France constructs his materialist version of social-epistemic rhetoric in dialectical opposition to other "dominant" pedagogies, including expressivist and cognitivist approaches: "Expressivism creates a discourse of self, in which the subject writes from a metaphysical position outside history and culture, as the privileged term of the communication process. Cognitivism deceptively models itself on science, especially structural (autonomous) linguistics and cognitive psychology, assuming a mantle of neutrality that raises knowledge above the social and political contention inherent in discourse" (21). One of the central problems with these dominant pedagogies is that they are "uncritical," teaching "students to subordinate themselves to institutional authority while preserving the appearance of individual freedom"(4).[18]

In dialectical opposition to expressivist and cognitivist pedagogies, France articulates a pedagogy based on materialist rhetoric that requires students to write critical essays about their own oppression at the hands of dominant ideologies. Materialist social-epistemic rhetoric is necessary because culture in general indoctrinates students to accept the dominant ideology as if it were inscribed in nature, not the product of ideological processes; and dominant composition pedagogies (expressivist, cognitivist) are deeply implicated in these larger cultural processes since they teach students that the only effective uses of language are those that reinforce dominant ideologies. A materialist writing pedagogy, then, teaches students to "uncover the discursive means by which dominant social groups confirm or 'naturalize' their dominance and by which subordinate groups contest or delegitimize asymmetries of power" (France 1994, 22). And the way students uncover these discursive means is through critical writing.

Although France dislikes the places assigned to students by dominant writing pedagogies, he himself, nevertheless, assigns students places, and it is from the defined orientation of these inevitably subordinate places that students compose critical writing. While one-dimensional rhetorics require rational writers and readers, two-dimensional, dialectical (oppositional) rhetorics require oppressed writers and sympathetic readers (since the oppressors themselves would be ambivalent, curmudgeonly, or manipulative). Most students in first-year composition, however, do not know they are oppressed; they are happy to participate in American education and culture. Yet from the perspective of two-dimensional, dialectical teachers, these students are simply duped by ideology. France describes the students who enter his writing classrooms as "subjects of a 'mass youth culture'" (France 1994, 3), alienated and insular (9), "culturally determined" (27), and "inclined toward a rhetoric of consensus" (30). Since materialist rhetoric, the foundation upon which France builds a new composition pedagogy (in dialectical opposition to expressivism and cognitivism), "contests the distribution of power inscribed in a text from the subject positions of those (i.e., 'slaves') excluded from power" (22), students must adopt these oppressed orientations in order to succeed in materialist critical writing.

For France, materialist rhetoric is not just another method for writing instruction, one to choose among others. It is our "responsibility," France argues, "to initiate students into the ongoing production of texts by enabling them not only to perform literary exegesis and effective composition but also to discern in texts—their own included—the material conditions of production, the historical role of a text in the cultural reproduction of (and resistance to) power" (France 1994, 27). A materialist rhetoric, then, "attempts to reverse the authorized axiology of the text as well as its distribution of power" (29); asks students to turn things upside down, reevaluating the text in the interest of the subordinate and nameless others" (30); and "recognizes those occupying subject positions incorporated in texts and their material, as well as discursive, subordination to structures of power" (36). A composition course that grounds its pedagogy in materialist rhetoric would treat "composition as a cultural process" (40) and would thus also be "dialectical," among other things, and France defines "dialectical" as "politically oppositional" (40).

One of the central problems with two-dimensional rhetorics is that when the entire world (material, individual, social, discursive, etc.) *has to be classified* as either this or that and nothing else, much of the complexity available to us in these contexts is lost to the artificial structure of theoretical opposition. Critical rhetorics, especially Berlin's social-epistemic rhetoric and France's slightly more materialist version of it, leave students with the understanding that their lives are conditioned and that they are oppressed but leave them with few strategies to improve their lives or ease their oppression.

THREE-DIMENSIONAL RHETORICS

When one-dimensional rhetorics are exposed as limited in scope or obsolete or potentially oppressive, and when two-dimensional rhetorics descend into counterproductive negative dialectics, there emerges a rhetorical need to mediate among competing (different, though not opposed) orientations. Kress explains that "in periods of intense change the problem is that the cultural dynamic is too great, so that critique is not the issue; the focus of intervention has to shift to the design of possible alternatives" (Kress 1995, 5). This is the function of three-dimensional dialectical mediation, to engage different orientations in productive contact in order to construct new orientations that transcend unifying one-dimensional rhetorics and critical two-dimensional rhetorics. Directed toward purposes of social mediation, three-dimensional dialectical discourses use rhetorical strategies such as deconstruction, dialogue, identification, critique, and juxtaposition, all of which engage orientations in positive and productive (not unifying or oppositional) ways.[19] Unlike the orientations performed in one-dimensional and two-dimensional rhetorics, the orientations performed in three-dimensional rhetorics are, in Davis's words, inessential.

Although I hesitate to associate three-dimensional rhetorics with post-modernism generally, one description of postmodernism is particularly relevant to this discussion of rhetorical dimensionality, Jean-Francois Lyotard's (1989) *The Postmodern Condition: A Report on Knowledge*, originally published in French in 1979 and translated into English in 1984. Lyotard offers postmodernism as an alternative to the "two basic representational models of society" that were prevalent during the first half of the twentieth century but which have their origins in the nineteenth century: "Either society forms a functional whole," as in Marcuse's one-dimensional society, or "it is divided in two," as in Marcuse's two-dimensional society (11). The first model, society as a functional whole, legitimates knowledge and action according to a grand narrative of emancipation. The second model, society as divided into two, legitimates knowledge and action according to a grand narrative of revolution.

Lyotard describes postmodernism generally as the "crisis of narratives" (Lyotard 1989, xxiii), or more accurately as an "incredulity toward metanarratives" (xxiv). Metanarratives (of emancipation and revolution) served numerous functions in modernist society, including the legitimation of knowledge and activity. If a given activity fit into the metanarrative structure, it was legitimate; if it did not fit, it was illegitimate, unethical, irrational, and so forth. One-dimensional and two-dimensional societies and their discourses rely on modernist metanarratives for their legitimating functions. Lyotard explains that in postmodernism, "The narrative function is losing its functors, its great hero, its great dangers, its great voyages, its great goal" (xxiv). Yet all of these "functors" remain, for example, in Marcuse's two-dimensional critique of one-dimensional society: the hero is the critical theorist, who has knowledge of contradictions; the danger is one-dimensional society and the closing of the universe of discourse; the voyage is the critique of one-dimensional society and its oppressive processes; the goal is two-dimensional, critical, thus free society. Lyotard explains that all activities may be judged according to their place in this metanarrative.

This legitimating metanarrative function, according to Lyotard, is being "dispersed in clouds of narrative language elements. . . . Conveyed within each cloud are pragmatic valencies specific to its kind. Each of us lives at the intersection of many of these" (Lyotard 1989, xxiv). Lyotard's clouds are metaphors for communities that develop their own localized narratives by means of heterogeneous language games (rule-governed rhetorical functions that both constrain and enable the generation of utterances). These narratives, even those that develop within relatively coherent communities, are by no means unified; like the language games that generate them, these local narratives are heterogeneous. In the larger context of social discourse, multiple communities compete for power in a process called "paralogy," a kind of rhetorical *agora* in which ideas and stories compete for explanatory power (60–67). In three-dimensional society, communities come into competitive contact in each instance of interaction, whether directly or indirectly, and the nature of this contact is determined by the purpose of engagement.[20]

During the late 1970s and 1980s, a number of scholars tried to "map" the field of rhetoric and composition (Berlin 1982; 1987b; 1988; Fulkerson 1979; Kameen 1980; Woods 1981). Although each of these maps plotted out slightly different boundaries, the effect was the same, to divide composition pedagogies into identifiable camps, each distinct and characterized by mutually exclusive tenets. Throughout the 1980s and 1990s, these maps remained enormously influential for both theoretical and pedagogical reasons. Yet even as early as 1987, Berlin would admit in the postscript to *Rhetoric and Reality* that his own epistemological taxonomy did "not prove as descriptive" after 1975 because of the "tendency of certain rhetorics within the subjective and transactional categories to move in the direction of the epistemic, regarding rhetoric as principally a method of discovering and even creating knowledge, *frequently within socially defined discourse communities*" (Berlin 1987b, 183; my emphasis). By then the social turn had begun and was becoming evident in rhetoric and composition scholarship.[21]

By the mid-1990s, some scholars whose approaches to composition research and pedagogy had been divided and conquered, especially by Berlin, made a conscious and concerted effort to *integrate* these sovereign camps into theories and pedagogies that would derive strength from diversity.[22] Early efforts to integrate theories Berlin had divided up include Sherrie L. Gradin's (1995) *Romancing Rhetorics* and Linda Flower's (1995) *The Construction of Negotiated Meaning*. In *Romancing Rhetorics*, Gradin (1995) argues that the most influential disciplinary maps (especially Berlin's) claim social characteristics for only one camp of composition pedagogy, divesting romantic expressionism, in particular, of its historical nature as a social, political, and rhetorical conception of language. But Gradin's attempt to resurrect expressivism presumes that, in fact, *social* pedagogies are best and that expressivism is *really* social-constructionist. Gradin does not, in other words, negotiate a new orientation in which the opposition (social versus expressivist) no longer holds true; she simply argues that expressivism has been misinterpreted. So the opposition remains in place, and Gradin slides expressivism into the category of social rhetorics.

In *The Construction of Negotiated Meaning*, Flower (1995) describes a social-cognitive theory of writing that accounts for the manifold practices that constitute every literate act, and Flower uses the key term *literacy* as a means to negotiate a new orientation toward writing theory and practice, one that integrates cognitive functions of the mind with social functions of culture and community. "Literate actions," Flower writes, "emerge out of a *constructive* cognitive process that transforms knowledge in purposeful ways. And at critical moments, this constructive literate act may also become a process of *negotiation* in which individual readers and writers must juggle conflicting demands and chart a path among alternative goals, constraints, and possibilities" (2), and every "constructive literate act is a social, cognitive, and rhetorical process (5). In one-dimensional rhetorics, arguments either express rational (acceptable) truths or irrational (unacceptable) falsies, and in two-dimensional rhetorics, arguments either critique oppression or manipulate the masses; in neither case is *negotiation* a legitimate goal (one should never negotiate with irrationality or oppression). Flower's social-cognitive theory of writing moves beyond the limiting constraints of one-dimensional (rational/irrational) and two-dimensional (liberatory/oppressive) rhetorics, looking instead toward dialectical negotiation and mediation as the driving forces of literate acts.

Literate acts are not rational or irrational, liberatory or oppressive; they are complex and do not value one element of their complexity over others, enabling and even necessitating a process of negotiation. Flower writes,

> Literate acts are sites of construction, tension, divergence, and conflict. They happen at the intersection of diverse goals, values, and assumptions, where social roles interact with personal images of one's self and one's situation, where individual rhetorical agendas mix with highly conventional practices. These metaphors—"interact," "intersect," "mix"—are by design inclusive, refusing to privilege one force over the other. That is because literate acts are often sites of negotiation where the meaning that emerges may reflect resolution, abiding contradiction, or perhaps just a temporary stay against uncertainty. (Flower 1995, 19)

One of the central tenets in Flower's social-cognitivist theory that enables three-dimensional dialectical complexity is the notion that orientations and the arguments (or literate acts) that emerge from them are never fully formed and stagnant. In a social-cognitivist rhetoric, orientations are always in the process of formation, as acts of thought and communication in social context. It is important, Flower writes, "to recognize fragmentation and contradiction within our own positions as individuals—but to still envision a constructive act that is more than the brush of discourses passing in the night" (Flower 1995, 41). "Meaning making," Flower contends, is not a rational or oppositional act; it is "a rhetorical act" that occurs "in the intersection between individual purposes and social uses surrounding literate acts" (42), in the "constant interaction of cognitive and social context" (43). Whereas one-dimensional rhetorics deny social forces in favor of the rational, and two-dimensional rhetorics deny individual forces in favor of a dynamic of domination and resistance, Flower's three-dimensional social-cognitive rhetoric views individual and social forces engaged in a constructive dialectic.

One of the key terms driving Flower's social-cognitive theory of writing, a term that is out of place in one-dimensional and two-dimensional rhetorics, is "negotiation," which Flower views as a "dilemma-driven and goal-directed effort" and, most critically, a "constructive process" (Flower 1995, 66). Since negotiation is a process, it inevitably also involves interpretation and reflection: we interpret our own goals in dialectical connection with social pressures and conventions, not just once but constantly, throughout the process of communication; and as we interpret, we also reflect on and revise our goals in response to our shifting conception of social forces. Negotiation, then, is part of a larger rhetorical process of meaning making in which goals and conventions, and many other aspects of the communication process, are in constant contact through evolving relationships (75–84). For Flower, then, viewing literate acts as processes of negotiation between individual writers and the social contexts in which they communicate enables a certain theoretical and practical complexity not possible in one-dimensional or two-dimensional rhetorics.

In *Community Literacy and the Rhetoric of Public Engagement*, based on her work with the Community Literacy Center in Pittsburgh, Flower extends some of her observations about social-cognitive rhetoric to the problems associated with writing in the public sphere, resulting in a methodology she calls an "intercultural rhetoric of public engagement" (Flower 2008, 5), or, more simply, "community literacy." Flower explains that community literacy is "a rhetorical practice for inquiry and social change," which has its theoretical roots in the work of John Dewey and Paulo Freire (16). Community literacy is marked by diversity in collaboration and dialogue across difference, and its goals are not only rhetorical but also practical, material. Flower explains,

> The community literacy I am hoping to document is an intercultural dialogue *with others* on issues that *they* identify as sites of struggle. Community literacy happens at a busy intersection of multiple literacies and diverse discourses. It begins its work when community folk, urban teens, community supporters, college-student mentors, and university faculty start naming and solving problems *together*. It does its work by widening the circle and constructing an even more public dialogue across differences of culture, class, discourse, race, gender, and power shaped by the explicit goals of discovery and change. In short, in this *rhetorical model*, community literacy is a site for personal and public inquiry and . . . a site for rhetorical theory building as well. (Flower 2008, 19)

When we value diversity, difference becomes generative as a source of intercultural inquiry, and diverse communities should not hope to achieve consensus at all times but must work to achieve understanding through discourse and interaction. As a generative source of inquiry, diversity grounds the construction of new identities and arguments (Flower 2008, 34–39). But this constructive impulse cannot be left to chance; it must be strategic or goal directed. Goals are often generated in collaborative planning in which community members adopt roles for discussion and seek "rival hypotheses" (54–60). Rival hypotheses are not simply accepted as an inevitable effect of diversity; rival hypotheses are sought because diversity is productive and generative. Community literacy, then, is actively dialectical and always three dimensional, always engaged in an inquiry process that leads to alternatives. In the next chapter, I focus more closely on three-dimensional dialectical rhetorics, (re)situating them within their classical function as topical arts.

Notes

1. Christopher Swift (2010) analyzes a debate between Marcuse and Theodor Adorno that occurred in the late 1960s (several years after the publication of *One-Dimensional Man*) regarding how to address the student revolts in France. According to Swift, Adorno argued that critical theorists should take a dialectical stance toward the revolts, engaging only in academic critique of the problem's historical development and ignoring the student activists' demand for practical (political, rhetorical) advice. Marcuse, on the other hand, was more sympathetic to the rhetorical needs of the student activists, though not to the extent that the students desired. Thus, Marcuse, while ultimately a philosophical dialectician, was willing to discuss practical matters with student activists. Adorno was not.

2. A similar view appears a few decades earlier in the work of Bakhtin, who associates practical rhetoric with monologic discourse and the aesthetic language of the novel with dialogic discourse.

3. I use *orientation* as a general term for a family of words that have similar meanings yet invoke specific contexts. As a general term, I prefer *orientation* to others because it comes with a spatial and temporal sense of positioning. *Orientation* also carries a performative sense since orienteering is the active process of navigating through difficult and unknown terrain using practical, social knowledge and available tools. However, specific contexts might call for other, more specific terms. In one-dimensional rhetorics, for example, terms like *reason* and *rationality* are often invoked to describe effective orientations in the invention and judgment of arguments. *Reason* and *rationality* are avoided as key terms in two-dimensional and three-dimensional rhetorics. *Ideology* is a kind of orientation often invoked in two-dimensional rhetorics and occasionally in three-dimensional rhetorics but not at all in one-dimensional rhetorics. In many two-dimensional rhetorics, especially those arising out of Marxist social theory, the dominant culture creates ideology by means of institutions like schooling and work in order to mystify the subordinate class's relationship to the real world, leading to false consciousness. Thus, one would expect to see the term *ideology* at play in two-dimensional rhetorics, not the more general term *orientation*. In three-dimensional rhetorics, where mediation is the goal of communication, *ideology* occasionally appears in its postmodern sense of multiple and competing systems of ideas, but more often terms like *perspective* or *point of view* are invoked in order to signal the possibility of negotiation. Thus, although I prefer *orientation* as a key term here, there are certainly rhetorical situations that would encourage the selection of a different terminology. In those situations, the appropriate key terms should be invoked.

4. I am struck by the similarity between Burke's notion of linkages that form orientations and Stuart Hall's notion of articulation, which he also refers to as "linkages" (Hall 1996, 141) that form ideologies.

5. I use the term *signification* instead of a more specific term like *language* because the methods of rhetoric encompass more media than words alone. James A. Berlin (1996) and Linda Brodkey (1996) use the same term for similar reasons.

6. Chaim Perelman and Lucie Olbrechts-Tyteca call this process of peeling off contextual exceptions in order to maintain the general coherence of an orientation "the dissociation of concepts" (Perelman and Olbrechts-Tyteca 1969, 411–59).

7. Orientations can take many different forms, as Burke's own definitional slippage indicates. But what interests me in the context of dialectical rhetoric is not the *reality* of orientations (whatever that is). What interests me is the *representation* of orientations in specific rhetorical acts. This sense of orientation (as representational) is not present in Burke's discussion of the concept, but this move is also not entirely

original on my part. I adapt it from Aristotle's discussion of ethos, which is not an objective quality of an individual but is instead constructed in each rhetorical act.

8. For a more detailed discussion of the relationship between identification and division in Burke's work, see Shane Borrowman and Marcia Kmetz's "Divided We Stand: Beyond Burkean Identification" (Borrowman and Kmetz 2011). Also recall that Burke's (1973) parlor metaphor in *The Philosophy of Literary Form* (109–110) exemplifies a "dramatic process" functioning through "dialectical oppositions" (109). Any document we encounter, whether the Constitution or a student's essay, is "a *strategy for encompassing a situation*" (109)—that is, a way of making sense of competing orientations.

9. When they function ethically, Mary Louise Pratt refers to these individual orientations as "safe houses," or "social and intellectual spaces where groups can constitute themselves as horizontal, homogeneous, sovereign communities with high degrees of trust, shared understandings, temporary protection from legacies of oppression" (Pratt 1991, 40). One-dimensional rhetorics support the ongoing functions of safe-house orientations, reinforcing coherence and strengthening bonds, which are critical to social progress.

10. Many composition textbooks use Toulmin's "layout" as a model for generating argumentative writing, though they do not always invoke Toulmin's method overtly. Two popular textbooks that directly invoke Toulmin's method are *Reading and Writing Short Arguments* by William Vesterman (2005) and *The Aims of Argument* by Timothy W. Crusius and Carolyn E. Channell (2008). Some recent scholarship also draws on Toulmin as inspiration for further developments in argumentative theory and practice, including the work of Lisa L. Hill (2000), Karen J. Lunsford (2002), Christopher Schroeder (1997), and Christa Teston (2009).

11. These terms are all defined and exemplified at length in the chapter "The Layout of Arguments" (Toulmin 1958, 94–107).

12. Schroeder, for example, critiques Toulmin and the various adaptations of his model in composition theory and practice, suggesting that "Toulmin's approach . . . functions to obfuscate the relationship between knowledge and its larger political and social arena" and "ignores or excludes the wider context in which the actual negotiations of power transpire" (Schroeder 1997, 103). Thus, in Toulmin's model, "ideological choices are camouflaged by separating the arguments from the social and political arenas from which they emerge" (104). While I agree with many of Schroeder's arguments against Toulmin, I believe some are misplaced. For example, Schroeder criticizes Toulmin for neglecting ethos, pathos, and style, which he considers "essential aspects" of "persuasion" (97), which is of course true; they are not, however, essential aspects of argumentation, which is the subject of *The Uses of Argument*.

13. Carl B. Holmberg (1977) calls all two-dimensional rhetorics dialectical. In dialectical rhetoric, then, "the adjudication would have one of the parties involved be convinced or converted that there is one and only one correct way to live" (234–35), thus "persuading one part of its wrongness while upholding the rightness of the other party" (236). The style of dialectical rhetoric must be "clear and correct," and the aim of persuasion is "conversion of experiencers who are 'incorrect' to the 'correct' view" (238). Raymie E. McKerrow's "critical rhetoric" is also dialectical, though he does not invoke the term himself. Critical rhetoric, especially as the "critique of domination," attempts to "unmask or demystify the discourse of power" (McKerrow 1989, 91).

14. Feminism, Marxism, critical pedagogy, and cultural studies all have two-dimensional and three-dimensional varieties, but the early articulations of the social turn tended to draw from the two-dimensional varieties of these theories. There are

many different discursive arenas (sites of struggle) in which the two-dimensional critique of ideologies occurred (and still occurs) in composition studies, including race, ethnicity, class, gender, sexual preference, media, culture, politics, and so on.

15. Although Berlin was not the first person in composition studies to describe a socially oriented theory of epistemic rhetoric, he did coin the term *social-epistemic*, and his "Rhetoric and Ideology in the Writing Class" (Berlin 1988) is also the best-known articulation of this general approach.

16. In "Composition's Ideology Apparatus" (Sanchez 2001), later reprinted as a chapter in *The Function of Theory in Composition Studies*, Raul Sanchez (2005) critiques Berlin's conception of ideology as false consciousness, and in "Ideology and Critique in Composition Studies," I quibble with certain aspects of Sanchez's critique (McComiskey 2002a).

17. It would not be until his *Rhetorics, Poetics, and Cultures* that Berlin (1996) would hint at the idea that students should compose texts representing their own ideologies rather than just critique other people's (dominant) ideologies (128–29, 136, 173), but it is only a hint.

18. France also critiques the poststructuralist pedagogy described in early editions of David Bartholomae and Anthony Petrosky's *Ways of Reading*, suggesting that the critical-writing assignments and readings assign students the place of idealist textual critic, not materialist political activist. France writes, "Texts or textual practices are never inherently political; they become so only in the ongoing struggle to reproduce or contest material power," a struggle Bartholomae and Petrosky largely ignore (France 1994, 17). But later in the book, France invokes poststructuralist reading practices for his own purposes (23), and these practices do not look all that dissimilar to those described by Bartholomae and Petrosky.

19. Holmberg argues that three-dimensional rhetorics are "rhetorical," which he opposes to dialectical rhetorics. "Rhetorical rhetorics" do not judge one side as correct and the other as incorrect; instead, they seek "a balancing of views" (Holmberg 1977, 236). The style of rhetorical rhetoric is enthymematic and ambiguous, and the persuasive intent is not to convert but to instill in all parties a sense of empathy and a will to collaborate (238–39). Obviously, I disagree with Holmberg that three-dimensional rhetorics are not dialectical because I see more possibilities for dialectic than mere dualistic opposition. I agree with Holmberg, however, when he suggests that the "verbal means of balancing" perspectives became "*a communicative necessity*" when "two [or more] ways of life began to interact" (237–38).

20. It is important to realize that while one-dimensional society is made up of a single, unified orientation from which all legitimate discourse emanates, and two-dimensional society is made up of two or more (though usually two) opposed orientations that enable critical dialectic, three-dimensional society is not necessarily made up of three orientations. Dimensionality has less to do with the number of orientations engaged than it has to do with the nature and function of engagement among orientations. Thus, three orientations in oppositional contact are engaged in two-dimensional discourse, and two orientations in mediative contact are engaged in three-dimensional discourse.

21. In a response to Berlin's "Rhetoric and Ideology in the Writing Class," published in a subsequent issue of *College English*, Linda Flower (1989) argues that Berlin's "ideological thumbnail sketch" (765) of cognitivist rhetoric masks complexities that make it similar to social-epistemic rhetoric, both ideologically and epistemologically.

22. In another context (review of *Literacy Matters*), I called this impulse "the new integrationist movement" (McComiskey 2002b, 751), but I have since discovered that integration is not new. In fact, it is almost as old as the journal *College Composition*

and Communication. In the third issue of *CCC* (published in October 1950), Kenneth Oliver laments that proponents of the major pedagogical approaches at that time would not engage each other: traditionalists or formalists taught grammar and correctness; semanticists taught the negative workings of propaganda in media discourse; and communications specialists taught reading, writing, speaking, and listening for "social purposes" (Oliver 1950, 3). According to Oliver, these three theories, each sovereign and all mutually exclusive, had turned "freshman English" (as of 1950) into a "one-legged, wingless bird" (3). He explains,

> No one of these three, "communicators," general semanticists, nor formalists, seems to see the whole problem with anything approaching a full awareness of its proportions. It is as though the freshman study of language was a two-legged bird. A few scattered intelligent observers began noticing, some twelve or fifteen years ago, that the bird was hopping along awkwardly upon one leg of grammar, and occasionally flapping an ineffective cultural wing. "Look," they said, "that leg isn't sound; let's teach the bird to hop on the other one." So they bound up the grammar-leg to keep it out of the way, and made the bird to walk upon the other leg. And incidentally, saying that the poor bird could not fly anyway, they also bound its wings. "Wow," they confidently exclaimed, "the bird will stay on the ground where he belongs, and will hop along much faster. Also, it may never discover the yen to fly. So much the better; it will be less apt to fall and may hop in a straighter line. (Oliver 1950, 4–5)

Oliver comments, then, on the meaning of the metaphor (as though it were not itself perfectly clear):

> All three approaches seem to me to be incomplete and inadequate to the needs either of the individual student or of man as a social-cultural being. . . . The need is to teach our bird to use both legs and wings as well. Anything else is woefully limited and unworthy as an objective for college students. . . . No one "school" of freshman teaching in the field of our native language can lay honest claim to complete adequacy. There is still a very real need for the development of a well rounded and integrated course. (Oliver 1950, 5–6)

So much for the new integrationist movement. Integration is old. And Oliver is right. (Interestingly, Berlin cites Oliver's essay in *Rhetoric and Reality* [1987b, 109], but he only criticizes Oliver for favoring literary over persuasive discourse. Berlin never mentions Oliver's plea to integrate theories of composing.)

4

THREE-DIMENSIONAL
DIALECTICAL RHETORICS

In chapter 3, I described three dimensions of rhetoric (unifying, critical, and mediative) and how dialectic functions, or does not function, in each dimension. There I treated all three dimensions of rhetoric relatively equally with a brief theoretical characterization and at least one example each. In this chapter, however, I shift to a more detailed treatment of three-dimensional (mediative) dialectical rhetorics, not because they are better than the other varieties but because they have received less attention in rhetoric and composition scholarship. Three-dimensional dialectical rhetoric is the strategic art of mediating among different orientations in specific rhetorical situations and discursive contexts, thereby constructing new orientations in the process, and one crucial aspect of its strategic quality includes a set of topics (*topoi, loci*, places, etc.) for the invention and arrangement of mediative interventions.[1] These dialectical topics guide our mediations among different orientations, and they include deconstruction, dialogue, identification, critique, and juxtaposition.

But before I begin my discussion of three-dimensional dialectical rhetoric as a strategic, topical, and mediative art, I want to return to John Muckelbauer, Victor J. Vitanza, and Byron Hawk. As I explained in chapter 2, these three scholars critique dialectic (with no adjectival modification), but their critique is actually relevant only to philosophical dialectic. Thus, the first thing I want to do in this chapter is to explore how Muckelbauer's affirmative invention, Vitanza's sub/versive historiography, and Hawk's complexity theory might actually provide theoretical grounding for three-dimensional dialectical rhetoric.

AFFIRMATIVE, SUB/VERSIVE, AND COMPLEX
THREE-DIMENSIONAL DIALECTICS

Three-dimensional dialectical rhetorics are not implicated in critiques of philosophical dialectic. Whereas philosophical dialectic operates through negation by means of thesis-antithesis-synthesis,

DOI: 10.7330/9780874219821.c004

three-dimensional dialectical rhetorics operate through mediation by means of deconstruction, dialogue, identification, critique, and juxtaposition. It is true that Muckelbauer's affirmative invention, Vitanza's sub/versive historiography, and Hawk's complexity theory all challenge philosophical dialectic in their own ways; however, it is also true that affirmative invention, sub/versive historiography, and complexity theory form part of the theoretical grounding for three-dimensional dialectical rhetorics. In this section, I return briefly to Muckelbauer's (2009) *The Future of Invention*, Vitanza's (1997) *Negation, Subjectivity, and the History of Rhetoric*, and Hawk's (2007) *A Counter-History of Composition*, exploring their usefulness in the development of the theory and practice of three-dimensional dialectical rhetoric.

I argue throughout this chapter that three-dimensional dialectical rhetoric is a strategic and topical art and these themes emerge prominently as Muckelbauer develops his argument throughout *The Future of Invention*. Muckelbauer's (2009) notion of strategic invention does not imply the sorts of strategies associated with traditional rhetoric: delineate your purpose, analyze your audience, and generate arguments that address both effectively. Drawing from Gilles Deleuze, Felix Guattari, and Jacques Derrida, Muckelbauer explores the strategies of an itinerant traveler, such as a Sophist or a nomad, which reveal "an affirmative sense of repetition that indicates, in Derrida's terms, a 'strategy without finality,' an inventive strategy that does not have a predetermined goal, but does not proceed blindly" (Muckelbauer 2009, 80). Argument and persuasion are most often teleological, having a clear purpose and goal; however, the end product of affirmative invention is less overtly teleological and more exploratory. Although three-dimensional dialectical rhetorics can function teleologically, they are also very comfortable traveling with Sophists and nomads in the space of singular rhythms. Juxtaposition, for example, places different discourses in close proximity with no commentary, and the result of juxtaposition is usually a feeling of discomfort or dissonance, not epistemic conviction or a will to act in a certain way. This feeling of discomfort or dissonance mediates the juxtaposed discourses in an indirect, affirmative, affective way, as a traveler might mediate the spatial experience of an unfamiliar place or a Sophist might mediate the epistemological contact of different belief systems. Thus, affirmative invention is strategic in a nonteleological sense, and three-dimensional dialectical rhetorics often draw from these same nonteleological strategies.

Three-dimensional dialectical rhetorics are not only strategic but also topical, and Muckelbauer explores inventional *topoi* in the context of affirmative invention. Since affirmative invention secretes singular rhythms from dialectical appropriations and negations, Muckelbauer begins with a dialectical problematic. In Aristotle and throughout the classical corpus, the *topoi* are never fully explained or operationalized (other than the general listing of their forms and contents as places). Most scholarship on the classical *topoi* points out the tension between the unclear metaphor of *topos*-as-place and the unhelpful notion of *topos*-as-void. This scholarship then works to overcome the problem by filling in the *topoi* with additional contents or clarifying aspects of their history. These additions and clarifications, however, emerge directly from the dialectical tension between place and void, making these scholarly elaborations only critiques or syntheses, not affirmative inventions. Affirmative invention regarding the *topoi* would, according to Muckelbauer, be "less concerned with gaps and overcoming and more concerned with producing connections" (Muckelbauer 2009, 127).

Although George A. Kennedy points out that Aristotle never defines *topoi* in the *Topics* or in the *Rhetoric* (Aristotle 1991, 45), Muckelbauer finds a rich description of *topoi* in a text not typically studied by rhetoricians, the *Physics*. In this text, Aristotle explains that place (*topos*) "possesses an active power" (Muckelbauer 2009, 130). Thus, scholars miss the point of the *topoi* when they simply fill the void with historically specific contents. The *topoi*, Muckelbauer points out, are not inactive containers (pure form) or lists of acontextual content; they are active and generative forces of invention: "Part of the inventive character of *topos* is its capacity to respond immanently to the body that it simultaneously demarcates" (132). Thus, Muckelbauer concludes, the "concept of *topos* articulated in [the *Physics*] recommends a generative theory of place that emphasizes immanence, responsiveness, and connectivity" (133). A nonaffirmative use of the three-dimensional dialectical topics (deconstruction, dialogue, identification, critique, and juxtaposition) might be to think of a purpose and audience and then employ these *topoi* in a teleological effort to argue or persuade. An affirmative use of these topics might be to generate topical form and content simultaneously (though not dialectically in the philosophical sense of the term) in the act of invention itself. Here, form, purpose, and content swirl around in a cloud of discourse until shapes begin to emerge. Only when nascent shapes emerge should the active and intentional process for forming begin. Although three-dimensional rhetorics may allow for nonaffirmative uses of *topoi*, their affirmative use in generating singular rhythms is also highly valued. Linda Flower's notions of community literacy and intercultural rhetoric, for example, could not function fully or effectively in a discursive environment of purely teleological (nonaffirmative) communication. However, once affirmative invention reveals possible alternatives, negotiation (via role playing and community dialogue) then begins the process of shaping these alternatives into rhetorical performances that lead to positive change in real communities.

In *Negation, Subjectivity, and the History of Rhetoric*, Vitanza (1997) argues against histories of rhetoric that negate "others" (thirds, middles) in the interest of monological (The History of Rhetoric) and oppositional (revisionary histories of rhetoric) grand narratives. In place of The History of Rhetoric and revisionary histories of rhetoric, both of which negate (thirds, others, and middles), Vitanza offers what he calls sub/versive historiography as part of a more general "third sophistic," or a sophistic attitude toward recovering "others" (thirds, middles) from prior silence or negation (denegating them, without subsequently negating). The History of Rhetoric is based on a logic of construction and negation, and revisionary histories are based on a logic of negative deconstruction and negation, but sub/versive historiography is based on affirmative deconstruction and the constant desire to link (denegation, or the negation of negation). Although Vitanza associates dialectic with grand narratives of rhetorical progression, ignoring or negating parts of every thesis and antithesis with each new synthesis, I argue that the sub/versive historiographical strategies described by Vitanza as methods for a third sophistic support three-dimensional dialectical rhetorics, especially sub/versive identification and affirmative deconstruction.

Vitanza argues that association and its dialectical strategy, identification, can be politically problematic because in the positive act of identifying we must also disidentify (or negate). Vitanza writes, "The principle of identification by way of division is perhaps best summed up as congregation by segregation" (Vitanza 1997, 123). But Vitanza does not then negate identification altogether; instead, he appropriates it for a sub/versive third sophistic. Vitanza writes, "I, instead, identify with the third man/woman, or the excluded middles. What Derrida calls the trace" (21). Thus, Vitanza argues against "metaphysical identification," which functions according to a logic of "noncontradiction" and a politics of the "excluded middle" (38), and he argues in favor of third sophistic, sub/versive identification, a positive association with thirds, middles, and others. Sub/versive identification refuses to negate other subjects by ignoring or disparaging them but instead constantly identifies, links, and collects in a process of subjective expansion. As I will explain, three-dimensional dialectical rhetorics also employ strategic identification as a means of association, not negation (although I believe, contra Vitanza, that negation serves important functions in the larger communicative landscape).

According to Vitanza, the dialectical strategy of deconstruction can be as politically problematic as the structuralist discourses it is intended to challenge. The structuralist History of Rhetoric negates through silence, and deconstructive revisionary histories of rhetoric negate through recovering structuralist binaries and then simply reversing them, privileging what had once been negated and negating what had once been privileged. However, as with identification, Vitanza does not simply negate deconstruction; instead, he appropriates it for a sub/versive third sophistic. Vitanza offers affirmative deconstruction as a sub/versive, third sophistic methodology that subverts the political problems associated with the negation characteristic of structuralism and negative deconstruction. Drawing especially from the work of Derrida, Georges Bataille, and Gayatri Chakrovorty Spivak, Vitanza describes affirmative deconstruction as an attempt to "move outside of the binary (machine)" (Vitanza 1997, 50) and into a third subject position (105). In order to find this extrabinary (or trinary) location, we must "attend to the abject, the other in ourselves and in other selves" (105) to call out "to the other so as perhaps to pass out of the binary" altogether (219). Vitanza calls this drive to transcend binaries a "third sophistic" since binaries account for ones and twos and affirmative deconstruction seeks (nonbinary) threes, or, more generally, "some more" (236). Vitanza explains that "*one* and *two* are signs of negation; '*some more*' is a nonrepresentational sign of nonpositive affirmation" (236). Finally, Vitanza writes, "What '*some more*' would do, then, is to speak the unspoken, the Forgotten, the not yet divulged," engendering in us "a search for a desiring (machine) of a third position" (236). Deconstruction, the three-dimensional strategy for dialectical rhetoric, resembles affirmative deconstruction since its goal is not to negate through silence or reverse existing binaries (and then negate again); its goal is to destroy the forces of opposition that construct binaries in the first place, regardless of their particular politics. The result of three-dimensional deconstruction, as I will explain more thoroughly later in this chapter, is a third orientation from which new understandings emerge outside the limiting logic of binary oppositions. Flower's strategy of intercultural dialogue resembles affirmative deconstruction in its effort to negotiate (not negate) multiple literacies. Through public dialogue and collaborative inquiry, the rhetorical mediation of cultural differences generates new alternatives and avenues of change that would be effaced within unifying or oppositional rhetorics.

Hawk is far less pedantic than Muckelbauer and Vitanza in his rejection of dialectic. The problem with dialectic, according to Hawk, is not how oppressive or dangerous it is—but how *simple* it is. Hawk argues that the emerging landscape of digital communication technologies requires a composition pedagogy that is "post-dialectical" (Hawk 2007, 7, although the term appears numerous times throughout the book), based on complex vitalism rather than opposition and negation. Complex vitalism is postdialectical because it maps "complex interrelationships" across multiple differences. Here, somatic experience, affective intuition, and cognitive understanding interconnect in a "local moment" and become even more complex as connections proliferate into webs (113–16). These interconnections are enabled through multiple agencies. Complexity and interconnectedness are not new. Even in the *Encomium of Helen*, written during the fifth century BCE, Gorgias (1972b) recognizes that language connects body, mind, and soul with the force of a drug and that the very sight of a warrior strapping on armor causes fear and flight, even before any real danger is imminent. Sight and language, among many other agencies, have always connected somatic experience, affective understanding, and cognitive knowledge. However, first, our (post-Gorgian) obsession with simple structures (linear logics, oppositional dialectics) limits our ability to perceive, understand, and communicate complexity; second, the emergence of digital technologies since the 1990s throws complexity in our faces and forces us to deal with it.

Simple dialectics construct oppositions and negate "Others" (people, experiences, discourses, knowledges, and so on) through thesis, antithesis, and synthesis. However, three-dimensional dialectical rhetorics are complex: they recognize multiple sources of difference and generate productive interconnections through mediation and negotiation. These mediated differences may be difficult to map and engage since they take the shape of complex webs rather than simple lines or binaries, but this is our lot in the twenty-first century. For Flower, the whole point of community literacy is the generation of rival hypotheses, webs of competing discourses about local problems that emerge from complex interrelationships across multiple sites of difference. Intercultural dialogue is the strategy that constructs these complex webs of discourses, revealing structures of omission and oppression that may be masked by unifying and oppositional rhetorics.

As I will explain in chapter 5, the complex connectivity enabled by recent technologies, especially the development of Web 2.0, cannot be adequately understood in linear rhetorical terms or oppositional dialectical terms. Complex connectivity is best understood as the mediated negotiation among multiple differences, and three-dimensional dialectical rhetorics are best suited to engaging complex connectivity because they do not rely on linear or oppositional structures. For Hawk, the point of a "post-dialectical method" is "to map points of intervention, insertion, or connection" (Hawk 2007, 201), which is also the point, I argue, of three-dimensional dialectical rhetorics (a conjunction that causes an obvious problem of terminology). However, if Hawk is generally *post*-ing philosophical dialectic, and there are other forms and functions of dialectic that are not philosophical, then it is inevitable that complex dialectics, like three-dimensional dialectical rhetorics, are perfectly compatible with the method that Hawk calls "post-dialectical."

Three-dimensional dialectical rhetoric is a complex, affirmative, strategic, and topical art compatible with affirmative invention, sub/versive historiography, and complex vitalism despite Muckelbauer's, Vitanza's, and Hawk's conscious rejection of philosophical dialectic. In the next section, I explore in more detail three-dimensional dialectical rhetoric's qualities as a strategic and topical art, describing five *topoi* for the mediation and negotiation of complex differences, including deconstruction, dialogue, identification, critique, and juxtaposition.

THREE-DIMENSIONAL DIALECTICAL RHETORIC AS A STRATEGIC AND TOPICAL ART

Edward Said (1983) tells us that theories travel, and when they do, they enter new contexts and evolve to reflect the different historical interests (economic, political, social, cultural, material, etc.) of these new contexts. The theories and methods of topical invention in dialectic and rhetoric have traveled. During the classical period, they were exemplified in preSocratic and sophistic writings (such as Gorgias's [1972a] *Defense of Palamedes*); they were hinted at in Plato's middle works (especially the *Phaedrus*); they were systematized in Aristotle's works on language (commonly called the *Organon*); and they were made pragmatic for Roman education in the anonymous *Rhetorica ad Herennium* and in the works of Cicero and Quintilian. Throughout the rest of its history, topical invention in dialectic and rhetoric drifted the way of the wind in each discursive or historical context it entered. When dialectic and rhetoric were in disciplinary favor, theories and methods of topical invention were taught and used; but when dialectic was subsumed under the guise of one-dimensional logic, or when rhetoric was relegated to style or elocution, theories and methods of topical invention were ignored or even shunned. Both David L. Vancil (1979) and Frank D'Angelo explain that during the eighteenth century, topical invention disappeared almost completely, "except for purposes of formal debate" (D'Angelo 1984, 66). The *topoi* (or *loci*) reemerged during the nineteenth century in composition textbooks, presented as methods for paragraph development, and later, in the twentieth century, as "patterns of organization" for essays (66).

Part of the problem with understanding the historical trajectories of topical invention (whether in dialectic or rhetoric or both) is the determination of exactly what a topic is. In "Up from Theory," Michael Leff explains that the concept of topical invention throughout its history has been "ambiguous and multi-faceted": "Topics sometimes referred to modes of inference, sometimes to aspects of the subject under consideration, sometimes to the attitudes of an audience, sometimes to types of issues, sometimes to the generic headings of rhetorical material, and sometimes to several of these alternatives" (Leff 2006, 205).[2] But since past dialecticians, rhetoricians, and teachers of these arts were mostly interested in the *practice* of topical invention, few (with the possible exception of Boethius) theorized the nature and function of topics in dialectic and rhetoric generally (205–07). Even Aristotle, who discusses *topoi* at length in both the *Topics* and the *Rhetoric*, does not define them or theorize their place in argumentation beyond briefly mentioning their function as tools that generate material for enthymemes (Yarbrough 2004, 78–81).[3]

The revival of the rhetorical tradition in rhetoric and composition during the 1960s and 1970s also saw a revival of interest in the classical theory and practice of topical invention.[4] According to Edward P. J. Corbett, this revival was due in part to a shift in composition studies from a product-centered approach to "the renewed emphasis that teachers of writing have given recently to the *process* of composing" (Corbett 1986, 43). Composition scholars during this time began to teach the classical topics (mainly Aristotle's) as a tool for invention in their writing classes and subsequently, especially during the late 1970s, developed heuristics of their own, perhaps recognizing the situated (thus obsolete) nature of certain ancient *topoi*, or perhaps feeling the ancient *topoi* were too diffuse in form and function to be useful in a modern classroom. Many of these newer heuristics drew from contemporary rhetorical theories, such as Richard E. Young, Alton L. Becker, and Kenneth L. Pike's tagmemics, Kenneth Burke's pentad, and Stephen Edelston Toulmin's layout of arguments.[5] Although rhetoric and composition has not lost its interest in developing new inventional heuristics (a quick search in CompPile reveals a steady stream of scholarship about them), there has in the last decade been a renewed interest in the classical *topoi* as a means for rhetorical invention.[6] J. P. Zompetti (2006), for example, resurrects the use of Aristotle's common topics for modern argumentation, explaining that they are useful in helping students locate and structure arguments and develop critical thinking skills; they also help teachers of argumentative speech and writing develop their pedagogies for invention beyond drills and exercises.

Some existing definitions of *topoi* and topical invention center on their generative nature alone. Karl R. Wallace, for example, describes a "system of *topoi*" as "an orderly way of searching for meaningful utterances" (Wallace 1972, 395). More useful descriptions situate the generative power of topics in the context of audiences and rhetorical situations. For example, Janice M. Lauer defines topics as "resources for inventing arguments that include lines of reasoning, types of evidence, and appeals to audiences" (Lauer 2004, 162).[7] Corbett, referring specifically to Aristotle's *topoi*, defines them as "devices enabling the speaker to find those arguments that would be most persuasive in a given situation" (Corbett 1986, 45). But the best definition for my purposes here, in the context of three-dimensional dialectical rhetorics, is one that includes a strategic dimension in the employment of *topoi* as inventional tools. Ruth Anne Clark and Jesse G. Delia call topical invention "strategic verbal choice-making" and "strategic message formulation" (Clark and Delia 1979, 187). The *topoi* themselves, then, are "general strategic approaches to be adapted to specific communicative needs" (195), and their rhetorical goal (which makes them strategic and not just generative) is "to elicit the same forms of reasoning in others" (195).[8] This is the whole point of dialectical mediation—to encourage in others a spirit of complementary negotiation (otherwise the one gives in and the other does not).

One of the most interesting and complex articulations of a modern theory of strategic inventional *topoi* is described by David Fleming in "Becoming Rhetorical: An Education in the Topics." Fleming argues that what rhetoric needs in order to mediate between its theoretical and practical discourses are more effective "rhetorical metadiscourses" and that "one long-standing focus of rhetorical metadiscourses has been the 'topics'" (Fleming 2003, 95). However, the classical theories and practices of topical invention tend to be incoherent and unhelpful to modern students, and, as Fleming points out, "Most modern topical theories have taken the form of either highly focused hermeneutic tools for the analysis and criticism of texts or rudimentary checklists for essay writing in school" (106). As a remedy to this problem (i.e., the need for a strategic theory of topics but the lack of an adequate model for modern students), Fleming describes his own "theory of the topics," which includes "five broad topics of argument: 1) circumstantial knowledge; 2) verbal formulae; 3) common sense; 4) models of textual development; and 5) logical norms" (105). Fleming explains,

> In looking at any particular argumentative occasion or text, we see first the circumstantial knowledge surrounding it: the people, places, events, and *history* of that situation. . . . Next, there are verbal formulae, recurring linguistic patterns that make up the discursive repertoire of a particular community and are always being adapted and deployed in particular discursive situations. . . . Third, there are topics that give us access to common sense itself, that collection of truths, presumptions, values, and preferences . . . that is operative in a community. . . . Fourth are the conceptual patterns and structures that organize everyday argumentative thinking in a community. . . . Finally, there are topics that reinforce deep-seated *logical* knowledge: general warrants, rules of inference, and other "universal" principles that authorize arguments of various kinds. (Fleming 2003, 105–06)

Fleming further argues that the classical *topoi* functioned in the broader context of civic education, and his own system of topics returns to that ancient model, placing his updated *topoi* in the context of a modernized *progymnasmata*, which emphasizes practice in acquiring skill (Fleming 2003, 106–16). Fleming's modern theory of topical invention is strategic because it extends the generative power of *topoi* into civic education, giving topical invention a social (or qualitative), not just generative (or quantitative), purpose.

   Although I like Fleming's new theory of inventional topics for civic education, it does not (nor was it intended to) serve the more specific goals of three-dimensional dialectical rhetorics, in which rhetorical purposes center around the mediation of different orientations in particular rhetorical situations and discursive contexts. The topical strategies I present in the remaining pages of this chapter return both dialectic and rhetoric to their classical forms as strategic, topical arts (as Fleming and Ruth Anne Clark and Delia do), yet I formulate these topical strategies specifically for use in three-dimensional dialectical rhetorics. There are five topics I will describe, and each presumes, first, the contact of at least two (often more) orientations in rhetorical and discursive context and, second, the purpose of strategic mediation. These topics are deconstruction, dialogue, identification, critique, and juxtaposition.[9] Each discussion of a particular topic below includes a theoretical and practical treatment of the dialectical strategy followed by an interpretation of a student's essay I believe exemplifies the strategy in use. These essays were written by students in my advanced composition classes at the University of Alabama at Birmingham. The assignment that prompted the essays, Communities and Contact Zones, is reproduced in Appendix A, and the essays themselves are collected in Appendices B through F.[10]

The strategies associated with three-dimensional dialectical rhetorics have found a comfortable home in the context of digital communication technologies, which emphasize linking, connecting, and joining, and I explore this claim more thoroughly in chapter 5. In this present chapter, however, I argue that these strategies have become so thoroughly enmeshed in the general communication landscape that they are now indispensable to all composing, including the writing students do in school. As technologies evolve, communication in general becomes more and more complex since the process of evolution is additive rather than substitutive. In "Negative Spaces: From Production to Connection in Composition," Johndan Johnson-Eilola (1998) argues that even when we teach academic writing, students still must develop skills in connective (linking, joining) composition. Composition's obsession with the creative processes and original products of writing makes it difficult for the field to see the increasing value of making connections among discourses and cultures. Despite the profound influence of postmodernism and social construction on the field in general, rhetoric and composition has held firmly to certain traditional notions of text and authorship. Johnson-Eilola writes, "While we have come to value interconnection and dissensus in composition as it acts to construct texts and subjects, we often fail to reconsider the fundamental concept of what counts as a text. We value connection, but only secondarily. We still think of the text as a relatively coherent body of information with determinable bounds produced by an author of one sort or another" (Johnson-Eilola 1998, 18). Composition still emphasizes the production of unified texts. However, Johnson-Eilola argues, "composition theory and pedagogy must overcome a reliance on the idea of writing as *production* and look instead at ways for considering the values inherent in *connection* between texts and fragments [that are characteristic of] information systems such as the World Wide Web" (22). The fact is, Friedrich Krotz explains, we live in a world in which "digital media also change the other, already existing media (Krotz 2008, 25), and the rise of digital technologies has shifted strategies, such as the *topoi* associated with three-dimensional dialectical rhetorics, from the fringes of experimental writing (which is where Muckelbauer locates them) to the mainstream in the general communication landscape.

DECONSTRUCTION

When rhetorical situations call for the mediation of disparate orientations, one option speakers and writers have is to place these orientations into dialectical engagement for the purpose of dissolving the force of opposition that divides them. As a dialectical rhetorical strategy, deconstruction dissolves the forces of opposition that maintain orientations in mutually exclusive relationships. Deconstruction is traditionally viewed as a strategy for textual analysis, so its application to culturally salient texts, whether printed or spoken, is natural. However, prominent anthropologists and sociologists (such as Clifford Geertz and Richard Harvey Brown, to name just two) argue that culture and society themselves are texts to be read and interpreted like any other (printed, spoken) texts. Thus, cultures and societies in general, plus the texts produced by and within them, fall inside the scope of deconstructive rhetorical strategies. Deconstructive strategies can serve both two-dimensional and three-dimensional rhetorics, though they have historically been employed in composition studies as two-dimensional strategies for critical writing.

In two-dimensional rhetorics, deconstruction is primarily a strategy of textual criticism, unraveling the structural assumptions upon which an opposing orientation's salient texts are founded, revealing the rhetorical character of their truth claims, and invoking the supplement (the "Other" orientation and its alternative texts) as a challenge to the sovereignty of the opposing orientation. This critical form of deconstruction received a great deal of attention in the rhetoric and composition community from the late 1980s through the end of the 1990s.[11] *Deconstruction* also appears as a key term in rhetoric and composition's best reference volumes, published during the latter half of the 1990s, where it is usually defined as a critical methodology with sociopolitical implications. In the *Encyclopedia of Rhetoric and Composition*, for example, Thomas Kent defines rhetorical deconstruction as textual criticism that dismantles oppositional hierarchies and articulates the aporias that texts conceal (Kent 1996, 166–67). In *Theorizing Composition*, Barbara Heifferon and Phyllis Mentzell Ryder suggest that deconstruction in composition has been directed at exploding binaries and undermining privileged concepts (Heifferon and Ryder 1998, 79–83). And in *Keywords in Composition Studies*, Peter Vandenberg explains that deconstruction is most often invoked in the service of politicized critical writing (Vandenberg 1996, 58–61).

As Brooke Rollins (2006) points out, however, it was the very *critical* emphasis of deconstructive rhetoric during this time that planted the seed of its own demise. Critical methodologies (one of which was two-dimensional deconstruction) dominated rhetoric and composition from the late 1980s through the 1990s because of the powerful influence of social-epistemic rhetorics and critical pedagogies. Rhetorical methods based in deconstruction could be used to question traditional assumptions and challenge the *status quo*, thus serving the functions of ideological criticism very well. However, Rollins points out that Derrida's own skepticism of deconstruction's political uses, combined with the fact that other theorists (Karl Marx and Michel Foucault, for example) seemed to provide a more methodologically useful and politically friendly framework for critical rhetoric, contributed to the near disappearance of deconstruction in composition scholarship after the turn of the twenty-first century.

However, two-dimensional, critical rhetorics are not the only province in which deconstruction is methodologically useful. In three-dimensional rhetorics, deconstruction becomes a more complex and affirmative rhetorical strategy, defining the orientations involved in any given rhetorical situation and dissolving the forces of opposition members of these orientations invoke in order to maintain their own sovereignty and strengthen the differences that define each orientation's boundaries. Three-dimensional dialectical deconstruction has a positive, affirmative (not just negative, critical) inflection: its task is not to reverse binary structures but to construct new orientations no longer founded on old oppositions. Christopher Norris points out that "deconstruction is not simply a strategic reversal of categories which remain distinct and unaffected. It seeks to undo both a given order of priorities *and* the very system of conceptual opposition that makes that order possible" (Norris 1982, 31); deconstruction "inverts the opposition and cuts away the ground of its very meaning" (35). David Kaufer and Gary Waller agree, but state the matter more pragmatically: "Subversion won't meet with lasting success unless there is a constructive plan with which to follow it up" (Kaufer and Waller 1985, 75). In "Rhetoric after Deconstruction," James Arnt Aune argues that "no communication can ever be fully present to itself, for it is always already marked by the play of difference and deferral of meaning which is language" (Aune 1990, 256), and this play of difference and deferral of meaning does not always take the form of binary structures and may even resist the logic of opposition. Three-dimensional deconstruction, as a strategy for dialectical rhetoric, is thus never complete until the very foundation that supports the force of opposition is dissolved, unable to do the conceptual work of holding orientations in mutually exclusive relationships.

One of the primary strategies deconstructionists use to dissolve forces of opposition is to trace the presence of the "supplement" in a text or orientation, understand its hierarchical arrangement in a system of values, and then invoke the "mark," an alternative term or concept that inhabits the gaps (or "aporias") among competing terms (Leitch 1963, 169–78). In traditional Western hierarchies (man/woman, bourgeoisie/proletariat, straight/homosexual or nonmonosexual), the first term is privileged, natural, inevitable, and the second term supplements (emphasizes by means of opposition) the meaning of the first term. Deconstructive criticism demonstrates that the privileged term is always already constituted by the supplement, though many texts and orientations do not often overtly invoke the supplementary term or concept. Thus, deconstructive criticism (whether two-dimensional or three-dimensional) begins, in these cases, with a constructive move, invoking the supplement and then tracing its absent-presence throughout the text or orientation. In its final move, only three-dimensional deconstructive criticism seeks an alternative concept, the mark, that throws into crisis the competing terms and the force that defines them as opposed, creating a new orientation from which interpretation and rhetoric can proceed.

In *Writing and Difference, Of Grammatology*, and *Glas*, among other works, Derrida (1976; 1978; 1990) argues that the language of a text does not derive meaning through reference to signifieds, realities, or truths. Rather, the language of a text derives meaning through a chain of signifiers linked together by a system of conceptual differences. There is, thus, no extralinguistic, existential truth that can be verified by observation or experimentation and upon which meaning rests. Truth itself is a rhetorical construct (created and maintained only within the boundaries of a text) that disintegrates when the epistemological foundations of the oppositions (opposed or competing orientations) that link signifiers together are called into question. As a three-dimensional strategy for dialectical rhetoric, then, deconstruction analyzes particular discourses as linguistic constructs, and it lays bare the rhetorical methods by which appeals to truth are made, showing that the truth of any discourse is a ruse. The goal of deconstruction is not resolution (as in thesis-antithesis-*synthesis*) but only the revelation that the force of opposition maintaining orientations in mutually exclusive relationships is linguistic, rhetorical, discursive, not real, and thus collapses in on itself when questioned. This collapse is the impetus from which new orientations arise.

Although deconstruction does, in the end, construct new orientations in which two or more orientations collapse together without the force of opposition there to do its work, these new orientations are in no way more true or less subject to deconstruction than the orientations that have collapsed. Orientations that result from deconstructive criticism, due to the very nature of language and symbol systems, generate new forces of opposition between themselves and other orientations, opening themselves up to further deconstructive strategies. While this endless process of deconstruction and construction may seem frustrating at first, writers and speakers should take heart in the understanding that new knowledge is generated in the process.

Lindy Owens's Deconstruction of the Force of Opposition between College and Family Orientations

As a three-dimensional strategy for dialectical rhetoric, deconstruction dissolves the forces of opposition that define orientations as opposed and maintain them in competitive relationships. Three-dimensional deconstruction invokes the supplement or the mark, terms that are suppressed in one-dimensional rhetorics in order to mask their hierarchical structures. Invoking the supplement or the mark demonstrates that oppositions, when challenged, have no viable epistemological or ethical foundation. Lindy Owens (whose essay, "The Grass Is Greener," appears in Appendix B) uses deconstruction in order to dissolve the force of opposition between her own college orientation and her sister Amber's family orientation, which intersect in a context of discourses about early adulthood. Lindy shows that the supplemental terms for both orientations (*college* for the family orientation and *family* for the college orientation) invoke the same marks (fear and jealousy), making these two orientations, in the end, not all that different. Fear and jealousy then become the basis for a new orientation Lindy and her sister share, an orientation that mediates their differences and reveals common ground since the force of opposition is no longer there to do its divisive work.

Lindy begins her essay recognizing three distinct orientations—her own college orientation, her sister Amber's family orientation, and a transitional orientation—represented in the Facebook status updates of her friends. Lindy wonders if she is happy remaining in her college orientation, and she wonders if those who have family orientations (or are transitioning into them) are happy, too. This transition represents for Lindy the constant deferral of meaning for one of her key terms, *happiness*. One thing Lindy knows for sure is that her sister's family orientation is completely foreign to her: Lindy hands Amber a bottle of cold formula, she has trouble translating baby Jackson's dialect, she doesn't recognize an expression of discomfort in Jackson's eyes, and she doesn't burp Jackson enough. In the material world of her sister's family orientation, Lindy feels inept and untrained, smiling at Jackson's "bug-eyed stare" without recognizing it as a sign of pain.

Despite Lindy's awkwardness coming into contact with her sister's family orientation, she nevertheless consciously acknowledges the situated terministic screen she uses in her description of the encounter. Lindy writes, "In describing my own reactions to my sister's household, I know I sound like an inexperienced jerk. But the truth is I really wasn't prepared to have an up close and personal view of the domestic life for a few years, maybe even a decade. I haven't decided yet if I want to get married and have kids." Lindy lacks experience with "domestic life" and is unsure if becoming a wife and mother is the right path for her in the end. One thing is certain: Lindy wants to be happy. But, Lindy writes, "I'm just not sure if, for me, starting a family is the path to happiness."

Lindy's current orientation is dominated by the material and social context of college life, and her apartment reflects a "college-centric atmosphere." The apartment is always dirty and noisy, and Lindy has four other roommates, one of whom installed a stripper pole in his room. There are pets and choking hazards, so few kids are ever brought to Lindy's apartment for a visit. Yet the dirt and the noise and the eccentricities of her roommates are attractions for Lindy. She always has friends available for conversations, and when she does need privacy, Lindy just closes the door to her room, and headphones and a shot of whiskey drown out the noise well enough. Lindy's college-student orientation gives her (or *legitimates* for her) the freedom to do whatever she wants whenever she wants to do it, especially taking unplanned road trips, drinking, and sleeping late. Lindy writes, "It is a life with little responsibility and few rules. We fend for ourselves and rarely take other lives into consideration."

Lindy recognizes, however, that we do not always simply choose our orientations. There are social pressures that condition our choices of lifestyle, and there are consequences to making choices not socially sanctioned. Lindy wants to be happy, and she is happy, but lately she has begun to feel pressure. Lindy is not sure she is ready to start a family. "Yet," she writes, "I feel this slow pressure from all around me to do just that." Lindy hears, for example, that her "biological clock is ticking," that she may "not be as desirable" after a certain age, that, like expired milk, she might "go sour," that she might live a "life of loneliness" and "become the crazy cat lady." These are fears Lindy has regarding her orientation, and they are social fears, propagated by media and friends. And Lindy is, at times, jealous of her sister Amber's family and the "depth of emotional attachment" Amber feels toward her children. Yet Lindy also knows that, although her sister has followed the socially sanctioned path, Amber, too, feels certain fears and is jealous of Lindy's freedom.

Although Lindy acknowledges many of the differences between Amber's family orientation and her own college orientation, Lindy also recognizes that these differences disappear when she invokes each orientation's marks, the terms and ideas floating around in the *aporia*, that the supplemental oppositions (family/college and college/family) mask. Lindy's sister Amber has lived the American dream: she got married, had kids, and is presently raising a beautiful family. But she started a family at a young age and now struggles with finances and health insurance. Having lived according to the dominant social mores, Amber remains jealous of Lindy's freedom, missing late-night parties and random road trips. Lindy lives the college dream—takes interesting classes and parties with friends. But Lindy lacks the depth of emotional connection her sister feels for her kids, so her freedom comes with a price. In an interesting twist, Lindy reverses the poles of orientation: "Maybe if I hadn't been so stubborn in my last relationship, I would be with my future husband and we could be planning our lives together. Maybe if my sister had not gotten pregnant, she could have gotten her design degree and gone into commercial art." But Lindy is not satisfied with this thought experiment, asking, "Would either of us be happier?"

Early in her essay, Lindy explains how completely different her sister's family orientation is from Lindy's own college orientation, yet when Lindy begins to explore the marks, the ideas that these opposed orientations both mask, such as fear and jealousy, the distinctions between these orientations begin to break down. For Lindy, our choices of orientation and lifestyle often come down to fear: "Fear is the motivation," Lindy writes, "fear that we are living our lives the wrong way, that someone else has already figured out the secret to happiness, and that we'll never discover the secret ourselves." In the end, Lindy admires her sister for the choices she has made, and she respects Amber for overcoming her fears and resisting the temptations that stem from jealousy. Yet it was this process of recognizing these suppressed elements in both orientations (fear and jealousy) that made Lindy realize her sister really isn't that much different from her. So the "dreams" Lindy and her sister have lived so far are not really ideals, orientations that should be privileged above all others; they are processes through which people pass on their way to other orientations, seeking what is always deferred, eternal happiness, yet also finding satisfaction in the process, a situated kind of happiness satisfying in its own way.

DIALOGUE

When rhetorical situations call for the mediation of orientations, one option speakers and writers have is to enter disparate orientations into a process of dialogic interaction. As a three-dimensional strategy for dialectical rhetoric, dialogue integrates orientations, maintaining certain elements of each as sovereign, yet merging other elements, creating a space in which orientations can change and adapt to each other.[12] In dialogue, speakers and writers, through a kind of rhetorical osmosis, breach the force of opposition that maintains orientations as different, allowing for filtered mutual influence on dialectically engaged orientations. According to Gregory Clark, "The purpose of [dialogic communication] is to enable people to develop a shared understanding of their common experience in an interaction that becomes . . . more than the sum of its individual participants because the shared knowledge that emerges from it cannot be reduced to what each one of them separately knows" (Clark 1990, 3). Dialogue tests the limits of the force of opposition, creating a whole made up partly of the sovereign orientations and partly of the newly formed interaction. Other modes of dialectical engagement avoid any kind of mutual influence among orientations; however, mutual influence is the very soul and substance of dialogic interaction.

In *Saying and Silence*, Frank Farmer (2001) points out that Mikhail Bakhtin's general theory and method of dialogics is antithetical to the theories and methods of one-dimensional rhetorics. Following a discussion of truth and dialogics in *Problems of Dostoyevsky's Poetics*, Farmer writes, "Again we sense Bakhtin's hostility to what he once called theoretism, but now refers to as 'philosophical monologism,' that abstract plane of reasoning that promotes truth as something capable of excluding human beings altogether" (Farmer 2001, 17). Although a general sense of dialogue can serve one-dimensional rhetorics, as it does in van Eemeren and Grootendorst's (2004) notion of critical discussion, Bakhtin's sense of dialogics cannot serve one-dimensional rhetorics since there is always a social other who conditions every utterance. Bakhtin's dialogics, as a dialectical strategy, serves three-dimensional rhetorics when the social other or "outsider" is "kindly, benevolent, affirming, generous, and gift-bestowing" (Farmer 2001, 96). However, as Farmer suggests, "If the gaze of our outsiders is an unrelievedly critical one" (108), the dialectical strategy of dialogic interaction may simply reveal the necessity for two-dimensional critical rhetoric, foregoing intentional interaction altogether (though Bakhtin and Farmer would say all communication is dialogic and the problem would need to be addressed *through* dialogics).

In *The Dialogic Imagination*, Bakhtin describes language as inherently dialogic, mediating the interaction of speakers and listeners and forcing mutual influence. Utterances are never made in a social void; they are always contextual, always inflected with the complicated contexts that surround them (Bakhtin 1981, 276–77). Since language itself is inherently dialogic (and thus dialectical), any speaker who uses language with the appearance of monological structure or function must have added this monological appearance artificially. In particular, poetry and, interestingly, rhetoric, according to Bakhtin, are actually dialogic in function but create the appearance of monological structure. Bakhtin writes, "All rhetorical forms, monologic in their compositional structure, are oriented toward the listener and his answer" (280). Dialogic rhetoric (both three-dimensional and dialectical), then, is the material manifestation of negotiated meaning, of mutual influence between speaker and listener, writer and reader.

Just as rhetorical language is oriented toward an audience, all language, regardless of function or form, is oriented toward a response, and this response inevitably influences the shape and function of any utterance, making all language dialectical. According to Bakhtin, "In the actual life of speech, every concrete act of understanding is active: it assimilates the word to be understood into its own conceptual system filled with specific objects and emotional expressions, and is indissolubly merged with the response, with a motivated agreement or disagreement" (Bakhtin 1981, 282). Bakhtin continues,

> Thus an active understanding, one that assimilates the word under consideration into a new conceptual system, that of the one striving to understand, establishes a series of complex interrelationships, consonances and dissonances with the word and enriches it with new elements. It is precisely such an understanding that the speaker counts on. Therefore his orientation toward the listener is an orientation toward a specific conceptual horizon, toward the specific world of the listener; it introduces totally new elements into his discourse; it is in this way, after all, that various different points of view, conceptual horizons, systems for providing excessive accents, various social "languages" come to interact with one another. The speaker strives to get a reading on his own word, and on his own conceptual system that determines this word, within the alien conceptual system of the understanding receiver; he enters into dialogic relationships with certain aspects

of this system. The speaker breaks through the alien conceptual horizon of the listener, constructs his own utterance on alien territory, against his, the listener's, apperceptive background. (Bakhtin 1981, 282)

For Bakhtin, mutual influence may not be a conscious rhetorical strategy employed by speakers and writers in the process of persuasion. Mutual influence happens always and everywhere language is used because language derives meaning from the effects of shifting contexts.

In "Bakhtin's Rhetoric," Jon Klancher (1989) describes two dialectical rhetorical strategies based on Bakhtin's dialogic theory of discourse. First, rhetors should develop a critical sense of how the actual (social, dialogic, polyphonic) nature of language is masked by rhetorical strategies that give the discourse an appearance of monological structure and function. This skill will enable rhetors to "show how . . . social languages can be found and articulated within what appears as a largely univocal or 'monologic' sphere of public discourse" (84). Second, rhetors should develop a productive sense of how dialogic language is represented in style. Klancher writes, "Styles of writing and speaking signal ideological investments" (92), and rhetors should be familiar with the "sociopolitical signals" (92) associated with a wide variety of styles. And in "Liberal Education, Writing, and the Dialogic Self," Don H. Bialostosky (1991) also examines Bakhtinian rhetorical strategies as they relate to the writing classroom. Here he suggests that teaching writing requires that we familiarize students with "specific other voices in relation to which they may define their own voices" (18). Bialostosky points out that "other voices for Bakhtin give our voices their occasions and provocations, their reasons for saying one thing rather than another, their differences that make them distinguishable and audible among the many voices in the forum" (20).

Pedagogical applications of Bakhtin's work to composition usually result in critical attention to other writers' voices and the productive development of students' own voices through stylistic experimentation with paraphrase, parody, and imitation. However, there are other applications of dialogics, not based on the linguistic surface structure of utterances, that are also useful, especially since, as Geertz (1973) and Brown (1989) suggest, cultures can be interpreted as texts. For example, just as utterances are created in response to other utterances, so orientations are created in response to other orientations, and as orientations come into contact, they alter their style and structure, integrating elements of other orientations into the fabric of their own without losing their general functions. Through these and other pedagogical strategies, students learn about the dialogic nature of language and the role signification plays in mediating diverse orientations. Through dialogic interaction, speakers and writers influence, and are influenced by, other orientations, creating a shared understanding that can serve as a foundation for productive communication.

Emily Etheredge's Dialogic Interaction between Homeless and Family Orientations

As a three-dimensional strategy for dialectical rhetoric, dialogue integrates certain aspects of orientations while maintaining the sovereignty of each orientation in other respects. Emily Etheredge (whose essay, "Infiltrating Our Home with Love," appears in Appendix C) uses dialogic interaction to demonstrate how both she and Phillip, a local homeless man, adapted their orientations to allow for integration, enabling the two to live together peacefully and productively without altering their orientations completely. Emily's and Phillip's orientations were initially structured by a context of discourses that framed loving families as stable (and therefore good) and homeless individuals as unstable (and therefore bad). Working in and through this initial discursive context, Emily used three-dimensional dialogic interaction to reframe her relationship with Phillip, resulting in a mediation of orientations marked by partial adaptation rather than opposition.

Emily begins her essay describing a mission trip she took to Peru during which she struggled to adapt to the new culture. What made the trip a wonderful experience was the knowledge that, when it was over, Emily would return to her "completely unchanged" home, her "tight-knit" family, and her "crisp and clean" bed. The trip to Peru was exciting because of the complete stability Emily experienced at home, and that stability enabled Emily to focus on the work of the mission and on the experience of a new culture. This sense of stability, however, was disrupted by an email Emily received from her father explaining that "my family had opened our home up to a young guy my dad had met through his job at the Jimmie Hale Mission," a local homeless shelter and food bank. The young man, Phillip (not his real name), had spent a year in jail and was homeless upon his release, so Emily's family made the decision to let Phillip stay in their home until he could get his feet on the ground. Emily's orientation, dominated by a sense of stability represented in her close family relationships and familiar material surroundings (and reinforced, at the time, by the temporary instability of the mission trip), was thrown into crisis, and Emily was forced to decide how she would respond.

Emily's initial reaction to the crisis of instability was, in the vocabulary of dialectical rhetoric, two dimensional, oppositional, and critical. Emily explains that "the words in the email [in which her father revealed the plan for Phillip] seemed to contain venom for I became very angry that our family had taken in a charity case and allowed a 'bum' to come and invade my territory." This man, "who had made unwise choices throughout his life," was a threat to Emily's stability at home, and this threat made her focus only on the "changes" (which has a negative meaning here, contrary to "stability") "that would ensue upon his arrival." Emily explains, "I wanted to protect my *status quo*," and the most effective way to justify her negative reaction to Phillip was to frame his orientation as diametrically opposed to her own. Phillip was a bum, a charity case, a thief, a creep, and a stranger. Emily was the opposite of all of these qualities and thus the opposite of Phillip.

Their first encounter was by phone, and it did not go well. Emily called home about her delayed departure from Peru, but it was Phillip who answered. Philip expressed excitement at finally meeting Emily, but Emily explains that she only wanted to give him a piece of her mind and "emphatically share [her] feelings upon returning to the States." Emily asked to speak to her mother and explained that she was excited to see everyone except "the stranger" named Phillip. Although Philip spoke only kind words to Emily, she had already fully "paraphrased," in Bakhtin's sense, the life of a man she had not met, and this paraphrase was aggressively monological, ignoring, masking, and eliminating all dialogic possibilities.

In any dialogic interaction is an initial meeting of orientations during which differences are apparent, and it is the recognition of these differences that, if the three-dimensional dialectical impetus is present, leads to a gradual process of integration. Emily's language shifts noticeably when she begins to describe her second encounter with Phillip. As Emily exited the plane, she ran to her loving family and embraced them. Emily writes, "Amidst all the hugging, I noticed a young, timid, and unsure individual awkwardly standing in the shadows of my reunion." Emily had already decided to despise Phillip; nevertheless, since he would be living in her home, Emily decided she "might as well let him know [her] name," and she gave him a "quick side hug." Phillip's rough exterior (Emily's own mental image of this bum and thief) was not at all what she perceived in the airport; the person she had constructed in her mind was not the person standing before her. Emily writes, "He was not at all how I had pictured him, and the gruff exterior of his voice I had heard on the phone days earlier melted away when I saw that he wanted to feel accepted by someone. His eyes contained a lifetime of pain that I would more than likely never understand. My worst experience in life would seem almost laughable to someone like him, and I immediately felt that I had terribly misjudged him."

What event had tilled the ground in preparation for this seed of reversal? It was Emily's reflection on her trip to Peru, during which she had worked to create relationships with people she did not know or understand, and who probably had misjudged Emily as a "typical American" or "spoiled." Although Emily may have been misjudged, she was nevertheless able to convince her Peruvian hosts that she was not as they had presumed. This sense of cross-cultural understanding, a kind of empathy that surprised Emily, prepared the way for dialogic interaction between Phillip's and Emily's orientations. This exposure to "Other" voices and the kinds of misunderstandings that can happen in cross-cultural (multivoiced) circumstances gave Emily the linguistic and social tools she would need to open up the possibility of dialogic understanding and communication with Phillip.

The starting point of dialectical interaction for Emily and Phillip was the recognition of what each could gain from mutual interaction. Emily writes, "[Phillip], who had been raised without a family full of laughter or support, was entering our hearts and learning what it felt like to be loved and accepted. For us, we were learning what it was like to live with someone from a completely different background and how to adjust to someone who had never experienced the support of a family." In the paragraph that follows this recognition, Emily illustrates the progression of dialogic interaction between Phillip and her family. First, Phillip is frustrated that Emily's socks have gotten mixed up in his laundry; then Phillip holds hands and prays before dinner and has time for sharing; then stories of old memories, Emily explains, "f[eel] strange knowing Phillip had not been there"; and finally, Phillip becomes the "older brother figure" in Emily's life. Subsequent events show dialogic integration without the total loss of sovereignty for Phillip's or Emily's orientations. Emily's mother cooks from scratch, but Emily is delighted with Phillip's Hamburger Helper meal because it comes from his heart and represents his way of life. Phillip is honored to receive gifts at Christmas, gifts that Emily and her family have chosen carefully, especially for Phillip. Here recognition of difference and adaption lead to a productive life together, which would go on for three years.

In the end, Emily recognizes that it was the "*blending*" of backgrounds (Phillip's and Emily's) that "made the entire decision to have him come and stay with us completely worth it." And Phillip's presence in her

household taught Emily "to love and accept people who weren't necessarily raised in the same environment." While other three-dimensional
strategies involve a kind of reaching into other orientations for the
material of dialectical rhetoric, dialogic interaction is marked especially by a slow progression of adaptation based on response to context.
Emily's integration of certain aspects of Phillip's orientation into her
own, and her willingness to allow Phillip to integrate certain aspects of
her orientation, resulted in a rich cultural experience for both individuals, who, in the process of dialogic interaction, never lost the structures
and contents of their original orientations.

IDENTIFICATION

When forces of opposition are grounded in what Chaim Perelman
and Lucie Olbrechts-Tyteca call the "dissociation of ideas," one option
speakers and writers have, when discursive contexts and rhetorical situations call for mediation, is to reconnect these apparently disparate ideas
and their orientations through strategies of identification. In *The New
Rhetoric*, Perelman and Olbrechts-Tyteca describe dissociation as "techniques of separation which have the purpose of dissociating, separating,
disuniting elements which are regarded as forming a whole or at least
a unified group within some system of thought: dissociation modifies
such a system by modifying certain concepts which make up its essential
parts" (Perelman and Olbrechts-Tyteca 1969, 190). Strategies of dissociation serve the purposes of one-dimensional and two-dimensional rhetorics, separating out from a single orientation all ideas that seem incoherent or contradictory. Dissociative rhetorical strategies, then, create and
reinforce the sovereign identity of a single orientation and emphasize
the forces of opposition that divide this orientation from others.

Perelman and Olbrechts-Tyteca (1969) describe "processes of association" as "schemes which bring separate elements together and allow
us to establish a unity among them" (190), and this is the central function of identification.[13] Identification, one of Burke's key concepts in
A Rhetoric of Motives, resolves differences among orientations that have
been constructed through habitual dissociation, and it serves as a framework within which more specific strategies of dialectical association
(such as metaphor) might be articulated. Burke argues that the sovereignty of any orientation, as a unique locus of principles and motives,
does not make this orientation immune to the associating rhetorical
power of identification (Burke 1969, 27). According to Burke, identification is "a dialectical device" that is marked by "the shift to a higher

level of generalization" (20).[14] Burke describes identification as a process whereby two or more orientations perceive a union of interests despite their unique qualities. Burke writes,

> A is not identical with his colleague, B. But insofar as their interests are joined, A is *identified* with B. Or he may *identify himself* with B even when their interests are not joined, if he assumes that they are, or is persuaded to believe so.
>
> Here are ambiguities of substance. In being identified with B, A is "substantially one" with a person other than himself. Yet at the same time he remains unique, an individual locus of motives. Thus he is both joined and separate, at once a distinct substance and consubstantial with another. . . . Two persons may be identified in terms of some principle they share in common, an "identification" that does not deny their distinctness.
>
> A doctrine of *consubstantiality*, either explicit or implicit, may be necessary to any way of life. For substance, in the old philosophies, was an *act*; and a way of life is an *acting-together*; and in acting together, men have common sensations, concepts, images, ideas, attitudes that make them *consubstantial*. (Burke 1969, 20–21)

And later, Burke continues, "Any specialized activity participates in a larger unit of action. 'Identification' is a word for the autonomous activity's place in this wider context" (Burke 1969, 27). As a general framework for dialectical strategies aimed at association, identification encourages speakers and writers to examine the differences among orientations and seek principles (structural, experiential, conceptual, etc.) that lurk at higher levels of abstraction than the orientations themselves.[15] These principles often take the linguistic form of figuration. Diane Davis (2010) explains that, for Burke, "there can be no identity without identification, and there can be no identification without figuration, without the suasive force of meaningful figures" (21).

Like Burke, Lawrence Grossberg (1979) also links figurative language in general, and metaphor in particular, with the associative functions of dialectical rhetoric. Drawing from Frederic Jameson's *Marxism and Form*, Grossberg asserts that "it is only through the use of figurative language that the contradictions found in a world of humanity's own creation can be constituted, expressed, and potentially overcome" (244). And, Grossberg continues,

> Metaphorical language rests upon the knowledge of what each of the opposing terms is or means. The fundamental shock that is the mark of the metaphor rests upon this ground: One can appreciate the explosion of meaning that occurs when the two discordant universes of meaning are brought together. . . . Out of this destruction of the ordinary sense and reference of the world of language, out of this clash of semantic fields,

and through the twist of meanings given to each of the terms, people are momentarily transposed into a new universe. Through the medium of the semantic tensions of the ordinary world, new possibilities of existence are opened. (Grossberg 1979, 244)

In fact, Grossberg goes so far as to call all dialectical rhetoric metaphorical in nature: "Dialectics is, fundamentally, a form of creative fabrication, using language metaphorically to transcend immersion within the world of everyday life" (Grossberg 1979, 244). Dialectical rhetoric, then, is epistemic in the most powerful sense of the word: "Dialectics, in the form of metaphorical language, reveals that the problem of contradiction is not a problem of reality, but, rather, a problem of and for symbol-using creatures in their attempt to make sense of experience" (244–45). As a three-dimensional dialectical strategy for mediating orientations, poetics and metaphor transcend the force of opposition that maintains orientations in mutually exclusive relationships, viewing opposed orientations from the perspective of alternative orientations (higher or just different) in which the force of opposition itself is not present or valid. Metaphors connect distinct orientations for the dialectical purpose of creating integrated knowledge.

In *A Poetic for Sociology*, Brown also claims that certain stylistic devices, metaphors in particular, are not just decoration but are, in fact, associative and epistemic: "To hold that metaphors are meant to convey intelligible meanings is to reject the view that they are merely a decorative or emotive use of language; or conversely, it is to suggest that style and emotions themselves convey cognitive content" (Brown 1989, 82). From this point of view, metaphors in particular aid in the process of engaging oppositions in productive dialectical contact: "Metaphoric thinking requires a 'double vision' that can hold an object in attention simultaneously from two (or more) points of view and, in so doing, *create* it as *that* particular object of experience. In such a 'stereoscopic vision' we can maintain the interchange between two systems or levels of discourse" (83–84). Metaphor, in this sense, is specifically three dimensional and dialectical because, as Brown points out, "metaphors are our principal instruments for integrating diverse phenomena and viewpoints without destroying their differences" (79). He adds that "by transferring the ideas and associations of one system or level of discourse to another, metaphor allows each system to be perceived anew from the viewpoint of the other" (81). Yet Brown's view of metaphor is not purely idealistic; he extends the epistemic effect of metaphor into the material world as well. If language can construct reality, Brown suggests, then it can also alter existing realities by inflecting them differently (Brown 1989, 98; Burke [1966b] makes a similar argument in "What Are the Signs of What?"). Metaphors, in other words, are particularly effective instruments for shifting our cognitive viewpoints as well as our perceptions of reality, thus opening our minds to greater affectability by means of identification.

Orientations engaged dialectically through three-dimensional identification are most often resolved by reference to other (different or more abstract) orientations in which the force of opposition that maintains each orientation in a mutually exclusive relationship is no longer recognized as valid or relevant. Seeking common substance as the grounding of identification is a general strategy for association that transcends oppositional discourse, and the poetic associations characteristic of metaphorical and analogous argumentation connect more specific aspects of different orientations, opening up new spaces for productive three-dimensional dialectical engagement.

Ashley Henderson's Identification of Latin American and African American Orientations

Identification, as a three-dimensional strategy for dialectical rhetoric, (re)connects dissociated ideas, seeking new levels of abstraction at which the forces of opposition that divide orientations are no longer relevant; it transcends forces of opposition and creates new orientations. Ashley Henderson (whose essay, "The Constant Power Struggle," appears in Appendix D) describes her desire to transcend economic competition among Latin Americans and African Americans with the common and transcendent notions of family and religion, creating a new and cooperative orientation in which the two ethnicities can live productively and appreciate the other.

Ashley begins her essay writing about the recent increase in populations of Latin Americans and African Americans in the United States, suggesting that power could be gained if these populations were to work toward common goals. However, she says, "There is always an indescribable tension that resonates between the two cultures" (and Ashley repeats the word *tension* throughout the essay to describe the relationship). This tension stems primarily from economic interests, especially since the increase in Latin American populations means competition for jobs formerly associated with African Americans. Ashley writes, "The African Americans feel that the employer will choose White people just because they are White or the Latin Americans because they will work for less pay. Tension is created because it seems to African

Americans that Latin Americans have come to this territory and taken all of the jobs." Whereas African Americans have made great strides in their relationships with European Americans, many African Americans feel a growing tension with Latin Americans since Latin Americans are now fighting for the same resources that were hard won by African Americans during the civil rights era. Even when it comes to education, the tension stems from increased populations laying claim to limited resources. Ashley explains that when educational resources are spread too thin, especially in inner-city environments, dropout rates increase, hurting the entire population, not just one small group. According to Ashley, "Both Latin Americans and African Americans have valid issues, but there is simply not enough money to go around for the matter to be handled effectively and fairly; therefore, it stirs the tension." And it does not alleviate the situation that, among Latin American and African American populations, dropouts often become gang members, fueling the flames of hatred among the rival groups.

Yet this tension between Latin American and African American populations is particularly troubling for Ashley since she is "of African American descent" but also would love to immerse herself in Latin cultures and languages without "feeling as though I am being judged for my desires and ethnicity." Ashley believes family, religion, and culture are three concepts that can transcend the economic tension experienced between Latin American and African American groups, moving them toward identification. For "both Latin American and African American cultures," family "is the glue that holds everything together when nothing else is intact," and these families tend to be matriarchal and extended. Ashley explains that "a strong belief in the Christian faith is just as important as family to Latin Americans and African Americans." Although each ethnicity centers around a different religion, the fact is, Ashley explains, that "the act of attending church and having God as the center of their lives is a sacred and most prized tradition" that has the power to make the tension between ethnicities cease. The problem is that "there is not a constant reminder of religion in their daily lives." In addition to family and religion, Ashley sees dialectical intersections among Latin American and African American groups related to culture. Both ethnicities have unique dances and foods all Americans, regardless of heritage, enjoy. Ashley relates these transcendent categories metaphorically, suggesting that Latin Americans and African Americans are "like fraternal twins: although they do not look alike, they think and act alike; but they are not the same identity and their differences show up sooner or later."

Ashley uses identification and metaphor to transcend the differences among Latin American and African American cultures. And the inability of some to stop their violent ways genuinely makes Ashley sad: "If we could stop using violence to try and solve everything, we would be able to see that together we will be a stronger force, not separate. Throw pride out of the window." Working together as a single group, Latin Americans and African Americans will be more likely to achieve their dreams and aspirations than if they fight among themselves, and a meeting of national leaders from both ethnicities might inspire local groups to find ways of transcending divisive issues, such as economic competition, and identify with common qualities, such as family, religion, and culture.

CRITIQUE

When rhetorical situations and discursive contexts call for the mediation of disparate orientations, one option speakers and writers have is to appropriate selected aspects of these orientations through critique. Jeff Rice points out that appropriation is valuable to rhetoric precisely for "its recontextualization of previous forms and meanings" (Rice 2007, 54), and digital communication technologies enable and reinforce appropriation as a productive *topos* for writing.[16] This recontextualization increases discursive complexity, since, as Mark C. Taylor points out, "The process of appropriation results in an internal proliferation of differences" (Taylor 2001, 137). Rice writes, "All writing involves some degree of theft, particularly when writing is introduced into the digital, an area that relies to a great extent on the 'borrowing' logic associated with appropriation" (Rice 2007, 57). As a three-dimensional strategy for dialectical rhetoric, critique appropriates the useful aspects of available orientations in order to address and solve complex rhetorical problems. Critique, depending on how it is defined and employed, can serve two-dimensional and three-dimensional rhetorics. In two-dimensional rhetorics, critique is used to expose and judge abuses of power that result in the subjugation of certain orientations, and the rhetorical process of two-dimensional critique ends with this negative judgment.[17] In three-dimensional dialectical rhetorics, critique evaluates orientations generally (not just negatively) and then appropriates the aspects of each orientation deemed valuable in the service of a positive, practical goal. Thus, in three-dimensional dialectical critique, there is a clear movement beyond evaluation not present in two-dimensional critique.

Though considered a later member of the Frankfurt Institute for Social Research, having worked directly with Theodor Adorno, Jurgen

Habermas was skeptical of the two-dimensional Marxist methodologies employed by his predecessors there. Toward the end of volume 1 of *The Theory of Communicative Action*, Habermas (1984) explains that the "critique of instrumental reason," practiced by founding members of the Frankfurt Institute, "denounces as a defect something that it cannot explain in its defectiveness because it lacks a conceptual framework sufficiently flexible to capture the integrity of what is destroyed through instrumental reason" (389). The critical methodologies employed by members of the Frankfurt Institute, particularly Adorno and Max Horkheimer, force these critical theorists into a limited understanding of complex social problems since certain elements of these problems inevitably fall outside the scope and ken of Marxist critical discourse. Habermas's own work is methodologically eclectic, appropriating strategies equally from highly politicized Marxist critical theory and more pragmatically (less politically) oriented speech-act theory, depending mainly on his rhetorical purpose in articulating a general theory of communicative action. This is the spirit of appropriation in three-dimensional dialectical critique.

In three-dimensional (appropriative) critique, speakers and writers leave disparate orientations intact, ignore the forces of opposition that maintain different orientations in mutually exclusive relationships, and use critical strategies to select useful elements of each orientation depending on the exigencies of particular situations. Breaking away from the two-dimensional critique associated with the Frankfurt Institute, members of the Birmingham Center for Contemporary Cultural Studies (BCCCS), responding to the pressures exerted by postmodern theory during the late 1960s through the 1980s, assume all representations are constructed in a variety of ways and for a variety of political purposes, and individuals occupying different subjectivities can intervene in the processes of representation, both critiquing existing representations and creating new ones. In "What Is Cultural Studies Anyway?" Richard Johnson (former director of the BCCCS) says that "culture" is a process whereby subjectivities produce and consume representations (Johnson 1987, 46), and this process is always dialectical.

Stuart Hall (also former director of the BCCCS) situates postmodern cultural studies in the intersection of social anthropology, or the explication and analysis of identifiable sets of everyday beliefs, and literary studies, or the explication and analysis of artifacts from high culture (Hall 1980, 15–47). Because postmodern cultural studies operates in this dialectical middle ground, it is able to make productive use of the helpful methodologies from both disciplines without tying itself down to the stifling political investments of either discipline. In "Notes on Method," Paul Willis argues that cultural studies borrows "thick description" from anthropology as a useful methodology but discards its implication in anthropology's positivist desire for objectivity and system. Positivist ideologies prevent anthropology from adopting active political stances, and these ideologies can be countered with consciously articulated "theoretical confessions" (Willis 1980, 90). Further, Raymond Williams's (1961) *The Long Revolution* and Richard Hoggart's (1957) *The Uses of Literacy* both apply literary methods of close reading to cultural artifacts while consciously discarding literary studies' elitist focus on high culture that prevents it from comprehending social structures and effecting social change. While practitioners of postmodern cultural studies believe social anthropology and literary studies yield useful methodologies for the critical study of culture, they also reject (or ignore) anthropology's positivism and literary studies's elitism, thus opening up the possibility to effect political change through critique. It is in this dialectical appropriation of the useful elements of literary studies and anthropology that the work of cultural studies derives its political power.

If "culture is ordinary," as Williams suggests (Williams 1993, 5), then so is critique, for critique and culture go hand in hand—they always have and always will. Jere Paul Surber explains,

> It is difficult to imagine a time at which human beings were satisfied with the conditions of their lives. It is equally hard, if not impossible, to conceive of a state of affairs either natural or cultural to which every person or group would give its unqualified assent. In fact, the most archaic narratives we have, from mythologies to founding religious texts, to the earliest histories of world civilizations, are full of conflict, opposition, and revolt against established order. Since the beginnings of documented human association, human culture and its implicit critique seem to have developed hand in hand. (Surber 1998, 1)

Critique is not radical. It is not a practice limited to fringe subcultures. Critique is ordinary.

Yet to speak (or write) of critique as though it is a coherent, unified methodology is quite simply wrong. While all methods of critique may share the most general aim of evaluation, each orientation, with its own unique sets of beliefs and goals, gives rise to a different sense of critique (methods, objects, and outcomes). Surber writes, "Each type or style of cultural critique is founded on certain assumptions, proceeds more or less methodically from that foundation, and implies definite judgments about the nature, values, and ends of what is being criticized" (Surber 1998, 1). Thus, there is no transcendental critique, no unbiased or objective orientation from which the questionable subjectivity (or error) of all other orientations might be determined. All critique is situated, historically and culturally, and what some critical theorists call "transcendent" criticism is an illusion of the worst kind, the unfounded presumption of transcendental superiority where none exists.

Three-dimensional dialectical rhetoricians use critique not as a polemical tool but as an appropriative tool. Three-dimensional critique ignores the force of opposition that maintains orientations in mutually exclusive relationships, selecting useful elements from each orientation depending on the exigencies of particular situations. Johnson defines critique in relation to culture, broadly conceived, as a pragmatic process based in appropriation: "I mean critique in the fullest sense: not criticism merely, not even polemic, but procedures by which other traditions are approached both for what they may yield and for what they inhibit. Critique involves stealing away the more useful elements and rejecting the rest. From this point of view, cultural studies is a process, a kind of alchemy for producing useful knowledge" (Johnson 1987, 18). Here Johnson refers not to critique in the polemical (two-dimensional) sense of illuminating other orientations' deficiencies but to critique in the three-dimensional dialectical sense of appropriating strengths from various orientations and leaving weaknesses behind. Two-dimensional critique reaches negative closure; three-dimensional dialectical critique reaches forward to new integrative possibilities.

Orientations engaged through three-dimensional appropriative critique lose their sense of opposition because of the integrative force of a pragmatic rhetorical goal. A full understanding of the material contents and social commitments of every orientation engaged is useful, of course, but not necessary since appropriation invests all appropriate practical methods with new contents and commitments in the process of their use. Here speakers and writers choose their methods from those available, regardless of the original orientation, depending on their usefulness in an immediate situation and for a particular purpose.

Wade Harrison's Appropriative Critique of a Military Orientation for the Practical Purpose of Surviving a Prison Term

Critique, as a three-dimensional strategy for dialectical rhetoric, is driven by pragmatic rhetorical goals. Through appropriative critique, aspects of each engaged orientation are accepted or rejected based on their usefulness in the service of a pragmatic end. Wade Harrison's (whose essay, "Jumping in the Car," appears in Appendix E) practical goal of surviving hard time in prison drives his appropriation of military and prison orientations. By the end of his sentence, the process of appropriation had nearly become one of full acceptance, but Wade was paroled before that process took complete control of his original orientations.

Wade begins his essay with a brief description of the idyllic family and social orientations he enjoyed throughout most of his elementary and secondary education. Wade's family was middle class, educated, engaged, and religious. Wade himself was athletic and popular—until the accident that changed his life and ripped these orientations away from him, at least for a time. Although Wade did not intend to harm anyone, he was nevertheless responsible for the loss of two lives. Wade expected to be sentenced to prison. He knew his prior family and social orientations would not serve him well there (and, in fact, could create grievous problems for him), and he also knew his trial would take place sometime in the distant future. Thus, in order to gain practical survival skills for life behind bars, Wade enrolled himself in military school. Two and a half years after the accident, Wade went to trial and was sentenced to "five years in state prison." Over two years of military school gave Wade what he calls "military bearing," which in itself was not much of a benefit since he "went to prison looking exactly like a cop." However, there were other qualities Wade acquired in military school, qualities that reduced his problems in prison and may well have saved his life:

> I did, however, have a few things I acquired at military school going for me. As a former drill sergeant, I was accustomed to keeping a stern look on my face, a "mean-mug," as inmates would call it. Also, I had been body-building for a while because it was easier to command people when they thought you could manhandle them, and because I'd long known that I was going to prison. And lastly, I had been training as a fighter for all the same reasons, so I was no stranger to confrontation. In fact, I had a black eye and a gash on my cheek when I walked into prison my very first day. Along with a little luck, these traits were the only reasons I could think of as to why no one tried to swindle me when I was new to the system, when I was "green."

Wade's Beaver Cleaver and *Saved by the Bell* family and social orientations had been supplemented, intentionally, for practical purposes, with completely different orientations that helped to condition his demeanor and behavior in prison.

Wade's pragmatic goal of survival amid random violence and mental disturbance became his motivation for assimilation and reinvention. Wade explains, "I entered prison like a scientist on a mission; I had to research every minute aspect of this culture if I was to learn how to behave." What appeared to be random acts of violence, early in

Wade's stay, made him realize very quickly that he "was a long way from Presbyterian private school." Wade's inexperience with the language of prison life earned him the nickname *Sir*, but he was lucky it did not earn him a far worse fate. With time, Wade began to understand the language of his fellow inmates, and he used it more and more with accuracy and confidence. Eventually, however, Wade would face a dangerous situation when he was committed to fighting another inmate who was bigger and more violent than this high-school favorite son. Wade grabbed a weapon and was, in his words, "getting ready to die" until this fight was "extinguished" by the presence of another inmate, who whisked Wade away, possibly saving his live. This inmate, however, was a white supremacist, which immediately threw Wade into a crisis of conscience. His practical drive to survive, however, left him aligned with those who had saved him.

Wade had come to "exemplify prison culture." He "looked and talked like a convict." But he also never *fully* accommodated the prison orientation; he accepted and used only those methods of interaction that would ensure his survival. Wade, for example, explains that he "never joined any gangs or engaged in any criminal behavior," which would have indicated a complete reversal of orientation, a complete acceptance of a prison orientation to replace all other orientations. Toward the end of his stay in prison, however, things began to change, and Wade's survival instinct began to dominate his very existence. Wade writes, "Towards the latter part of my sentence, I started to look less like a Presbyterian schoolboy, less like a highly decorated cadet, and less like the youngest in an ideal American family. I started to look less like a good person, and more like a son of a bitch." Things that had once bothered or scared Wade began to amuse him as they had the other inmates earlier in his stay. Wade writes, "I remember the moment I realized how much I'd changed. I was asleep when a sissy on the bunk next to me erupted in screams. Just like on my first night in prison, someone was attacking the guy with a razor blade. I knew why he was being attacked because, for no particular reason, I knew everyone's business. At first, I was pissed because the fiasco was keeping me awake. Then I almost started to laugh at the sound of his girlish pleas—almost." Although Wade was profoundly changed by his experience in prison, he never fully lost his family orientation, though he did come close. Yet if he had not critically appropriated other orientations, first military and then prison, his very life would have been in jeopardy. Dialectical appropriation, for Wade, was nothing less than a survival skill, and he has come through that experience able, now, to appropriate other positive orientations and to recover the family and social orientations he nearly lost.

JUXTAPOSITION

When rhetorical situations and discursive contexts call for the dialectical engagement of disparate orientations, one option speakers and writers have is to juxtapose these orientations for the purpose of exploiting the force of opposition that divides them. In juxtaposition, speakers and writers use rhetorical strategies to embrace, as a productive energy, the force of opposition that maintains different orientations in mutually exclusive relationships. Here the force of opposition is left fully intact, as are the mutually exclusive identities of the orientations themselves. Rice argues that juxtaposition creates new knowledge not possible in traditional approaches to communication: "Juxtapositions among ideas as well as word and image prompt assumptions and inferences absent in most argumentative or narrative writing" (Rice 2007, 74). These assumptions and inferences are the products of juxtaposition, and juxtaposition is integral to "media-based rhetorics" (78). Hypertext is one aspect of digital communication technologies that explicitly uses juxtaposition as a rhetorical strategy "in ways that print cannot accommodate" (80). Clearly, juxtaposition has been used as a rhetorical strategy for many centuries, from Zeno's paradoxes to Marcel Mauss, Richard Huntington, and Peter Metcalf's uses of juxtaposition to preserve indigenous cultures from biased anthropological representation. Nevertheless, rhetorical strategies related to juxtaposition have certainly found a comfortable home in digital communication, and especially in hypertext.

As early as the 1980s, several influential figures in composition studies were recognizing the importance of juxtaposition in writing (though they did not often call it *juxtaposition*). In *Embracing Contraries* and "The Uses of Binary Thinking," Peter Elbow (1993) describes effective cognition as the ability to collect many conflicting orientations, hold them in mind, and tolerate their ambiguity without immediately seeking resolution. Elbow calls this the "both/and perspective," which is more generative of creative thought and writing than the dominant either/or perspective. David Bleich (1988), too, argues for a "double perspective" on language and literature, offering both/and thinking as an antidote to modern culture's debilitating obsession with the ideology of individualism. Finally, Grossberg argues, "[Dialectics] is not a simple assertion of the coexistence of opposites within contradictions. Dialectics is thinking precisely about the way in which opposition or difference produces identity" (Grossberg 1979, 236–37), and "dialectical thought attempts to understand some phenomenon through its existence within a web of contradictions" (237). Interestingly, while Elbow, Bleich, and Grossberg articulate similar perspectives on binary thinking, Bleich and Grossberg do so in the service of social ideologies and Elbow does so in the service of individualist ideologies.

In juxtaposition, according to Brown, "None of the participating subperspectives are treated as precisely right or precisely wrong. Each is a voice, or position, which, in interacting with the others, contributes to the development of the whole" (Brown 1989, 211), and "the juxtaposition of logically incongruous frameworks forces upon us an awareness which is deeper than the denotative surface of what is being told" (216). In juxtaposition, then, multiple orientations are placed in close proximity, and their oppositional interplay produces meaning deeper and more significant than the sum of the orientations themselves; there is, however, no mutual influence since each orientation, despite dialectical engagement through juxtaposition, retains its own identity, its own sovereignty as a unique orientation. Thus, for example, when sociologists' points of view conflict with the points of view of their subjects, Brown recommends that these conflicts remain unresolved in textual representations. "Social reality," as Brown calls it, is messy; it never abides by the laws of one perspective. Positivist sociology describes only those elements of social reality that fall within the purview of its epistemology and methodology and discards the rest as irrational or subjective. But three-dimensional dialectical sociology explores and represents conflicting points of view because "they are the substance of the social reality that is described" (62). Brown explains that "various voices do not cancel each other out, nor is truth limited to those points on which they agree; instead, much as characters in a play, each voice enriches the others, each contributes to the dialectical construction of more and more comprehensive *meta*-perspectives" (Brown 1989, 69). In progressive (not positivist) ethnographic texts, anthropologists and sociologists often simultaneously represent interpretations by members of the culture under study and academic interpretations of the same social structures and processes, leaving aside any attempt to gain control of (or colonize) the total discourse through some kind of metacommentary.

The social world ethnography purports to describe is messy, fraught with tension and hierarchies, and marked by flux and competition. In *The Interpretation of Cultures*, Geertz recognizes this difficult representational role of recent ethnography:

> Ethnography is thick description. What the ethnographer is in fact faced with . . . is a multiplicity of conceptual structures, many of them superimposed upon or knotted into one another, which are at once strange, irregular, and inexplicit, and which he must contrive somehow first to grasp and then to render. . . . Doing ethnography is like trying to read

(in the sense of "construct a reading of") a manuscript—foreign, faded, full of ellipses, incoherencies, suspicious emendations, and tendentious commentaries, but written not in conventionalized graphs but in transient examples of shaped behavior. (Geertz 1973, 9–10)

A shift has taken place, then, in the very conception of the representational work ethnography does: its task is no longer to "make sense of" social chaos, selecting and describing those elements of culture that best fit the ethnographer's narrative; its task is to represent social chaos in all of its nonlinear, contradictory forms.

In *Anthropology as Cultural Critique*, George E. Marcus and Michael M. J. Fischer take the revision of positivist ethnography described by Brown and Geertz one step further. In the ethnographic strategy Marcus and Fischer call "defamiliarization by cross-cultural juxtaposition," "The idea is to use the substantive facts about another culture as a probe into the specific facts about a subject of criticism at home" (Marcus and Fischer 1986, 138). Marcus and Fischer explain that "this technique entails using detailed ethnography of cultures abroad, with special care not to remove them from their contemporary situations, as a critical and comparative probe for some equally intensive project of ethnography *at home*" (157; my emphasis). Thus, while Brown and Geertz shift the emphasis of ethnography away from the objectivity of the researcher and toward the lives and needs of the subjects, Marcus and Fischer turn the object of ethnography toward their own cultures, beginning with ethnographies of others as a means to defamiliarize our own cultures and reveal aspects of them we may not initially be able to recognize. Marcus and Fischer explain,

> What we have in mind is an ethnographic project pursued within a domestic context that from its inception has a substantive relationship to some body of ethnography elsewhere. . . . The latter serves to give the former a framework or strategy of analysis that would not otherwise be achieved. The dual tracking of ethnographic cases and experiences thus characterizes a repatriated project of ethnography from the fieldwork through to a text of cultural criticism, which like some experimental ethnography, may employ ethnographic detail and rhetoric, but may not be in any conventional sense simply an ethnography. . . . Cross-cultural juxtaposition works dialectically in all phases of a project of critical ethnography: there are critiques at both ends, of both societies. (Marcus and Fischer 1986, 162–63)

Three-dimensional dialectical rhetoricians, then, use defamiliarizing ethnography and cross-cultural juxtaposition in order to shed light on their own cultural situations and the situations of their audience members in ways that may not be accessible without juxtaposition.

Adrian Fitchpatrick's Juxtaposition of Medical and Maternal Orientations

The three-dimensional strategy of juxtaposition exploits the force of opposition, exaggerating it for a variety of rhetorical purposes, often creating an orientation that tolerates opposition as a condition of existence. Adrian Fitchpatrick (whose essay, "The Journey to Motherhood," appears in Appendix F) juxtaposes an objective, statistical, medical orientation regarding premature birth with her own orientation as the mother of a premature child. Adrian makes no effort to comment on the differences between these orientations, though she does graphically highlight their differences by italicizing the medical orientation. In the process of juxtaposition, Adrian shows that both orientations need not exclude the other; in fact, they can coexist, though opposed, without need of resolution or interaction.

Adrian begins her essay with a description of her marriage and her subsequent transition into another life role, wife. This new role soon brings the possibility of yet another new life role, mother, but there are complications. Adrian writes, "My pregnancy was anything but a 'normal' pregnancy and there was absolutely no glamour." Although Adrian had heard many stories of the annoying pains of pregnancy and the beauty of childbirth, her own experience with pregnancy was marked by fear and potential loss. Her research into the risks associated with premature birth highlighted for Adrian a disconnection: she was researching about and for *her* baby, but the doctors who had written the articles and websites she read were talking about babies, *any* babies, or an average of all babies. Although at first Adrian did not like the impersonal, objective tone of the research she was reading, she also, in some ways, found it comforting that they were not personalizing their findings for her son, which would have been too difficult to read. Journals and websites provided Adrian information about premature babies, and Adrian herself was able to personalize that information, to say that a percentage is not the reality of her baby. A percentage is only a number, not a child with a beating heart. And, in fact, Adrian's baby did beat the odds; Brayden was not a statistic.

Adrian uses the dialectical strategy of juxtaposition to illustrate her experience as a wife and mother but also as an informed parent, and juxtaposition, in the end, represents her own acceptance of these two very different orientations, medical and maternal, toward premature birth. Toward the end of Adrian's essay, the italicized sections simply recount milestones in Brayden's development, and Adrian continues to reflect on her own conflicting feelings as a parent. Thus, with no direct commentary on the orientations placed side by side throughout this essay,

Adrian uses juxtaposition to emphasize the force of opposition between medical and maternal orientations, illustrating the possibility of productive coexistence without the need for resolution or integration.

The five students whose essays I discuss throughout this chapter chose to use three-dimensional dialectical strategies to mediate orientations that, on the surface, appear opposed, irreconcilable, incommensurable. These orientations are not essential social structures, though they certainly do have material qualities; they are evolving structures performed in the act of dialectical rhetoric. If composition studies is to recover dialectic as the counterpart of rhetoric (or *more*, as part of a unified art, dialectical rhetoric), then it must also recover dialectic in its classical sense as a strategic and topical art, and those topics should reflect a discursive context (not classical at all) that is shaped by, and that shapes, the full range of available communication technologies.

Notes

1. I should point out that almost all communication, not just three-dimensional rhetorics, is in some respect strategic. One-dimensional rhetorics use rational argumentation as a rhetorical strategy to convince reasonable audiences to hold probable (socially coherent) beliefs. Two-dimensional dialectical rhetorics use oppositional critique as a rhetorical strategy to unveil the mystifying and oppressive power of ideology. Three-dimensional dialectical rhetorics use topical mediation as a rhetorical strategy to negotiate among orientations in context.

2. Fifteen years before Leff's comment, Walter Jost expressed a similar view of the polysemy of the topics. According to Jost, the "history of the topics is notoriously slippery (as is well known, the term has a dozen or more meanings and applications)" (Jost 1991, 3). He then tries to "simplify" the concept with a definition: "Topics are 'places' the rhetor turns to—or less metaphorically—are ideas, terms, formulas, phrases, propositions, argument forms and so on that the rhetor turns to in order to discover what to say on a given matter" (3). Yet when we think about teaching and writing, questions arise: Which ideas? All ideas? Which terms? All terms? Is there a difference between an idea or a term in general and an idea or a term that might serve as an inventional tool in the speaking or writing process? I certainly hope so, but Jost leaves these questions unanswered. Jost does, however, go on to argue that rhetorical theorists and teachers need to focus more on the specific (social) topics and less on the general (common) topics.

3. Stephen R. Yarbrough's (2004) treatment of the relationship between *topoi* and enthymemes is by far the best I have encountered.

4. See Tommy J. Boley (1979), Edward P. J. Corbett (1965), Richard Larson (1968), and W. Ross Winterowd (1973), to name just a few. In communication studies, the 1971 volume *The Prospects of Rhetoric*, a report of the National Developmental Project sponsored by the Speech Communication Association and edited by Lloyd Bitzer and Edwin Black, called for scholars to develop new systems of topics for modern rhetoric (Bitzer and Black 1971).

5. For heuristic adaptations of Young, Becker, and Pike's tagmemics, see James Kinney (1978), Charles Kneupper (1980), and Victor J. Vitanza (1979). For heuristic adaptations of Burke's pentad, see Philip M. Keith (1977; 1979) and Kneupper (1979). For heuristic adaptations of Toulmin's layout of arguments, see Michael L. Keene (1979) and Kneupper (1978).

6. Just since the turn of the millennium, there have been a number of reappraisals of the classical *topoi* and adaptations of them for modern rhetorical theory and practices. See David Fleming (2003), Carolyn R. Miller (2000), Sara Rubinelli (2006), Arthur E. Walzer (2000), Barbara Warnick (2000), Stephen R. Yarbrough (2004), and J. P. Zompetti (2006), for example.

7. Janice M. Lauer (2004) provides a comprehensive history of invention in rhetoric and composition, including ways in which topical invention intersected with other rhetorical methods and concerns.

8. Writing about Boethius, Eleonore Stump describes a topic as "primarily a strategy rather than a principle, . . . something like a basic recipe or blueprint, according to which one can produce many things the same in structure but different in detail and in material" (qtd. in Yarbrough 2004, 79).

9. These three-dimensional topics function much like the affirmative topics described by Muckelbauer (2009), as frameworks that evolve with contents in a relationship based on mutual generation. Their function, in other words, is "producing connections" (127), not limiting perception. These three-dimensional topics are also functional manifestations of what Gregory L. Ulmer calls *chora*, which he offers as the digital replacement (or supplement, depending on the work one is reading) of literate *topoi*. Whereas the *topoi* of classical rhetoric functioned to limit and classify argumentative options, the function of choral invention is to expand meaning and link different ideas into new sets (Ulmer 2005, 151, 185–86). This process of linking is necessitated by the context of hypermedia, which is structured as a system of nodes in a seemingly limitless network (Ulmer 1994, 27). The structure of choral invention is not prefabricated like the classical *topoi*. Instead, "choral writing organizes any manner of information by means of the writer's specific position in the time and space of a culture" (Ulmer 1994, 33). Since three-dimensional topics produce connections, then affirmative invention (Muckelbauer), sub/versive historiography (Vitanza), complex vitalism (Hawk), and choral writing (Ulmer) all support a theory and practice of the hybrid art I call *dialectical rhetoric*.

10. It is important to recognize that interpreting students' dialectical enactments complicates matters since interpretation adds another dialectical layer. In other words, in the process of interpreting Lindy's, Emily's, Ashley's, Wade's, and Adrian's dialectical mediations of various orientations, I have inevitably inserted my own orientations into the process. Other readers would insert their own orientations as well, resulting, perhaps, in a different account of the orientations performed and mediated by these five students. Nevertheless, all five students have read my interpretations of their essays (and in some cases asked for changes, which, of course, I made exactly as they requested), making my take on their essays at least close to what theirs might be.

11. Deconstruction, which emerged as an interest in English departments during the 1970s, was of little concern to composition scholars until the 1980s (with one notable exception: Sharon Crowley's 1979 article "Of Gorgias and Grammatology"). Barbara Heifferon and Phyllis Mentzell Ryder explain why:

> Compositionists distrusted deconstruction, not only because of its ties to potentially elitist literary theory, but also because the Derridean concepts of language and critiques of

metaphysics of presence threaten traditional assumptions of composition. Deconstruction not only disrupts time-honored concepts such as "unity and coherence," "organization or structure," "voice," "smooth transitions," and other theories such as "expressivism," but also disrupts the sense that meaning, authors, texts, and audiences are stable concepts. (Heifferon and Ryder 1998, 80)

If deconstruction subverted our best advice as writing teachers, what use was it as a framework for developing pedagogies? Linking deconstruction with critical writing enabled compositionists to draw from this methodology without disrupting too many of the traditional concerns of the writing class. See, for example, discussions of deconstruction by such composition scholars as Sharon Crowley (1979; 1985; 1987; 1989), Reed Way Dasenbrock (1988), Kathleen Dixon (1995), Randall Knoper (1989), Jasper Neel (1984; 1988, especially), Jean Reynolds (1999), and John Schilb (1989) (also see Maxine Hairston [1992] for an argument against critical deconstruction in composition).

12.   Gregory Clark (like Ann E. Berthoff two decades before, though he doesn't cite her work) views dialectic as a special form of dialogue: "The term *dialogue* can be used to describe any exchange of assertions and response, whereas the term *dialectic* is used to describe a particular kind of dialogue, one sustained exclusively for the purpose of constructing and revising knowledge that its participants can share" (Clark 1990, 19). While there is some historical precedent for such an interpretation (in Plato, for example), I prefer to view dialogue, or, more specifically, dialogics, as a dialectical strategy.

13.   Perelman and Olbrechts-Tyteca (1969) describe three argumentative strategies for association that can help to fulfill the more general goals of identification. These strategies include quasilogical arguments, arguments based on the structure of reality, and arguments establishing the structure of reality. Quasilogical arguments resolve apparent contradictions and incompatibilities among orientations through such strategies as definition, reciprocity, transitivity, and comparison (193–260). Arguments based on the structure of reality establish solidarity among orientations by invoking causation, ends and means, coexistence, and authority (261–349). Arguments establishing the structure of reality construct relations among orientations through example, illustration, analogy, and metaphor (350–410).

14.   For general treatments of dialectic throughout Burke's works, see Parke G. Burgess (1985), Timothy W. Crusius (1986; 1988), Elizabeth M. Weiser (2009), and James P. Zappen (2009).

15.   In *A Poetic for Sociology*, Brown (1989) articulates a similar argument to Burke's, writing that "only by assuming a higher order outside our paradigms are we provided the possibility of ordering the material that occur within them. . . . Higher-order structures are not essences or forms that we must know in themselves; instead, the very positing of them provides the implicit principles for the discovery and organization of what we already can apprehend" (225).

16.   Rice critiques the notion of topic (or *topos*) as "print-based": "The topoi have served print-based writing instruction by allowing students (and often instructors) the ability to work from a common repository of ideas" (Rice 2007, 33). On this basis, Rice rejects the use of *topoi* as rhetorical strategies in digital communication. Thus, Rice may object to my appropriation of appropriation for a topics-based rhetoric of both digital and print communication. However, I believe topics have little to do with specific ideas (let alone repositories of them) and everything to do with strategies, which are perfectly appropriate for use in any rhetoric, digital or print.

17.   Raymie E. McKerrow's notion of "critical rhetoric" is a case in point. McKerrow writes, "In practice, a critical rhetoric seeks to unmask or demystify the discourse

of power" (McKerrow 1989, 91), and, as such, critique "has as its object something which it is 'against'" (92). Thus, critique's purpose is negative, not constructive: "The task of a critical rhetoric is to undermine and expose the discourse of power in order to thwart its effects in a social relation" (98). While two-dimensional critique has its place in rhetorical practice, it is used as much to suppress as it is to liberate.

5
THREE-DIMENSIONAL DIALECTICAL
RHETORICS IN DIGITAL CONTEXTS

In chapter 4, I argued that three-dimensional dialectical rhetorics are increasingly influencing the larger communication landscape, including even the conservative discourses of academic argumentation, and I illustrated this argument through discussions of five essays written by students who adopted three-dimensional approaches to their essays about communities and contact zones. The assignment to which these students responded (see Appendix A) eliminates the possibility of a one-dimensional response, but it leaves the choice between two-dimensional and three-dimensional responses completely open. I am always surprised at how many of my students choose to approach their contact-zone topics from the three-dimensional perspective of dialectical rhetoric. But, then again, I really shouldn't be. The fact is, our present students have grown up in a newly emerging digital media ecology that emphasizes mediation and negotiation, not unification or opposition. Digital communication technologies have created a discursive context in which the strategies associated with three-dimensional dialectical rhetorics are relevant, useful, and productive.

In this final chapter, I look closely at how digital-communication contexts tend to function dialectically, emphasizing interaction, growth, process, complexity, mediation, and negotiation. I then examine each of the five *topoi* of three-dimensional dialectical rhetoric within the context of digital communication technologies. This examination reveals that deconstruction, dialogue, identification, critique, and juxtaposition are common rhetorical strategies in digital communication, and a conscious awareness of the functions of these strategies gives students more rhetorical control over their interventions in these contexts and others.

DIGITAL DIALECTIC

According to Michael Heim, dialectic is "the inner logic of differences [not oppositions] exposed over an extended period of exchange. . . .

DOI: 10.7330/9780874219821.c005

What more fitting support to dialectic could we have than the technological medium we call cyberspace?" (Heim 1999, 40). Here digital dialectics entail neither synthesis nor negation: "The challenge is not to
end the oscillation" of differences in dialectical engagement, but instead
it is to "find the path that goes through them. . . . [It] is an existential
process of criticism, practice, and conscious communication" (41). In
fact, without the philosophical imperative of negation, digital dialectics,
based on difference and experience, provide opportunities for orientations to evolve positively in response to contextual pressures. Carol
Gigliotti (1999) argues, "Pitting one method, one idea, one object, one
person, one culture against another for the purpose of cancelling one
of them out is, though efficient, not particularly healthy. . . . What is
needed is a dialectical process based on the goal of one position enlarg-
ing the other, offering it possibilities for improvement that an insider
might never have guessed" (52). This view of dialectic as amplification
(not negation) is particularly relevant, according to Gigliotti, in a "digital environment" (52). Since the goal of three-dimensional dialectical
rhetorics is mediation, not negation or opposition, orientations can
grow and change in digital contexts according to their own ethics.

Digital texts are always in process, rarely finished, and sometimes
only temporary. As three-dimensional dialectics are marked by growth
and change, so too are digital texts. In "Unfinished Business," Peter
Lunenfeld argues that "the business of the computer is always unfinished. In fact, 'unfinish' defines the aesthetic of digital media" (7).
While certain dialectics (philosophical especially) are characterized
by teleology, digital dialectics tend to eschew *telos* in favor of process.
Lunenfeld (1999) writes, "To celebrate the unfinished in this era of digital ubiquity is to laud process rather than goal—to open up a third thing
that is not a resolution, but rather a state of suspension" (8). Instead
of marching through history toward utopia, digital dialectics make us
meander through cyberspace, engaging cyberplaces as they emerge
in almost (but not quite) random patterns. Lunenfeld points out that
"there are always more links to create, more sites springing up every day,
and even that which has been catalogued will be redesigned by the time
you return to it" (10). Dialectic, in the context of digital communication
technologies, loses the requirement of *telos* (and thus negation) that
characterizes philosophical dialectic, making digital communication a
complex, three-dimensional context for dialectical rhetorics.

With an emphasis on process, digital dialectics (like three-dimensional
dialectical rhetorics) require constant mediation and negotiation. In
Life After New Media, Sarah Kember and Joanna Zylinska argue for a

"significant shift in the way new media is perceived and understood: from thinking about 'new media' as a set of discrete objects (the computer, the cell phone, the iPod, the ebook reader) to understanding media predominantly in terms of processes of mediation" (Kember and Zylinska 2012, xiii). Processes of mediation account dialectically for the evolution of technologies and their use in human interaction. In this endless dialectical process, Kember and Zylinska argue, "Mediation becomes a key trope for understanding and articulating our being in, and becoming with, the technological world, our emergence and ways of intra-acting with it, as well as the acts and processes of temporarily stabilizing the world into media, agents, relations, and networks" (xv). Mediation thus becomes our source of orientations in relation to the technologies we encounter every day, and these orientations (like all orientations) are formed in part through "differentiation" (xvi). Digital media are performative, and their dialectical mediations (and differentiations) of objects and events condition how the world is perceived. Kember and Zylinska explain that "mediation is not a spatialized thing or object but first of all a temporal phenomenon, a process involving human and machinic agencies" (64), and these agencies are always engaged in dialectical interaction.

While digital communication in general is a productive context for three-dimensional dialectical rhetorics, the addition of Web 2.0 applications to the larger structure of the Internet has complicated matters. The applications characteristic of the early World Wide Web (around 1994 to 2004) maintained a "distinct divide between content providers and content users" (Baehr and Lang 2012, 45) and consisted of an "enormous array of independent sites serving pages on request" (Dumas 2013, 59). Readers followed links from page to page depending on their own purposes (entertainment, information, etc.), and the nearly random logic of the link sometimes made it difficult to find certain kinds of content. In Web 2.0, companies offering specific Internet services have begun to integrate their sites so readers can click on a map icon to get directions to a local movie theater, for example. Social collaboration and networking sites (wiki, blog, and microblog sites; photo- and video-sharing sites) no longer provide content for surfing readers but provide platforms for users to produce and consume content, blurring the earlier distinction between writers and readers. Web 2.0 sites have become interactive, integrated, user-centered, collaborative, and mediated more thoroughly than ever before. Although the hardware infrastructure has changed little in the transition from the early World Wide Web to Web 2.0, the design of software has changed fundamentally, and the willingness of developers to integrate their proprietary functions has increased dramatically. Since Web 2.0 applications encourage and enable social networking, collaborative interaction, and the seamless integration of platforms, the most salient key word describing the functions of twenty-first century communication technologies is *connectivity*.[1]

Most forms of communication enable connectivity in some way. Andreas Hepp (2008) says that "connectivity is a general avenue of communication. It is not new or specific to electronic media or the internet" (42). However, with the rise of platformed sociality, facilitated collaboration, and integrated applications in Web 2.0, the effect of connectivity is increased exponentially, and the kinds of connections shift with the affordances, or material and rhetorical possibilities, of each medium (Hutchby 2001, 23–33). Friedrich Krotz points out that "media connectivity may be understood as an ever-thickening net of communication possibilities and communication flows of the people who, to an ever-increasing extent, live in a complex media environment" (Krotz 2008, 25). Just as all arts and technologies have positive and negative uses, so too does writing in Web 2.0 contexts (van Dijck 2013). Nevertheless, these contexts are here, and we would be fools not to deal with them in positive and productive ways, especially since careers for professional-writing graduates will certainly involve online publishing and will likely include writing of (or in) Web 2.0 platforms.

James E. Porter explains that Web 2.0 has caused a shift in professional writing from the "expert in content" model to the "expert networker and collaborator" model. Porter writes, "In the digital economy, what we come to think of as 'writing ability' is shifting in rather dramatic ways toward a community and collaborative notion of networked writing. The professional writer becomes more a creator of communities, of networks, than a creator of content" (Porter 2010, 188). Although print will not die out, it is true that professional writers with skills only in print composition will lack other skills currently in high demand. Print composition assumes a model in which the writer is the expert providing content for nonexperts. If professional writers are unable to compose as collaborators, as cocreators of content in user-generated folksonomies, they will soon find themselves unable to produce the kinds of documents driving the professional-writing industry right now. According to Porter,

> In the world of Web 2.0, information content development is determined by communities of users, ordinary end users who are not experts or domain specialists. For certain kinds of tasks—particularly for messy, complicated, and open-ended exploratory work and for solving wicked problems—the best option may be to get experts out of the way and to

design systems to include dynamic collaboration with nonexperts. . . . What if the job of experts is not to solve problems by themselves, but rather to design robust collaborative systems that allow diverse groups of users (experts and nonexperts alike) to pool community resources in order to solve problems? The notion of "expert" is shifting away from its traditional basis in "content knowledge" to another basis: expert as skilled social networker and collaborator. (Porter 2010, 189–190)

In writing contexts where communities of users generate content collaboratively, dissolving the distinction between expert and novice communicators, the task of professional writing shifts toward providing platforms for effective collaborative thinking and composing.[2] And three-dimensional dialectical rhetorics provide strategies for understanding, inventing, and designing integrated documents and sites for collaborative composition.

DIALECTICAL RHETORICS IN WEB 2.0

The qualities of digital dialectics and Web 2.0 discourses discussed so far—difference (not opposition), expansion (not negation), process (not object), mediation (not determinism), and collaboration (not monologue)—are all hallmarks of three-dimensional dialectical rhetorics. These hallmarks, along with the five strategic *topoi* discussed in chapter 4 (deconstruction, dialogue, identification, critique, and juxtaposition), highlight productive connections and enable writers to compose and consume content effectively in Web 2.0 contexts where the engagement of differences (linguistic, social, economic, cultural, ethnic, gender, and so on) proliferates.

Deconstruction

In 1998, six years before Tim O'Reilly popularized the term *Web 2.0* at the O'Reilly Media Web 2.0 Conference in 2004 (van Dijck 2013, 177), Johndan Johnson-Eilola (1998) argued that rhetoric and composition was inexplicably persisting in viewing writers as individual producers and readers as individual consumers of texts despite the powerful ideological influence of cultural studies and social construction on the field as a whole. Now a full decade after the O'Reilly Media Web 2.0 Conference, composition still persists in this view of writers and readers, despite the fact that Web 2.0 software technologies have collapsed traditional rhetorical distinctions like writer/reader, speaker/audience, and encoder/decoder into unified, integrated concepts like *users*, or the portmanteau *produsers* (Jenkins, Ford, and Green 2013, 182). Integrated terms like *users* and *produsers* understand participation in Web 2.0 platforms as irreducible to either production or consumption, thus dissolving the forces of opposition that maintain this outmoded distinction. Viewing the web as a platform and participants as produsers forces rhetoric and composition to reexamine some of its foundational structuring terms, searching through deconstructive methodologies for a new supplement or mark amid the ashes of archaic distinctions. Web 2.0 produsers are not "simply consumers of preconstructed messages"; instead, they are "shaping, sharing, reframing, and remixing media content in ways which might not have been previously imagined. And they are doing so not as isolated individuals but within larger communities and networks" (Jenkins, Ford, and Green 2013, 2). Since Web 2.0 has been recognized and described for at least the past ten years, it is not unreasonable to say rhetoric and composition has been slow to recognize its discursive characteristics and its influence on writing studies.

In the early World Wide Web, producers provided content and readers consumed it. However, as Craig Baehr and Susan M. Lang point out,

> In the transition to Web 2.0, more extensive and sophisticated interactions became possible, and the line between author and reader blurred. . . . Both authors and readers are now users, demonstrating a significant shift toward usability and accessibility in online publications. Wikis, blogging, and microblogging technologies, including MySpace, Facebook, and Twitter, have enabled readers to assume roles as collaborative authors in more structured authoring environments. Authors can and do write from desktop or laptop computers, mobile computing devices, and even basic cell phones. As a result, a multiplicity of discourses are now generated on the web (author centered, reader centered, collaborative, amalgative), in which users formerly known as "readers" can participate. (Baehr and Lang 2012, 47–48)

While composition teachers still maintain clear distinctions between writing and reading, speaking and listening, encoding and decoding, the students who currently populate our writing classes more often understand composing as an integrated art of usage (or produsage), with no force of opposition dividing consumption from production. For these students, the opposition production/consumption has been so thoroughly deconstructed in their everyday media lives that they have to learn and apply this opposition's textual effects when they enter their composition classes.

Several Web 2.0 platforms useful for academic research blur traditional distinctions often maintained by writing teachers beyond their usefulness. The website Delicious, for example, is an interactive Web 2.0

application in which users tag, organize, and share online bookmarks, and they search other users' tags and bookmarks as well. As more and more information is found online, including academic books and journals, Delicious provides a platform in which users generate knowledge through produsage, simultaneously and dialectically reading, structuring, and writing web content. In "Being Delicious: Materialities of Research in a Web 2.0 Application," Collin Brooke and Thomas Rickert explain that "if research and writing are commonly held to be more or less separate activities, Delicious suggests the dissolution of such an easy distinction" (Brooke and Rickert 2011, 164). Unlike content-heavy sites in the early World Wide Web, "Delicious provides very little content of its own, beyond an assortment of help files, code snippets, and a consistent layout for site content. The vast majority of site content is provided instead by individual users, whose bookmarks are networked with each other's" (172). Within the Delicious platform, users bookmark sites useful to their research (academic or personal) and tag the sites with keywords and phrases. Brooke and Rickert point out that this single act of tagging is an integrated literacy: "While interpretive work is integral to this activity, so is the productive-expressive power of language" (173). Bookmarking and tagging in platforms like Delicious have become integral strategies for online research, and these strategies do not fit the traditional distinctions between writers and readers (speakers and listeners, encoders and decoders, etc.) that most composition teachers still maintain.

In "The Changing Space of Research: Web 2.0 and the Integration of Research and Writing Environments," James P. Purdy argues that Web 2.0 platforms such as *Wikipedia* and ARTstor directly challenge the "antiquated model of knowledge production" maintained in composition courses. This antiquated model "disconnects research from writing, artificially separates the academic from the nonacademic, and misrepresents how knowledge is created" (Purdy 2010, 48). For Purdy, "In Web 2.0, writing and researching activities are increasingly integrated both spatially and conceptually"; thus, "Web 2.0 technologies showcase how research and writing together participate in knowledge production" (48). *Wikipedia* is an example of an integrated researching and writing space in which users construct knowledge. What is most striking about *Wikipedia* as a Web 2.0 platform is not its status as a credible (or not credible) academic source but its "inclusion of writing as a natural part of research and its public display of how its research articles are written" (50). ARTstor is another Web 2.0 platform that integrates researching and writing into a single strategy for knowledge production, and, like *Wikipedia,* "promotes writing as a part of research processes" (53). ARTstor enables students and scholars to create image groups and store them in public folders where anyone can access the collected images and write and read notes composed socially and collaboratively by means of specific tabs. These notes are "savable and searchable, allowing users to search annotations and responses to images and making this writing part of the research archive" (54). By enabling this multimodal production of knowledge, Purdy explains, ARTstor "establishes a close connection between archival materials and writing about them, . . . and writing is an invited and expected part of working in the archive" (54). When composition students use ARTstor to its fullest capacity, they engage "explicitly the complex and recursive relationship" (54) between researching and writing in the process of knowledge production.

Delicious, *Wikipedia,* and ARTstor are not the whole of research and writing resources available in the larger communication landscape. Thus, these Web 2.0 resources should not constitute the whole of research and writing instruction in composition classes. However, they are important and prominent resources that simply cannot be ignored either. Brooke and Rickert explain that "learning to function within such environments is a necessary step we are called to by these newly emergent research opportunities" (Brooke and Rickert 2011, 174). And Purdy writes, "We should incorporate these technologies into writing instruction as objects of analysis and as writing and researching resources" (Purdy 2010, 48). Web 2.0 platforms for knowledge production are gaining in both popularity and credibility, so their presence in academia will only increase, and composition must take account of the ways in which these resources deconstruct the traditional distinctions between writers and readers, speakers and listeners, and encoders and decoders in the general process of knowledge production.

Dialogue

In digital communication, the proliferation of links among sites is so vast that thousands of orientations become locked in dialogic interaction. The deeply interconnected nature of digital media leaves few opportunities for one-dimensional argument. Digital communication tends to be responsorial, generating content through interaction with other media, other sites, and other people, adapting language to the call of others, filtering information, allowing for mutual influence. My own use of Facebook is an example of interaction and dialogue at work in a Web 2.0 context.

I joined Facebook in 2009 (according to my timeline), and I immediately became uncomfortable with the primary choice I was being forced to make: to friend or not to friend. The angst was so bad that I nearly deleted the page a month later. But I kept it because so many of my friends (real friends) from high school and work used it to keep in touch. In the end, I friended some people I shouldn't have and I didn't friend some people I should have. Nevertheless, there I am. You can visit my page, though there isn't much to see. Ben Davis, one of my Facebook friends (and a friend outside of Facebook), is a local high-school English teacher with whom I have worked for the past ten years in my university's National Writing Project site. It is absolutely true that when I am with Ben, my identity forms in relation to him, and my language use is the evidence of that formation. The same is true of our communication on Facebook but with one extension. When I respond to Ben's status updates, I am not only answering the call of the other, dialogicly, but I am also answering the call of the other's others, considering, for example, who might be lurking on his page and reading my comments. I am a smart aleck at heart, so many of my responsorial quips make fun of myself or situations referenced in a post. In one status update, Ben said he was "excited to work on another summer institute with Dr. McComiskey." He was obviously answering the dialogic call of others, not me (since he would never call me Dr. McComiskey). I responded, "Who?" Ben, and several of Ben's friends, many of whom I didn't know, "liked" the self-deprecating nature of the comment. My response to Ben's post relocated the dialogic interaction from Ben and his others to me as the other of Ben, and this humbling gesture struck a chord with some of his friends.

Another status update Ben wrote on his Facebook page elicited a response from me that was not "liked" by a single "friend," signifying, by Facebook's empirical standards, the dialogic failure of the utterance. Ben wrote, "Would someone please tell me why we are attacking Libya?" Some of Ben's friends responded with comments like "I don't know" or "It's crazy." But I responded, "To protect our nation's economic interest in canned fruits and vegetables." Ben wrote, "Huh?" and I responded, "You know the jingle: If it says Libya, Libya, Libya on the label, label, label. . . ." No one posted after that, so I apparently killed the dialogue. Although I was just trying to be funny, my comment was monological, not dialogic, in the sense that my answerability to Ben required that I account for his age and at least try to be sensitive to his political commitments. Ben is too young to remember the jingle, and even if he had gotten the joke, I am pretty sure he would have just furrowed his brow.

So Ben didn't "like" my comment. None of Ben's other friends "liked" my comment either because they were also too young to remember the jingle or believed that humor was an inappropriate response to the crisis in North Africa. Fast-paced communication + smart-aleck writer + misunderstood audience = dialogic failure (at least sometimes, and definitely this time). The platform provided by Facebook has built-in meters measuring dialogic success or failure. If an utterance (whether a status update or a response) calls out to others in a dialogic, interactive way, that utterance will generate many responses (first built-in meter) and receive many "likes" (second built-in meter). Most people who spend time on Facebook actually strive to communicate in the most dialogic ways possible, taking pleasure in generating responses and receiving "likes" because if they don't, they are simply "unfriended." Although Facebook is a good example of a Web 2.0 platform with functions that serve as built-in meters of dialogic interaction, many other social media sites also incorporate similar functions, like Twitter's retweets and trending values. In these cases and others, dialogic communication is encouraged by the design of the platform's interface, and monologic communication (like my Libya post) is discouraged by the structure of the interface.

Identification

The early World Wide Web was a fertile forum for the production and display of multimodal documents. In this context, visual rhetoric emerged as a concern for composition specialists who believed writing was just one medium in which rhetoric functioned. If composition specialists did not expand the scope of their pedagogies to include visual rhetoric, they would be left behind and forgotten, specialists in a medium no longer relevant to most public discourse (and even some sites of academic discourse). Thus, the incorporation of visual rhetoric into the disciplinary concerns of composition studies was itself an act of strategic identification. Yet most of the earliest discussions of visual rhetoric in composition studies took an oppositional approach to the subject, suggesting that critical *writing* could disabuse students of their susceptibility to visual manipulation, breaking unethical associations between images and oppressive ideas by developing critical consciousness (i.e., becoming conscious of the signifieds that hid behind their signifiers and the metaphorical vehicles that hid behind their tenors).[3] This early emphasis on critical writing about manipulative images soon gave way to explorations of how visual images could best be used in the total composition of technical documents, with specialists in professional communication particularly leading the way. During this time, professional writing scholars were forcing a shift from critical rhetorics of visual images toward architectonic rhetorics of visual design, drawing inspiration from interdisciplinary art and graphics scholarship.[4] Design shifted emphasis from interpreting images to creating balance and harmony among multiple elements on a page or screen. Architectonic design soon made its way into composition studies (supplanting critical visual rhetorics) as multimodal composition became more mainstream and not just the purview of technical fields. Interestingly, the emergence of Web 2.0 complicated this new emphasis on design. As Kristin L. Arola points out, "We need to acknowledge and engage with the fact that new forms of writing in Web 2.0 often exclude design" or "the purposeful choice and arrangement of page elements" (Arola 2010, 6).

In Web 2.0, the design of an interface is prefabricated and provided in the structure of the platform or application, so users do not generally engage in the architectonic design of most Web 2.0 sites. And, since regularization of design makes data more manageable and thus marketable, few options are given to users regarding the appearance of an interface. Critical visual rhetorics and the architectonic arts of design still have their place in composition pedagogy; however, if teachers want their students to communicate effectively in the context of Web 2.0, they must also include pedagogical attention to the arts of information visualization. Information visualization is, at heart, the identification among visual, verbal, and numerical signification, and Web 2.0 technologies aid in this process of identification. In "Information Visualization, Web 2.0, and the Teaching of Writing," Madeleine Sorapure writes,

> One effect of the outpouring of user-generated content in the blogs, wikis, tags, and tweets of Web 2.0 is to expand what had already seemed to be infinite: the amount of information available to us via the Internet. By inviting users to produce as well as consume content, Web 2.0 appears to be widening the gap between the amount of information we have available to us and our ability to process this information and derive value from it. However, we also find in Web 2.0 many new applications that can help us visualize and, literally, see and experience information in new ways. With the development of free, online, interactive visualization tools, the field of information visualization—or infovis—is being opened to diverse users and uses, particularly to novice users who want to visualize personally relevant information. Indeed, Web 2.0 is making infovis increasingly viable as a medium for organizing, exploring, analyzing, and creatively deriving meaning from the deluge of information that we face in our everyday lives. (Sorapure 2010, 59)

Although Sorapure does not neglect the critical evaluation of information-visualization software as carriers of ideological investments, she is also deeply committed to helping students learn to use information-visualization tools as means to discover strategies of identification amid media chaos.

If the drive to produce and consume content in Web 2.0 results in so much data that no single person could ever really know what all of it means, the only sensible way to approach this hoard of data is to abstract it into useful generalizations and then identify these generalizations with other generalizations. Web 2.0 tools for information visualization help people abstract useful information from masses of data to improve their abilities to discover new patterns, make sound decisions, and generate productive insights (Sorapure 2010, 61). Since information visualization is quickly becoming more accessible to public audiences for research and communication purposes, Sorapure points out, "Writing teachers can therefore take advantage of opportunities [to generate] new assignments, activities, and course goals" (63).

One particularly interesting site for information visualization is text visualization, which, Sorapure explains, represents large chunks of text through various means, sparking new ways to discuss and analyze documents or sets of documents. The most common example of text visualization is the word cloud, and Wordle is the best-known site for generating word clouds. In Wordle, users can enter text into the word cloud analytical engine and generate a graphic display of the words in the text. Words like articles, prepositions, and conjunctions are automatically omitted, and the rest of the words are large if they appear frequently and are small if they appear infrequently. Obviously, a word's size is not always an indication of its importance, but that makes for an interesting point of discussion about a reading assignment or a starting point of analysis for a draft of an essay. I have a colleague who made a word cloud of the entire text of F. Scott Fitzgerald's *The Great Gatsby*. When he teaches the novel, he introduces the word cloud, not as a representation of some truth or accuracy in the novel but as a way to talk about how important themes can emerge in language and how sometimes frequency does not correlate with importance (there are important themes in the novel, in other words, that have no representation in the word cloud). Although there is nothing true or accurate in word-cloud representations of large documents, this form of information visualization is a new way for students and writers to observe patterns in chunks of text and find associations among elements of those patterns. Exploring these abstracted associations gives readers and writers new ways to identify with the enormous amount of data found in the growing world of Web 2.0.

Critique

Three-dimensional appropriative critique (not two-dimensional oppositional critique) involves stealing away the best of an orientation and leaving behind the rest. This appropriative form of critique manifests itself most clearly in Web 2.0 digital-design practices in which general templates are used but then changed, allowing for creativity. Here critique is not the negative evaluation of poor design; it is the process of altering poor or unwanted design elements and accentuating positive traits for one's own purposes, producing complex intertextual connections in the process. In "Hacker Ethics and Firefox Extensions: Writing and Teaching the 'Grey' Areas of Web 2.0," Brian D. Ballentine (2009) argues that "grey-area" hacking (neither officially sanctioned nor intentionally malicious) teaches students not only the visual effects of writing and adapting code but also engages students in important discussions of ethics for writing in Web 2.0 contexts. Whereas the early World Wide Web consisted of pages designed and owned by writers to be viewed and consumed by readers, Ballentine explains that "the model design for Web 2.0 databases has been geared predominantly toward openness," and "because content owners have chosen to take a more hands-off approach to controlling access to their data, hackers/writers are seizing opportunities to produce any number of counter artifacts." Rewriting the code that structures interfaces and remixing digital content have become necessary literacy skills for Web 2.0 writers, especially since Web 2.0 platform providers intentionally design their interfaces to enable, not prevent, hacking, remixing, and appropriative critiquing. Ballentine explains, "Appropriation and intertextuality are inherent in writing" generally, but appropriation has been taken to new levels in Web 2.0 with the propagation of open-source ideology.

In his essay, Ballentine (2009) focuses on "two new Web 2.0 extensions—Web Developer and Greasemonkey—for the open source browser Firefox that . . . extend an unprecedented invitation to remix, hack, manipulate, and even sabotage content." Using the Web Developer extension for Firefox enables hackers to see the source code that structures a site or interface, and using the Greasemonkey extension enables hackers to write "action scripts" that load simultaneously with the source code, altering the page or interface on the hacker's computer only while leaving the original source code unaltered. In other words, this particular form of hack is only ever manifest on the hacker's monitor. It exists, thus, in the ethical "grey area" since the hack is neither officially sanctioned nor malicious or damaging to the original source code. Ballentine provides two examples of hacks using Web Developer and Greasemonkey. First, each time Ballentine deleted his browser's cache, he would have to reenter his full username into the university's email interface and then click the cursor in the password box to make it appear there. In order to make this email interface more user friendly, Ballentine used Web Developer to observe the code structure of each element in the interface and then used Greasemonkey's action scripts to insert his username and locate the cursor inside the password box each time he accessed his university email through Firefox. Second, Ballentine used Web Developer to observe the source code that inserted an advertisement for the cholesterol drug Crestor on the "Matters of the Heart" page in URL www.cnn.com/health. He then used Greasemonkey to alter that code and remove the ad from the page—but keep in mind this absence would occur only on his own computer monitor and nowhere else.

It is true that Web 2.0, more than the earlier World Wide Web, presents users with structured platforms for prefabricated networking, collaboration, and sharing that force a split between form and content (Arola 2010, 4). Yet Arola's response to "losing the means of production" in Web 2.0 writing is primarily critical and thus two dimensional. Arola writes, "In a Web 2.0 world where design remains primarily beyond a user's control, the interface seemingly functions in an arhetorical way; an interface that allows an easy post is a success. Yet as we know, interfaces do rhetorical work. If we are to critically engage with the rhetoric of the interface and critically engage with Web 2.0, we must pay attention to how Web 2.0 interfaces are shaping our interactions and ourselves" (7). For Arola, less power to design may lead to "less critical consciousness" (7). And one way for students to become more critically conscious of the structuring force of Web 2.0 templates is to have them "analyze the interfaces of Web 2.0" (13). Although Arola does offer her students the option to redesign sites and interfaces, they do so in separate files or with crayons and paper, not by working inside the code that structures the actual interfaces. Thus, Ballentine's approach to gray-area hacking is much more oriented toward three-dimensional dialectical rhetorics in which students appropriate positive design elements in Web 2.0 interfaces and alter those that do not serve their purposes as users. Ballentine is also quick to point out that this kind of hacking is not individualist. Hackers are social by nature, and the ideology of open-source programming requires that they share their successful hacks on user-generated sites like userscripts.org (Ballentine 2009). Hackers thus engage in appropriative critique and then share their appropriations with the larger hacker community.

Juxtaposition

Connectivity is one of the central rhetorical functions of digital media in general and of Web 2.0 applications in particular. In *Media Convergence: Networked Digital Media in Everyday Life*, Graham Meikle and Sherman Young discuss the ease with which traditionally different modes of media representation can now be integrated into hybrid genres that simultaneously serve multiple social functions and address multiple audiences. The social and collaborative connections enabled by media convergence are usually performed with no direct commentary on the nature or function of connectivity despite the obvious presence of different orientations inside the digital space of any platform. A Facebook page, for example, might integrate updates by friends (personal communication) and breaking news feeds (mass communication) with no formal distinction in their digital presentation (Meikle and Young 2012, 59). And multimodal assignments (assignments requiring intentional media convergence) are gradually filtering out from specialized courses in multimedia composition and into more mainstream writing courses like first-year composition. Thus, juxtaposition, or placing different discourses side by side without interpretation, can be a powerful strategy in digital texts, and rhetoric and composition must continue to take account of its uses in all communication media.

Holding differences clearly in view without directly mediating or negotiating them enables audiences to participate in creating the argument of a document, much as Aristotle's enthymemes would have functioned in his literate rhetorical world. An enthymeme has the general structure of a complete syllogism, but at least one of its premises is unstated and thus inferred by the audience. Enthymemes are persuasive because the audience participates in constructing the argument. Juxtaposition, as a rhetorical strategy, carries this same constructive force. Jeff Rice, for example, argues that juxtapositions "force reader interaction at levels traditional scholarly prose cannot" (Rice 2007, 74).

Although composition studies has been slow to accept juxtaposition as a legitimate rhetorical strategy, the fact is that juxtapositions are all around us in every difference we perceive that is not somehow reconciled in the mind. And Rice understands digital communication as grounded in juxtaposition as a fundamental rhetorical strategy. In *The Rhetoric of Cool*, Rice writes, "The nature of new media composition represented on the Web, TV, film, iPods, digital sampling, and elsewhere is the result of the complex juxtaposition of ideas, images, texts, and sounds" (Rice 2007, 76). Most people encounter these juxtapositions as unremarkable functions of their everyday digital lives, from news websites that distribute a broad range of content to social-networking platforms that represent in one space disconnected content from myriad social and professional sources. Yet composition teachers remain reluctant to allow students the freedom to communicate using this ubiquitous rhetorical strategy. Rice explains, "To read these new media applications as distinct from the research and compositional work done in the field is to deny the ways media shapes composition practically as well as ideologically" (Rice 2007, 77). Juxtaposition is ever present in new media communication.

However, as a *topic* for three-dimensional dialectical rhetoric, juxtaposition must not be random, as news feeds and Facebook timelines tend to be. Juxtaposition is an inherent quality of Web 2.0 platforms that encourage participation in spite of difference, yet the simple presence of juxtaposition does not make its use strategic, dialectical, or rhetorical. Here is where Rice and I part company, at least at first, since in *The Rhetoric of Cool* he argues that juxtaposition functions outside of rhetorical purpose. For Rice, traditional composition pedagogies, and the writing students do based on them, are driven by purpose, which is usually determined before outlines, thesis statements, and topic sentences can be composed. Rice explains, "Purpose operates outside of the associations that motivate juxtapositions because it is predetermined. . . . Once purpose is established, writing proceeds based on that initial vision or goal. Anything not initially conceived as relevant to one's purpose should be discarded" (Rice 2007, 83). For Rice, such strategies for the control of purpose limit a writer's "ability to juxtapose new ideas, concepts, or texts as they are encountered" (84). New media forms of composition, such as hypertext links, for example, forge open associations and do not follow a logic predetermined by purpose.

Rice correctly points out that "media production and idea formation are too complex to avoid conflicting beliefs or positions" (Rice 2007, 86); however, these conflicts, these juxtapositions, are never random. Even in hypertext, links are selected for a variety of rhetorical reasons. Rice bases his critique of purpose in writing on James McCrimmon's 1963 textbook *Writing with a Purpose*. Of course, rhetorical purpose now is not what it was in 1963, and I am sure Rice would not suggest it is. But McCrimmon is presented in Rice's book as the paradigm for purpose in writing. Yet even as recently as 2011 (and in *Kairos: A Journal of Rhetoric, Technology, and Pedagogy*), Beth Powell, Kara Poe Alexander, and Sonya Barton (2011) argued that purpose (among other things) is critical for students' success in composing multimodal documents. Also, even the linking strategies associated with juxtaposition can be purposeful without being random and can be expansive without being determinist. In *Multiliteracies for a Digital Age*, Stuart Selber (2010) points out that hypertext authors "project grids of possibility that influence user actions in central ways: they structure graphs that map the hierarchies of included information; construct tables of contents and headings that distinguish topics as primary, secondary, tertiary, and so on; and determine which places in a system constitute centers or homes. From these vantage points, users inherit authorial perspectives on how best to approach online information, and their movements from place to place are at least influenced, if not occasionally determined by the imposed structures" (171). Thus, juxtaposition is a purposeful strategy for three-dimensional dialectical rhetoric.

Interestingly, in his more recent book, *Digital Detroit*, Rice shifts his attitude toward juxtaposition, viewing it more as a productive rhetorical strategy than as a creative accident. Here Rice calls juxtaposition in networked writing "a rhetorical practice that allows for mapping" (Rice 2012, 174), or what Bruno Latour calls "reassociations" (175). Rice explains, "In this rendering of reassociations, social relationships are not contributors to or results of 'being crazy'; they are interests established among a variety of information, some of which could possibly appear schizophrenic at first glance because of the odd juxtapositions generated" (175). Although juxtaposition may at first appear "out of line with representational reality," the fact is that juxtaposition "manufactures a relationship out of a preliminary connection. The juxtaposition serves to generate a social, rhetorical act" (Rice 2012, 175). Here, I believe, Rice begins to describe juxtaposition as a *topos* for digital communication, though I am not convinced he would accept the term just yet. Digital environments encourage juxtaposition as a rhetorical strategy, and students who have learned to communicate through digital technologies, are comfortable with the reassociations and connections enacted (dialectically, rhetorically) through juxtaposition.

CONCLUSION

Dialectic and rhetoric have traveled, throughout history and throughout the pages of this book, sometimes as foes, sometimes as counterparts, and sometimes as collaborative partners in a hybrid art. In one-dimensional contexts, dialectic and rhetoric are usually viewed as separate arts, with dialectic generating and judging logical truths and rhetoric dressing them up in beautiful words. In two-dimensional contexts, dialectic and rhetoric are usually viewed as counterparts, both participating in probability (not truth), with dialectic spinning out strings of opposed arguments and rhetoric picking the strongest and making a case. In three-dimensional contexts, dialectic and rhetoric merge into a hybrid art, dialectical rhetoric, in which different orientations are mediated and negotiated by means of five *topoi*, deconstruction, dialogue, identification, critique, and juxtaposition. Unfortunately, three-dimensional dialectical rhetorics have received little attention in rhetoric and composition scholarship despite their increased relevance in the context of digital communication technologies. What Mark C. Taylor (2001) calls the "moment of complexity," partly an effect of digital and networked communication technologies, requires more options than just unifying and oppositional dialectics and rhetorics; it requires communicative options that emphasize negotiation, mediation, and linking, all of which entail openness and affectability. Interestingly, the youngest generation of students that currently populates our college composition classes has grown up utterly submerged in digital and networked communication technologies, and the rhetorical strategies associated with these technologies have also become critical aspects of more conservative discourses, such as academic argumentation.

Constructing dialectical rhetoric as a hybrid art, made more visible in the context of digital technologies, has itself been an act of dialectical rhetoric, mediating and negotiating two orientations that historically have been defined as fundamentally different or even opposed. Throughout this book, I have used deconstruction to dissolve the forces of opposition that cause dialectic and rhetoric to function as mutually exclusive (counterpart or oppositional) arts, and I have sought the marks, mediation and negotiation, that destroy the foundation upon which dialectic and rhetoric are constructed as different or opposed. I have used dialogic interaction to maintain the unique interests of both dialectic and rhetoric but also allow for mutual influence or rhetorical osmosis, recognizing the responsorial nature of orientations and the polyphonic discourses that populate them. I have used identification as a strategy to seek more general orientations and wider contexts that transcend the forces of opposition defining dialectic and rhetoric as mutually exclusive arts, and I have adopted dimensionality as a guiding metaphor in this pursuit. I have critiqued dialectic and rhetoric, appropriating rhetoric's useful interest in identification and dialectic's useful interest in distinction while discarding the rest (such as unethical manipulation and linear logic), and I have employed these selected concerns together in the service of a pragmatic goal, the construction of a hybrid art, dialectical rhetoric. Finally, I have juxtaposed dialectic and rhetoric diachronically, illustrating how they evolved as counterparts or oppositions and how composition studies (with the exception of Berthoff) recovered rhetoric without any significant connection to dialectic. In other words, throughout this book, I have used the strategies of three-dimensional dialectical rhetoric in order to conceive and describe three-dimensional dialectical rhetoric.

One-dimensional and two-dimensional rhetorics certainly have important uses, even in the emerging contexts of digital and networked communication technologies. When communities lose their identities (real or imagined) to the decentering and homogenizing effects of digital globalization (McLuhan and Powers 1989), only one-dimensional unifying rhetorics will be an effective means to reclaim identity and reestablish purpose. When social media platforms become so thoroughly regulated by market discourses that their drive toward the unification of desires becomes imbedded in their structures and process (van Dijck 2013), only two-dimensional critical rhetorics will be an effective means to call that unifying impulse into question. Technologies at times appear to be inevitable (evolving independently, out of our control) and inalterable (immune to critical discourse), but this is not entirely true. While there are certainly discourses that influence technological developments in powerful ways (such as corporate media and global markets), it is also true, as Graham Meikle and Sherman Young point out, that "end users also shape technologies" (Meikle and Young 2012, 26). Meikle and Young make it very clear that "technologies . . . are not unchangeable. Rather, they are contested systems that allow competing possibilities to be realized. Technologies are not inevitable, all-powerful forces that leave no room for alternative values and concerns. These are contests that we can be a part of, where we can shape technologies, but only if we confront those ideas and values with which we do not agree" (27). Critique is ordinary, even in the context of digital and networked communication technologies.

When digital communication technologies do not homogenize and decenter identities into global orientations (necessitating one-dimensional and two-dimensional rhetorics), these same technologies offer communicative affordances, or rhetorical possibilities inherent in the media themselves (Hutchby 2001, 23–33), for three-dimensional dialectical rhetoric, affordances previously difficult to achieve through print and broadcast technologies. These communicative affordances enable audiences (or, more accurately, produsers) to develop new social functions for communication that are, in turn, changing the very culture in which we live: "We can *organize* media content in new ways for ourselves and others (a 'read-tag' culture), we can *remix*, remake, and reimagine digital media texts (a 'read-remix' culture), we can *collaborate* on all of the above (a 'read-and-write-together' culture), and we can *distribute* or *share* what we've found or made (a 'read-share' culture)" (Meikle and Young 2012, 104). Surely these media affordances impose certain limitations on the social functions of communication as much as they open up new avenues, but as long as creative audiences have the power to mediate and negotiate (organize, remix, collaborate, distribute, and share) material for their own rhetorical purposes, the very technologies that offer these affordances will be open to productive, mediative discourses.

Although all three dimensions of rhetoric have their uses (and, of course, their respective abuses), I believe that three-dimensional dialectical rhetorics tend to function effectively in the widest variety of discursive contexts, including digital environments, since they can invoke dialectical contrasts in stagnant contexts and promote resolution and association in chaotic contexts. Thus, three-dimensional rhetorics should receive more attention from the rhetoric and composition community. This book, I hope, is a step in that direction.

Notes

1. New communication technologies enable connectivity, but humans connect. Some of the connections made by humans are positive and helpful, and these connections are aided by technologies such as social media, collaboration platforms, and cloud drives. Other connections are criminal and destructive, and these connections are aided by technologies such as worms, Trojans, and zombies. These destructive technologies, generally called *malware*, have the potential to cause great harm. In a 2009 report called *Computer Viruses and Other Malicious Software: A Threat to the Internet Economy*, the multinational Organization for Economic Co-operation and Development (OECD) explains that "malware can gain remote access to an information system, record and send data from that system to a third party without the user's permission or knowledge, conceal that the information system has been compromised, disable security measures, damage the information system, or otherwise affect the data and system integrity" (21). Unfortunately, malware is widely available on the Internet, easy to use from any computer, difficult to detect at the point of infection, and complicated to remove once installed and activated. The OECD calls those who design, sell, and use malware "malicious actors" (Organization for Economic Co-operation and Development 2009, 21), and the scope of their malicious actions is increasing as more and more kinds of devices (mobile phones, PDAs, and tablets) access the Internet and as more and more

means of access (wireless area networks, Bluetooth, broadband, and cloud drives) emerge and proliferate.

Connections made by "malicious actors" using malware can have devastating consequences, from economic (identity theft and corporate embezzlement) to personal (publication of medical records and disclosure of private communications). Thus, an entire industry has emerged in the fight against malware and its consequences. For example, firewalls prevent external searches from gaining access to certain areas of the Internet, and virus scans have real-time functions that block malicious software at the point of entry. These programs are designed to limit the infections and damage done by viruses and worms, among other threats. However, these safety measures also limit the very quality that makes the Internet so valuable today—its connectivity. The OECD points out that "security measures may also impede innovation and productivity. Those involved in improving cybersecurity sometimes tend to overlook that the reason why the Internet is so susceptible to security threats—namely its openness—is also the reason why it has enabled an extraordinary wave of innovation and productivity growth" (Organization for Economic Co-operation and Development 2009, 81). While security measures restrict malware by closing down potential entry points, they also close down uses of the Internet that may lead to creative, innovative, and productive connections. Thus, the OECD recommends that "total security is neither achievable nor desirable" (82).

Just as rhetoric can be a positive *techne* when used for ethical purposes and a negative *techne* when used for unethical purposes, so new technologies can be used ethically and unethically. While botnets, for example, enable connectivity among virus-infected computers, resulting in negative connections for all but criminals, other technologies enable connectivity that results in positive connections, encouraging social engagement, creative collaboration, and document sharing. These latter technologies that enable ethical connectivity form a rich context for three-dimensional dialectical rhetoric, which engages people and their orientations in productive connections.

2.   While Porter points out how professional writing has shifted emphasis since the introduction of Web 2.0, others see significant problems with communication in platformed virtual spaces. Although connectivity is usually stated as a positive quality of Web 2.0, the corporatization of social media platforms has turned connectivity into an insidious violation of privacy. According to Friedrich Krotz, "Commercialization may have the power to make the lifeworlds of the people irrelevant. This metaprocess [of media commercialization] thus may lead into a society that may with far greater certainty be described as a functional systemic network" (Krotz 2008, 28). "User data," Jessica Reyman (2013) argues, "is not merely a technology by-product to be bought and sold; rather, it forms a dynamic, discursive narrative about the paths we have taken as users, the technologies we have used, how we have composed in such spaces, and with whom we have participated" (516). Also, as Krotz points out, "Connectivity concepts and an understanding of society as a network frame the discussion, whereas topics like the economic dimension or the problems of cultural hegemony have largely disappeared" (13). Since Web 2.0 has seen the emergence of corporatization, concepts like network and connectivity tend to hide (or mystify) the hegemony that works in the shadows of Web 2.0. Thus, critical concepts like hegemony, and the concepts of culture that go along with it, must not be forgotten in our zeal for distributed subjectivities.

Some rhetoric and composition scholars have become so skeptical of the platformed sociality and interfaced design of Web 2.0 applications that they believe writing instruction should focus only on critique rather than production. Kristin

L. Arola argues that Web 2.0 creates a troubling split between form and content in which website developers create prefabricated platforms for user-generated content, and users upload their content with no concern for design. Arola writes, "If we don't want our students to become the invention of the template," then students (all students, not just professional writing students) must critically "analyze the interfaces of Web 2.0" (Arola 2010, 12) and the ways in which they produce certain subjectivities and discourage others.

3.   There are plenty of examples, but three of the best known are James A. Berlin (1991), Joel Foreman and David R. Shumway (1992), and Charles A. Hill (2004).

4.   Some of the scholars exploring architectonic design in professional writing include Ben F. Barton and Marthalee S. Barton (1993), Deborah S. Bosley (1992), and Charles Kostelnick (1990).

APPENDIX A

ASSIGNMENT SHEET

Communities and Contact Zones

As the title of this assignment implies, you have two tasks in writing your essay: first, to describe two different "communities"; and second, to describe what happens when those different communities intersect in a "contact zone."

Communities

Benedict Anderson (1991) argues that "all communities . . . are imagined" and "communities are to be distinguished, not [just] by their falsity/genuineness [or the reality of their existence], but by the style in which they are imagined" (6). Most communities have two components, boundaries and social bonds. A community's boundaries may be spatial (e.g., borders dividing cities, states, countries, continents) or conceptual (e.g., content/theme-oriented Internet chat rooms). But communities are not just places or concepts; they are also imagined social relationships or bonds. So, for example, an internet chat room is a community both by virtue of its common (cyber)space and because the individuals participating in the ongoing conversation imagine affinities with other participants. And we (all of us sitting in this room) are a community both because we meet every MWF for Advanced Comp and because we imagine ourselves to share certain desires and goals. Communities are not defined only by spatial or conceptual proximity; communities are also defined by each member's own articulation of a common social bond.

Contact Zones

Something interesting happens when different communities with different (or even opposed) values come into contact; they enter into what Mary Louise Pratt (1991) calls a "contact zone." Pratt defines a "contact zone" as "a space in which peoples geographically and historically separated come into contact with each other and establish ongoing relations, usually involving conditions of coercion, radical inequality, and intractable conflict" (34). Of course, Pratt has a rather narrow conception of "contact zones," so for the purposes of this assignment it will be more useful to expand Pratt's definition to include any two or more communities with different values coming into contact, the result of which involves some kind of tension or at least the recognition of difference.

The Assignment

In this essay, you'll describe two communities that have come into contact and whose contact has resulted in some sort of tension or recognition of difference. Your choice of communities is wide open. The most important thing to keep in mind, though, is that you are not just describing the communities (social bonds) and the contact (tension, difference) but also the spatial or conceptual arena (context) in which the contact takes (or has taken) place.

APPENDIX B

THE GRASS IS GREENER

Lindy Owens

My sister lives a very different life from my own. She is the mother of two children. I am a college student. While she is busying raising her children, I am wrapped up in my social life, school work, and the occasional relationship. Two distinct cultures have developed in each of our households, cultures which have caused me to wonder at times if the path I am walking is the right fit for me. Am I really happy with how my life is turning out? Is my sister happy with her life? I started to ponder these questions a few weeks ago during a visit to my sister's house in Huntsville.

Amber was busy feeding her five month old son while her two-and-a-half year old daughter ran around the living room, pulling out one toy at a time and then abandoning each one on the carpet for some new distraction. I was sitting on the couch, checking the Facebook status updates of my friends on my lap top, which sounded something like this:

> Meredith is hanging out with her hubby, watching Macie laugh at Barney.
>
> Stefanie can't wait til she's married!! TWO DAYS!!
>
> Emkay thinks that too much lace on the dress is likely to make her look like a poodle in white on the big day.
>
> Brandon is going to see my girl after work :)
>
> Holly got the ultrasound pics up, go check em out!!

I sighed in frustration as I looked at status after status detailing the romantic and familial developments of my friends' lives. At that moment, I was scheduled to attend five weddings in the summer, two of which I would be attending as a bridesmaid, and one was my sister's wedding. I was so sick of looking at color coordinated dresses and flowers, I wanted to scream.

Turning to me, Amber asked me, "Would you get some more formula from the fridge? I think he's still hungry." She set the empty bottle on the coffee table before us. I put my computer aside and headed to the kitchen to retrieve a new bottle from the refrigerator. Returning, I

DOI: 10.7330/9780874219821.c007

handed it to her cold. She gave me a blank look. "You have to heat it up," she said.

"Oh," I said and went back into the kitchen to pop the bottle in the microwave.

"Leave it in there for one minute," she called from the living room. I did as she told me, shortly returning with the warm bottle in hand. Amber took it from me, testing the heat of the milk on her wrist. Adjusting her son, Jackson, against her arm, she fed him the bottle. He slurped up his dinner happily. I watched them for a moment, conflicted thoughts running through my head. I wondered what he was thinking. River, my niece, came to my sister and patted her tiny hands on her mother's knees.

"Where 'oo go?" she said, speaking in some baby dialect that I had yet to translate.

"David will be back soon," Amber told River. "You want some juice-juice?"

Amber then turned to me and asked, "Would you finish feeding him so I can get her some juice?"

"Uhhh... sure," I said, not wanting to sound inept in the ways of feeding children. I was a girl after all. Weren't these domestic processes supposed to come naturally to me? She handed Jackson off to me with the bottle. I held him stiffly against my arm, bottle propped to his lips. Jackson looked up at me with a bug-eyed stare that seemed to say that he was very surprised about the taste of his milk.

"Is he supposed to look like that?" I called to my sister, who hurried back into the living room, perhaps expecting to find her child blue-faced and suffocating in the arms of her untrained and childless younger sister.

"Like what?"

"His eyes, they're like bugging out."

"They are not! He's supposed to look like that!" She retorted, indignant.

"'Kay," I said meekly and hid my smile. She rolled her eyes and told me it was time to burp him. She brought me a towel and then helped to rotate him on my shoulder so he had a nice view of the family pictures while he passed gas. I patted him gently on the back.

"He responds better if you jiggle him," she told me. So I attempted this "jiggling" she spoke of. Jackson rewarded me with a soft "brrrp." I tried to hand him back to Amber.

"Oh he's not done yet, try to get at least three out of him." Sighing, I put him back on my shoulder and jiggled him once more. This time it took a while. Jackson not only burped but vomited on my Text Smart t-shirt.

"Um, Amber?" I called to her in the kitchen. "Can you bring me another towel?"

"Oh, did he throw up?"

"Yeah. On me."

"Sorry, sometimes he misses the rag," she said, as if this was a daily occurrence. Hell, it could have been an hourly occurrence for all I knew. I hadn't really been around much when River was being weaned, but it seemed like her vomit had not achieved the projectile standard which Jackson displayed. She loaned me a shirt for the ride home and promised to wash mine in time for my next visit. I told her my thanks and silently reminded myself to wear a rain coat the next time I fed Jackson. After some fond goodbyes, I headed home.

In describing my own reactions to my sister's household, I know I sound like an inexperienced jerk. But the truth is I really wasn't prepared to have an up close and personal view of the domestic life for a few years, maybe even a decade. I haven't decided yet if I want to get married and have kids. I would like to be happy. I'm just not sure if, for me, starting a family is the path to happiness. Yet I feel this slow pressure building from all around me to do just that. A large number of my girl friends are getting married or are currently married and having babies. What is it about your mid-twenties that makes people think it's time to settle down? Sure, there's that whole biological clock thing to consider if you want to have kids. There also seems to be this idea that American women after the age of twenty three are suddenly not as desirable as they were the year before. Are we really like milk cartons, with expiration dates and the impending event of going sour? Am I running out of time to find someone, to prevent a life of loneliness and becoming the crazy cat lady?

When I go home, the setting at my apartment is quite a drastic change from my sister's house. I have four roommates, one of which has two pets (a dog and cat). Cleanliness in the apartment is dependent on whether anyone has felt the unlikely urge to clean, which is not often unless a party or finals kegger has been planned. The only time a child ever comes to our apartment is during the odd visit from my friend, Andrea, who has a daughter. Amber generally does not bring her kids to my place. I think the cleanliness issue factors into that decision. Or it could be the fact that one of my roommates has a stripper pole installed in his room. Obviously my apartment is a college-centric atmosphere. We don't consider choking hazards when leaving our stuff strewn around the apartment. Yet I am comfortable here in this dirty chaos. I have my friends close by if I want to talk to someone. If I need privacy, I can just go into my room. While quiet is not so easy to come by, I have adjusted to it with head phones and, if need be, a shot of whiskey. We don't have to plan our days around feeding schedules, naps, or the whims of children. We can go on a road trip if we want to; we can stay up all night drinking and in the morning sleep in. It's a life with little responsibility or rules. We fend for ourselves and rarely take other lives into consideration.

When my sister was pregnant for the first time, she went through a brief period of panic in which she thought her social and adventurous life was over. In a way, that part of her life which was focused around friends is over. Now other tiny lives are growing out of her life. She is fixed in place, yet she has to be flexible enough to bend around the events of her children's experiences. When I describe our crazy parties to her, she gets a wistful look on her face as though she misses that time in her life. But when I look at pictures of her with her children, I see an unadulterated smile which she has never worn before; there is pride and joy. Similarly, when I see the way she looks at her children, I cannot comprehend the depth of emotional attachment she feels in looking at what she has created. Does she feel owned by her children? Does she fear for their lives constantly? Is there some magical state of bliss that parents feel when they share a special moment with their children? These are things that I do not understand and I fear slightly, while I covet my intellectual journey and claim slight superiority for staying in school. Truth be told, I'm jealous of her. But that could just be me looking on the other side of the fence and assuming the grass is greener.

When I visit my sister, I can feel my father looking at me, wondering why I haven't found someone with whom to look at wedding rings. He's probably wondering if there is something wrong with me, if maybe he raised me the wrong way. It's okay. I sometimes wonder that too. Overall, I think I am ill-suited to a relationship with someone who wishes to overcome my personality and that seems to be the only option in the men I know. When I was younger, I thought that I wanted to have at least five kids. That was before I found out how painful child birth is and how much children change your life. There is this idea that has been planted in my brain, that if I had made different decisions in my past I would be happier now. Maybe if I hadn't been so stubborn in my last relationship, I would be with my future husband and we could be planning our lives together. Maybe if my sister had not gotten pregnant, she could have gotten her design degree and gone into commercial art. But would either of us be happier?

I hate the What If idea. I have no control over time. There's no way I could go back and change what I've done. Yet when I see my sister's cozy family, I start to wonder about these things. My sister says she lives in a state of fear at times, wondering if she'll get the child support from her ex in time, if Medicaid will really pay the hospital bills from her last pregnancy, or if she will be able to afford the wedding to her fiancé in the summer. I also live in a state of fear, though my fear circulates around making rent on time, passing my classes, preserving my relationships, and surviving therapy. I wouldn't say that either of our lives are ideal. The American dream suggests that there is an ideal to be reached, but I don't believe that. What is the point in looking at other people and wondering whether what they have is better than what I have? Fear is the motivation; fear that we are living our lives the wrong way, that someone else has already figured out the secret to happiness, and that we'll never discover the secret for ourselves. I know my sister is jealous of my freedom. I can go binge drinking Friday night without having to notify a baby sitter twenty four hours in advance, and the next day I can sleep in nursing a hangover. I'm jealous of my sister's family, my niece's little hands which spell out "I love you momma" on construction paper.

Apparently, I'm supposed to be enjoying the highlight of my life. I am young, beautiful, and free—the MTV dream. I think this dream is overrated. It's like living in a commercial for facial lotion which is supposed to magically keep your skin wrinkle free, yet the actors are turning fifty-five and wrinkles weigh their faces down like banana pudding. The commercial seemed so convincing in the beginning, when everyone was young and beautiful, when the announcers were saying, "You can be young forever too!" But now it's just sad and deflating. Maybe that's why girls my age start to get the wedding fever, because they start to realize that the commercial is ending. The real world is going to replace the Hollywood set. They have to find something that is painful and real but beautiful, childbirth.

I have a secret to share. Though I claim to be a feminist and I despise the shackles of holy matrimony, I do not want to end up alone. There are rules in each of these cultures described here: in my sister's world, she must always be in control (though it's impossible), and she must be strong to protect her children. In my world, the college culture, we must pretend that our freedom is highly coveted, that everyone wants to be us. The trouble is that the world I live in is transitory. I won't be in college forever. My sister is light years ahead of me, though the culture I live in says she is lagging behind.

APPENDIX C

INFILTRATING OUR HOME WITH LOVE

Emily Etheredge

There is an element of comfort with leaving something the way you like it and returning to have it completely unchanged. In the summer of 2006, as I said goodbye and boarded an airplane for a two-and-a-half week long mission trip to Peru, I felt comfortable that my tight-knit family would be there for me when I returned. My entire family consisting of my parents, brother and sister, and several friends came to the airport to bid me farewell. As I hurriedly crossed off my checklist of things I was making sure I had not forgotten, I noticed their faces expressing excitement that I was getting to have this opportunity but sadness at the idea of me leaving. I was sad to say goodbye, but I knew that when I returned, everything would be just as I had left it. I had even made my bed so that when I returned, it would seem crisp and clean. My first week in Peru was filled with many activities, and I barely had time to even think of communicating to my family back home about how I was doing. I knew they were anxious to hear from me, but I was unable to contact them until half-way through my trip. I finally had an opportunity to send a quick e-mail to my dad, and I e-mailed about all of the high points, the exciting people I had met, the Spanish words I was struggling with, and how I had a new ambition to become a world traveler. I briefly inquired about events happening at home and assured all of them that I loved and missed them. My father sent a reply almost immediately, and the majority of the e-mail was discussing the fact that my family had opened our home up to a young guy my dad had met through his job at the Jimmie Hale Mission. The guy had spent a year in jail, and my dad had continually visited him throughout the process. Upon his release, he had nowhere to go, so my family decided that he could come and stay at our home for a little while. Although I was enjoying my trip immensely, the words in the e-mail seemed to contain venom for I became very angry that our family had taken in a charity case and allowed a "bum" to come and invade my territory. I was also furious with my family for taking him in while I was gone, and I felt replaced by this individual who

DOI: 10.7330/9780874219821.c008

had made unwise choices throughout his life. Selfishly, I wanted to protect my *status quo*, and I focused on the changes that would ensue upon his arrival. "Was he staying in my room while I was gone?" "I better not come back and have anything stolen by this creep, and he better not be sleeping in my comfy bed." "Maybe Dad should let me e-mail him and give him a piece of my mind." These thoughts plagued me after reading the e-mail about some guy staying in our warm and cozy home and tearing down the very structure of happiness surrounding the ones I loved. I resigned that thinking about the situation while I was unable to do anything was pointless, and I would emphatically share my feelings upon returning to the States.

Traveling back home was a little more difficult than originally expected, and I was unable to return until three days after my originally scheduled arrival date. I was told by my group advisor that I needed to call home and inform my family that I would not be arriving for another couple of days and assure them that I was alright. I dialed my telephone number that I had known since I was a toddler, and I anticipated a comforting voice that I loved to answer and make all of the stresses of the situation melt away. On the second ring, an individual answered in a deep, gruff voice that I did not recognize. I immediately panicked thinking that I had somehow dialed the wrong number. "Is this Emily?" he asked. "This is Phillip. I am excited to meet you today," he said. I was furious. Why was he answering my telephone? He was not my family, and I did not want to talk to him. I barely answered his question because I was not excited to meet him, and I wanted to assure him that he could go ahead and start packing his useless belongings before I even arrived because he would not be staying long.

"Let me talk to mom" I ordered, and I waited to hear the warmth of my mother's voice instead of this stranger who was infiltrating my home. My mom and I talked for about ten minutes and I explained to her the situation and assured her I was excited to see everyone in my family in a couple of days. Everyone except the stranger, the stranger named Phillip.

Stepping off the airplane, my mind was filled with mixed emotions about leaving lovely individuals in another country I had grown to love, and the excitement of seeing loved ones waiting for me to come back to my lovely home. My family clustered together at the end of the walkway in the airport, and I immediately eyed them and sprinted to see them all. I rapturously hugged my mother, and I kissed my little sister on the cheek, genuinely feeling as if they had all grown more beautiful in my absence. Amidst all of the hugging, I noticed a young, timid, and unsure individual awkwardly standing in the shadows of my reunion. He wanted to be a part of the hugging but didn't know how or really if he should. As much as I felt I already despised this individual, I walked over and gave a quick side hug to him and introduced myself. If he was going to be living with us, I might as well let him know my name. He was not at all how I had pictured him, and the gruff exterior of his voice I had heard on the phone days earlier melted away when I saw that he wanted to feel accepted by someone. His eyes contained a lifetime of pain that I would more than likely never understand. My worst experience in life would seem almost laughable to someone like him, and I immediately felt that I had terribly misjudged him. He was seeking to be accepted and I was able to relate to him because I had just spent two weeks in a different country trying to find a common bond with people who had no idea who I was. I had come from a completely different background compared to the Peruvians, and they had more than likely judged me as a "typical American" or "spoiled," and for the first time since I had learned Phillip was coming to stay with my family, I understood a small sense of what he was going through.

The weeks after I returned home from Peru were filled with many adjustments. Not only was I adjusting to being back in my warm and cozy bed, but there was also a stranger in my home whom I was attempting to figure out. My parents decided to talk it over with everyone in the family about whether or not Phillip should be allowed to stay with us temporarily until he was able to gain some stability in his life. We all decided that it was in the best interest for him to be allowed to stay under the condition that he would abide by the rules of our home. My dad explicitly informed Phillip that whatever rules were relevant within our home also applied to him, and that he must also find a job and begin to acquire his G.E.D. Phillip wholeheartedly agreed to the arrangement, and while we were all sitting around in our living room, this individual, who had been raised without a family full of laughter or support, was entering our hearts and learning what it felt like to be loved and accepted. For us, we were learning what it was like to live with someone from a completely different background and how to adjust to someone who had never experienced the support of a family.

Since Phillip had been abandoned at an early age and spent the majority of his teenage years in homeless shelters, he had very strong feelings of ownership. He liked to have his possessions completely protected and was not a fan of sharing. Laundry was especially difficult, for he enjoyed having all of his clothing completely together, and if something that was not his got mixed in somehow, he would become agitated and not understand how that happened. A pair of my socks got mixed in with his laundry one day, and he came to me very frustrated that I had messed with his "stuff." I was completely oblivious to the problem and even laughed it off figuring that he was just being sensitive. "Get over it," I said. "It is a pair of socks and it won't kill you." For me, it was silly and ridiculous that he would be frustrated at something so trivial. I didn't realize that he had lived a lifetime of having to claim his territory because within the walls of a homeless shelter there is an absence of a home. As the days progressed, things became a little easier with Phillip living with our family. He seemed to fit in with the five of us and began adjusting to our routines as if he had been a part of them for a lifetime. We ate dinner together as a family, and before he could dig into his meal, he had to hold hands and pray with us. My dad always inquired about our various daily activities at the dinner table, and Phillip learned that he also had a time for sharing. The television shows we found enjoyable, he watched, and the movies we rented, he showed an interest in. We also sat around and told stories of old memories, gathered throughout the years, about how the pet goldfish miraculously died three times, or how we had a crazy great aunt that made any holiday exciting with her antics. Phillip would always laugh along as if he had been there during those moments, and whenever a story would be told it almost felt strange knowing Phillip had not been there. I was picked up form a date one night, and Phillip answered the door. He introduced himself and said, "Hi, I'm Emily's brother Phillip, come inside because I want to have a little talk with you." I had always been the eldest of my siblings, and it was a nice change of pace to have someone older than I was to take on certain responsibilities. I also enjoyed having an older brother figure in my life.

One evening, my parents decided to go out on a date, and Phillip decided he was going to make dinner for us at home. He went to the grocery store with my little sister and came back beaming with pride over the groceries he had selected. He took out a box of Hamburger Helper, and we all animatedly stared at the luscious looking casserole on the exterior of the box. "You can get food to look like that from a box?" my little sister asked. We had never eaten Hamburger Helper before because my mom had always thought everything was better if it was made from scratch, and the concept of getting dinner from a cardboard box was thrilling and unusual to us. It was as if we were eating a delicacy, for we had never been introduced to something like that, and Phillip enjoyed making it for us because he had grown up eating it. For him, it was unusual to eat something made from scratch, whereas we all tried his simple dinner and thought it was amazing. We also started listening to music while we unloaded the dishwasher to make the task more enjoyable, and as my siblings and I were all dancing around and singing to the songs, Phillip stood off to the side, unsure of what to do. After a while, we persuaded him to join us, and he began dancing in the midst of our kitchen. Something so simple became one of the most enjoyable evenings because we had allowed him to show a little of himself by making us dinner, and he had become more like one of us by letting loose and allowing himself to have fun.

The strangest intersection of Phillip coming to live with our family was during holidays. It was strange because for Phillip, a holiday represented just a normal day, whereas a holiday in our family was something to prepare for and get excited about. The time when most people have very established traditions that have carried on for generations can be stressful for even the closest of kin, let alone someone who is not even blood related. For our family, Christmas is one of the most enjoyable seasons; we genuinely love the holiday. My family buys a real Christmas tree, and we decorate it together with ornaments my mom has purchased for us throughout the years. We also decorate gingerbread houses, and every Christmas eve my dad reads "The Night Before Christmas" to all of us before we go to bed. It is a time we all cherish, and even as we have grown, we look forward to all of the events that lead up to Christmas day. Phillip went along with the majority of our traditions and explained one evening that he had not grown up loving Christmas quite like we had. For him, Christmas was sometimes just another day that lacked the magical presence of warmth and togetherness. He had even mentioned that one year he didn't receive a gift for Christmas. "You must have been awful to Santa," my little sister said after hearing he had not received anything. It was hard for my family to picture someone not enjoying Christmas day, yet here was this individual who had never experienced a holiday within a family setting. We all worked really hard to make sure that Phillip's first Christmas with us was special. We bought him a stocking and hung it next to the ones we had from our family, we carefully selected gifts for him that we knew he would enjoy, and we even allowed him to sit closest to our father and get the best view of the pictures as he read "The Night Before Christmas." Christmas morning, we all piled downstairs to uncover our gifts brought by Santa. Phillip stood in amazement that he too had a pile of things waiting for him, and he repeatedly asked, "Are these for me?" Much like a young kid realizing that he received the toy truck he had been hoping he would get, Phillip rapturously tore open each parcel in front of him with a newfound happiness. The joy of watching him unwrap each individual gift and grin with excitement was something our entire family cherished to experience, and that Christmas was one of the most enjoyable because the blending of Phillip's background with our tradition's came together in a family setting that made the entire decision to have him come and stay with us completely worth it.

Phillip lived in our home for three years, and during that time we all adjusted to join in the same community of a family unit. My family learned what it was like to live with someone who was raised completely different from us, and Phillip learned to live with a group of individuals who sought to care for him and propel him to be the best he could be. I had hated the idea when I had originally learned he was going to stay with us, and I felt angry he was going to infiltrate our home, yet I didn't realize that his presence completed us, and without him we wouldn't have learned to love and accept people who weren't necessarily raised in the same environment. I also learned to appreciate the fact that every-one tries to feel accepted in their own way, and whether it is a trip to another country or a trip to someone else's home, a made-from-scratch dinner or a dinner made from a box, we all seek to be understood for who we are and need to find someone to love us in spite of it.

APPENDIX D

THE CONSTANT POWER STRUGGLE
Ashley Henderson

> *I have a dream that one day this nation will rise up and live out the true meaning of its creed: "We hold these truths to be self-evident that all men are created equal."*
>
> —*Dr. Martin Luther King Jr.*

For generations, the issue of race has been the origin of numerous heated debates, senseless murders, and pure evil. It has torn this country apart through segregation, creating inferiority complexes in the minds of the people who were segregated. People, such as the late, great Dr. Martin Luther King, Jr., fought and died for a better tomorrow. These people wanted all people, not just African Americans, to be treated equally. Now, with the election of our nation's first African American president, the country has demonstrated that times have changed dramatically; however, ignorance still plagues the minds of some people.

The two largest minorities in this country are Latin Americans and African Americans. It is estimated by the US Census Bureau that currently there are 47.8 million Latin Americans in the United States, which is 15.5% of the total population (US Census 3). 13.0% of the total population is African American (Pew Research Center 17). Of course, these are the estimates before the tally of the 2010 census, so the numbers are likely incorrect. Nonetheless, both cultures, Latin American and African American, have many things in common. Each has suffered oppression and prejudice living in this country, and both share many similar values, such as family and religion. Family and religion are the most important values for each culture because there was a time when that was all they had. Also, many traditions have been passed through generations of these two ethnic groups, and they have now become American traditions. The traditions go hand-in-hand with the struggles each group has conquered, and since they share so many similarities, they should have a bond like none other. However, Latin Americans and African Americans do not have a close relationship. There is always an

DOI: 10.7330/9780874219821.c009

indescribable tension that resonates between the two cultures. In this paper, I will discuss the many important and rich values deeply rooted in Latin American and African Americans cultures and the contributions made to the United States by both groups. This discussion will lead into my hypothesis regarding why there is tension between the two cultures and my solutions to resolve the conflict.

THE GLUE

Family is the most important aspect of both Latin American and African American cultures; it is the glue that holds everything together when nothing else is intact. Most Latin American and African American families are very large, and they observe traditions that have been passed down through the years. In both cultures, the grandmother is the matriarch of the family, the noble one. She is the one who possesses all knowledge about life, love, sacrifices, and struggles. Most of the time, family dinners are held at her house; this is her way of keeping the family together and keeping it strong. It is rare for grandfathers to live as long as grandmothers, so over the years families grow extremely close to their grandmothers. All children, regardless of ethnic origin, do what needs to be done to ensure the well being of their grandmothers, both financially and physically. I estimate that 75% of Latin American and African American families allow their grandparents to stay with them once they get to an age where they are not capable of caring for themselves; or, if the grandparents are stubborn, the children let the grandparents stay at their own home, but the children take care of all the utilities, as opposed to sending them to a nursing home. Also, a lot of Latin American and African American households are multi-dwelling, where more than one family is living under one roof. This too strengthens the bond of the family. Without family, you have nothing, and that is what both cultures strongly believe.

THE PROTECTION

Another form of cultural tradition is religion. A strong belief in Christian faith is just as important as family to Latin Americans and African Americans. Both cultures mandate that children go to church to learn about the Bible and to give thanks to God for all he has done. As with all cultures, Latin Americans and African Americans have had issues regarding which religion to accept for themselves; however, the main thing that stays consistent in both cultures is the belief in Christianity. This belief is important because having faith in God is what got the ancestors of both cultures out of horrific time periods, and it continues to protect them daily as they challenge unjust racial barriers. Although they do not always practice the exact same religion, the act of attending church and having God as the center of their lives is a sacred and most prized tradition. Almost all Latin Americans and African Americans, from the thugs to the priests and preachers, take religion seriously. Tension seems to cease between Latin Americans and African Americans once they are reminded of their religion, as if they have been slapped into common sense with a Bible. However, there is not a constant reminder of religion in their daily lives.

THE SPICE OF LIFE

Latin Americans and African Americans have brought many traditions to this nation. Numerous dances and foods are credited to both cultures. Salsa is the most famous dance deriving from Latin culture. It involves swift movements of the hips to a fast-paced beat, and Salsa dancers wear sexy clothes. The Tango is another Latin dance, and it has been nicknamed "The dance of love." The Tango is a sensual dance, again, using hips as the key point of movement. Both dances have been incorporated into the current dance trends here in the United States. African Americans brought a lot of rhythmic dances that originated in Africa. They use the beat of a drum to move their bodies with its rhythm. African Americans have made hip hop dance popular in the United Sates. Last, but certainly not least, food has to be the most notable tradition throughout both Latin American and African American history. The Latin American communities brought us tacos, salsa, queso, and a variety of spices. African Americans, too, are noted for the flavorful seasoning they have brought to the United States. To go along with the seasoning, African Americans also introduced their favorite foods, such as fried chicken and barbeque. Each one of the two ethnic groups is praised and will always be remembered for their numerous contributions of their traditions to the United States. The similarities in everything for both cultures are parallel, from family to traditions. They are like fraternal twins: although they do not look exactly alike, they think and act alike; but they are not the same identity and their differences show up sooner or later.

THE TENSION

Although these ethnic groups share many positive similarities, they have one dark issue that plagues both communities—they do not get along well. There is this unspoken, therefore indescribable, tension between the two ethnicities once they are joined together. They have to come in contact with one another on a daily basis, and you can feel the tension once you are in the presence of a mixed group or community. Back in the 1960's when Latin Americans and African Americans where fighting against a single oppressor, it was the struggle that united the two. As years passed, the Latin American population began to grown. Things changed and immigration from Latin countries became extremely common. Latinos began to swarm into the United States, both legally and illegally, to make a better living for themselves and their families. They wanted to experience the freedom this country promised; they wanted to establish businesses, make money, and go to school. Latin Americans, newly immigrated, were willing to make that happen by any means necessary. They began to do the jobs we spoiled Americans no longer wanted to do, and they were willing to work for a cheaper price. Soon, Latin Americans became the hot commodity in the work force, where originally it was African Americans who held those jobs. According to the 2000 US Census, the Latin American population had grown from roughly 9 million in the 1970s to nearly 35.3 million in just 30 years. Therefore, the jobs in America for African Americans have gone from slim pickings to extremely slim pickings. For employers, the choice is a White person, a Latin American, or an African American. The African Americans feel that the employer will choose White people just because they are White or the Latin Americans because they will work for less pay. Tension is created because it seems to African Americans that Latin Americans have come to this territory and taken all of the jobs.

For African Americans, the main issue stopped being just about Black and White relations and the fight for equality. Now, it has become a power struggle between Latin Americans and African Americans because numbers speak volumes as to who is in power; and according to the numbers, Latin Americans are steadily rising. African Americans feel they will be oppressed again. They have a fear of being replaced or overlooked by the government and thus of being treated unjustly again. Then there is the issue of educational funding from the government for minorities and inner city schools. There is not much funding to go around, so not only is tension rising between the two ethnicities due to a lack of jobs, but also because all people want the best for their children. It is obvious that some Latin Americans will need extra funding to teach their students English; however, African Americans feel slighted because they could use the extra funding as well to teach literacy to those students who come from homes where literacy is not emphasized.

Neither race condones dropping out of high school, but if the resources are not there to provide a good educational background, the likelihood of high school dropouts increases. Every year, the number of drop-outs is steadily rising among high school students. Both Latin Americans and African Americans have valid issues, but there is simply not enough money to go around for the matter to be handled effectively and fairly; therefore, it stirs the tension.

With the existence of high-rising tension and high levels of high school drop-outs between the two races, violence emerges among Latin American and African Americans. Most famously in the streets of Compton, California, both ethic groups have created street gangs and recruit or offer a home to young men who are looking for a place of acceptance. All gangs believe they run a particular section of the city and the other gangs are not allowed to trespass in their territory. These gangs invite violence. Latin American and African American gangs have been against each other since the emergence of gangs; and this constant tension has been the cause of numerous deaths in relations to race and gang affiliation. Again, some of this tension goes back to the lack of jobs and African Americans feeling that Latin Americans have taken their source of income and invaded their territory. Both minority groups want to be in control. Both are trying to ascend from the bottom of society's social ladder to the top. When competition is present, all of the history, the struggles, the family values, the traditions, and the common bonds between Latin Americans and African Americans disappear along with their respect for each other.

CONCLUSION

All of this tension between these two ethnicities affects me directly because I am of African American descent, but I love the Spanish language and all of the cultures surrounding the language. I would love to submerse myself in a Latin country one day without feeling as though I am being judged for my desires and ethnicity. It hurts me to wake up to news of more gang violence or to hear Latin Americans and African Americans arguing in the streets over who should and should not be there. It is childish to me. Everybody has a place in life, and God made us all different for a reason.

Violence begets violence and solves nothing. It is truly sad that the two cultures, who are alike in so many ways, cannot befriend one another. If we could stop using violence to try and solve everything, we would be able to see that together we will be a stronger force, not separate. Throw pride out of the window. Realize what our ancestors fought, bled, and died to achieve and how disappointed they would be because of our actions. Our ancestors' blood, sweat, and tears were not just shed so that African Americans could be treated equally by White people; they were shed so that all people would treat all other people equally, to come together as one and work hard to accomplish dreams and aspirations. The dream was to try hard in school and at work to become a force to be reckoned with. I say there should be a national meeting of all powerful people in both ethnicities. That would include, at least, President Barack Obama and First Lady Michelle Obama, Los Angeles Mayor Antonio Villaraigosa, Justice Sonia Sotomayor, and plenty more activists. They should come together and discuss different ways of handling the issues of allocating money needed to better the school systems for both races. Then local groups should organize smaller meetings throughout their communities to tutor children and build centers for both races to learn and excel together. Maybe if we start there, the economic tension will subside because both Latin Americans and African Americans will be equally qualified and seeking the same range of pay. Then the words of Dr. Martin Luther King Jr. will ring true for all who hear: "I have a dream that one day this nation will rise up and live out the true meaning of its creed: 'We hold these truths to be self-evident that all men are created equal'." He marched, fought, and died for all of our communities to see a better tomorrow.

WORKS CITED

"Hispanics in the United States." *US Census Bureau*. 2006. Web. 29 March 2010.

"Population by Race and Ethnicity, Actual and Projected: 1960, 2005 and 2050."

Pew Research Center 2005. Web. 29 March 2010.

APPENDIX E

JUMPING IN THE CAR

Wade Harrison

I was born the youngest in a typical middleclass family of four, my father a dentist, my mother a teacher. We were Presbyterians, and my father was a deacon, my mother the choir leader. I attended a small Christian private school until eighth grade, when I moved to public school. By eleventh grade in public school I was excelling at sports; I was voted class favorite, and I was in love with my girlfriend, the homecoming queen. For most of my youth, I had lived an existence that mimicked corny television shows. I had Beaver Cleaver's family and a social life that rivaled the stars of "Saved by the Bell." So when I got into a car accident that killed my girlfriend and her best friend, my world turned inside out.

Charged with Involuntary Manslaughter, I enrolled in military school and left town to await my trial. Surprisingly, I was at military school for two and a half years before I was finally called to court. The trial wasn't what I had expected. Because the circumstances of the wreck were clear, the trial was not a debate of what happened that night, it was an eight-hour evaluation of my character. Fortunately, I had reputable witnesses, mostly military commanders and professors, who spoke positively enough on my behalf that the judge gave me a light sentence. He sentenced me to five years in state prison.

I figured I was as ill prepared for prison as any nineteen-year-old boy could be. Years of military school taught me to conduct myself with "military bearing." I walked with my shoulders back and my chin held high. I talked with authority and exaggerated correctness. My haircut was a high-and-tight, and I didn't have any piercings or tattoos. I went to prison looking exactly like a cop.

I did, however, have a few things I acquired at military school going for me. As a former drill sergeant, I was accustomed to keeping a stern look on my face, a "mean-mug," as inmates would call it. Also, I had been bodybuilding for a while because it was easier to command people when they thought you could manhandle them, and because I'd long known

DOI: 10.7330/9780874219821.c010

that I was going to prison. And lastly, I had been training as a fighter for all the same reasons, so I was no stranger to confrontation. In fact, I had a black eye and a gash on my cheek when I walked into prison my very first day. Along with a little luck, these traits were the only reasons I could think of as to why no one tried to swindle me when I was new to the system, when I was "green."

For the most part, the prison culture I was soon immersed in was the exact opposite of everything I had been trained to embody. I had some assimilating to do and quickly if I was going to survive this place. With this necessity for personal reinvention in mind, I entered prison like a scientist on a mission; I had to research every minute aspect of this culture if I was to learn how to behave.

My first troubling discovery was that prison was not the physical environment I had envisioned. It wasn't like the movies, where inmates are segregated from each other in two-man cells with locked doors at night. The prison I was assigned to did not even have cells; it had dorms, and each dorm was a little longer than a basketball court. There were four dorms in the entire prison, each of which contained two rows of seventy-five bunk beds. They resembled homeless shelters more so than my preconceived image of prison cells. This was immediately disturbing for one overwhelming reason: there was nothing separating me from potential enemies when I slept.

Sure enough, my concern was validated on my very first night at Frank Lee Correctional Facility. I awoke in the middle of the night to the screams of someone's victim. A few bunks down from me, a man was being attacked by someone with a razor. The razor filleted the skin on the arms he was protecting himself with. There was blood everywhere, and his screams sounded like that of a hysterical woman. The other inmates roared with laughter at the sound. Before long, the lights turned on and several officers rushed into the dorm. The officers then beat both the attacker and the victim with nightsticks until they were unconscious. I didn't sleep the rest of the night. I was a long way away from Presbyterian private school.

My first few days in prison felt like life on another planet. People did not look or behave like anything I was accustomed to. Most inmates were so muscular they looked like football players. Many were covered in menacing tattoos, and everyone moved very slowly. Nobody had anywhere to be, so movement never had a purpose. Swift actions only occurred when there was a fight, and even the fights were like nothing I had ever seen. Prison fights were explosions sparked from the tiniest squabbles, and most of them seemed to come completely without warning.

I was a new foreign body in a place I didn't fit in yet, and everyone was aware of this. There was never any privacy anywhere, so I was always in the midst of hundreds of onlookers. I could feel that they were all conscious of my every action, but nobody stared at me either. Inmates hardly ever made eye contact at all. Instead, they would casually glance in my direction or look at me out of the corner of their eye as they whispered something to each other.

Before long, because everyone at Frank Lee had to do a job, I was assigned to the yard crew. This was an opportunity for me because it required me to be around the same people every day, allowing me to hear how they communicated and what they talked about. As far as Ebonics was concerned, I might as well have been listening to Chinese physicists discuss nuclear fission. The vernacular of most inmates was so incoherent to me that I thought I would never understand the words. On the rare occasions when I did make out the words they were saying, I didn't know their intended meaning most of the time.

On my first day in the yard crew, an older inmate approached me with a question: "bla bla bla bla?" I, of course, had no clue what he was saying, so I instinctively responded with "sir?" He seemed confused for a split second before he burst into laughter. Then he tapped his buddy and mumbled something like this to him: "bla bla bla bla . . . *sir?*" And they both started laughing so hard that one of them was rolling on the ground. Whenever he would catch his breath, he'd cry out "*sir?*" and start laughing again. I made my first mental note-to-self: don't call another inmate sir. I never did it again either, but everyone called me "Sir" from then on.

Almost everyone had a nickname in prison. Most nicknames came about because of something funny, and they were rarely flattering or eloquent. For example, there was an older man who was hit in the face by an eighteen-wheeler when he was running after a ball in the street as a kid. After brain surgery and facial reconstruction, he was left with a large indention on the left side of his face. Everyone called this man "Dent," and this was how he introduced himself too. Another man with a colostomy bag was called "Shitbag." The obese man on the bed next to me answered to "Fat Matt" without blinking an eye. I was thankful Sir caught on before I did anything really embarrassing.

The more people called me Sir, the more I began to hear the lingo directed at me. Ebonics was becoming clearer to me, and I even started to understand what most of the prison words meant. Most of the terms seemed to have no rational English correlation to their intended meaning, while some of them were downright ironic. "One time" meant a "five-O" was near. A "five-O" was a correctional officer, or cop. "Oh now" meant "hey there." "Turning" was the same thing as fighting. "Buddy" was *always* used to describe someone's gay lover, his "fuckbuddy," while "partner" was *always* used to describe a platonic friend. The strange list went on forever, and there were as many words in the prison dictionary as Webster's. I had learned a second language.

I didn't need my understanding of prison lingo to learn that ninety percent of fights at Frank Lee happened in one of two places, the basketball court or the "weight pile." I sucked at basketball, so the court was of no concern to me. The weight pile, however, was another story. I had to maintain my physique if I was to deter predators from "trying" me (trying to swindle or rape me). But every day at the weight pile was a gamble. In a prison with six-hundred inmates, our small workout area was a cesspool of testosterone and animosity, with everyone trying to get their own routine in.

I was at the weight pile as usual one day when I got careless. I started exercising on a bench-press that someone was already using. A black guy covered in tattoos was sitting about twenty feet away when he called out to me: "Oh now lil' bwa! You jus' gone take my shit like dat?" I put the weights down and stared at him for a second as I sat up on the bench and processed what he'd said. Everyone looked at me, and time seemed to stop as the next five minutes lasted an eternity. A lot was going on in his two sentences, and I was still unfamiliar enough with the lingo that I had to translate the words in my head. His posture and tone of voice were obviously aggressive. But what was he saying? "Oh now lil' bwa . . . Hey. There. Little. Boy." That was all the translating I had to do, the rest didn't matter. To call me "little" was derogatory in itself, but "boy" was a fight word in prison. Short for "fuckboy," boy was a term used to describe someone who would get raped and robbed without ever defending himself. It was time for me to fight or welcome my new reputation as a fuckboy.

As soon as I understood what was said to me, I stood up and raised my fists to my chin. The sight of this made everyone at the weight pile stand up simultaneously. It was then that I noticed all ten of them were black guys covered in tattoos. A closer look revealed that those tattoos all had the letters "GD" in them. Gangster Disciples comprised the largest gang in prison and, as the saying goes, I could have shit a diamond. But this was the reputation building moment I had been waiting on, so I grabbed a small weight for a weapon and got ready to "turn like good gas."

Just as I was getting ready to die, Wes and Dirty, two large white men I had never spoken to, approached the scene. The weight pile was a simple structure, a hut with a chain-linked fence nailed to its four posts. Even though Wes was the biggest white man in the prison, it was still daunting to see him nonchalantly grab the fence and rip the nails from their post. "ping, ping, ping, ping, ping!" The nails fell to the concrete as Wes and Dirty stepped into the arena. Wes stepped in front of me and spoke casually to the man who had been yelling at me. The tattoo on his back was in full view to me now; it was a giant flaming cross with a large swastika in the middle. "What's going here?" The guy was calmer now as he responded, "Nothin', man, but you need to tell your potna', Sir, to chill out." Wes then put his arm around my shoulder and led me away.

That fight had been extinguished, but there were coals burning now. Yet again, my whole life had turned around in an instance, an instance I mentally diagramed for the rest of the day. The GD's were sure to attack me in my sleep sometime in the near future. Along with the rest of the prison, the white supremacists now considered me one of them since they had saved me, and if I rejected them it would be an insult. If I rejected them, the GD's wouldn't be my only concern. Wes had intentionally waited until the last second to step in so that he could see whether I was going to fight and so everyone could see that he saved me. I now had a reputation as a fighter who was backed by the white supremacists, but none of that mattered if I couldn't make it through the night.

My "rackmate" at that time was Heard, the leader of the prison's GD's, so I was not excited to see a big grin on his face when I approached our bunk that night. Judging from his cocky smirk, I figured he was going to pick a fight with me as soon as he spoke. But the first thing he said was "You did a'ight out there today, lil' Sir." I was more than willing to let the word "little" pass as I was blown away by his friendly tone. "You mean, you don't want to fight me?" The conversation that ensued ended with him telling me: "You straight, Sir. I'ma chill dem niggas out for you." Sure enough, Heard chilled those Gangster Disciples out for me, and it was smooth-er sailing from then on. I had become part of the crowd now. Sir was no longer the new guy.

I eventually came to exemplify prison culture as much as the men around me did. I never joined any gangs or engaged in any criminal behavior, but I certainly looked and talked like a convict. I was weighing in at 196 lean pounds because I worked out every day without any problems. After my altercation with the GD's, Wes told me I needed to "jump in a car" if I was to use the weight pile without having to watch my back. A "car" was a group. In this context, jumping in the car meant that I needed to workout at the same time the Aryan Brotherhood did. Because all of the equipment on the weight pile would be occupied by them, I wouldn't have to worry about crossing any enemies. Most of the white supremacists were the closest things I had to friends, and they were okay with me not joining them since I had proven two things: I would defend myself, and I was not a snitch.

I knew they didn't consider me a snitch because they all smoked weed around me. When Frank Lee got a new warden, the rules became lax for a while. Lax rules meant that more people were getting high and homosexual behavior was becoming more open. Instead of raping boys, "ass-bandits" (sexual predators) had "sissies" (willing boyfriends). And high people meant happy people. Oddly, the inmate population was a lot more peaceful when left alone. However, when the warden got settled in, the rules became strict and the population became violent again. There was a noticeable drop in morale when the drugs got scarce and the sissies became scared to walk around selling themselves. Prison started to feel more and more like prison as the tensions rose.

We were treated like animals in a cage, so we started behaving like it—not because we wanted to out of resentment but because we were forced to for survival. The animalistic environment eventually gave me what felt like a sixth sense. I couldn't see dead people, but I could sense when something was awry. There was something about doing time in the same enclosed environment, with the same events and people, that made men stop thinking rationally and start behaving instinctively. Like birds in the jungle when a lion approaches, I could stop chirping mid-sentence when I sensed trouble brewing in the distance.

Prison was a world that ran on hate and ego, where the big fish ate the little. The strong were respected; the weak were rejected. Homophobia and racism had a stake in the actions of every man, regardless of his prejudice or lack thereof. Selfishness was the warrior ethos, and anyone who wasn't looking out for number one was being dominated by someone more powerfully egocentric and malicious. Towards the latter part of my sentence, I started to look less like a Presbyterian schoolboy, less like a highly decorated cadet, and less like the youngest in an ideal American family. I started to look less like a good person, and more like a son of a bitch.

I remember the moment I realized how much I'd changed. I was asleep when a sissy on the bunk next to me erupted in screams. Just like on my first night in prison, someone was attacking the guy with a razor blade. I knew why he was being attacked because, for no particular reason, I knew everyone's business. At first, I was pissed because the fiasco was keeping me awake. Then I almost started to laugh at the sound of his girlish pleas—almost.

After a year and a half of incarceration, my family had become increasingly concerned about me. They had long since quit worrying over my safety, but now they were concerned for the person I was becoming. I no longer pretended to behave like a prisoner; my mannerisms and countenance were now naturally like that of a convict. I no longer had to consciously decipher the prison terminology when it was spoken to me because it was no longer my second language; it was my first. When my family came to visit, they would tease me about using "dog" as a transition word in conversation. Sometimes they couldn't understand what I was telling them because my terminology seemed nonsensical. But they understood me when, after eighteen months of prison, I told them I had been granted parole.

My mother hugged me and cried for several minutes after I'd told her. When she finally caught her breath, she kissed me on the forehead and said, "It's about damn time, *Sir*. You're starting to sound like an idiot."

APPENDIX F

THE JOURNEY TO MOTHERHOOD

Adrian Fitchpatrick

Daughter. Sister. Granddaughter. Friend. These are titles that defined me. Then in 2004, those titles expanded to include "Wife." For the first time, I was separating from my original identities and venturing into new and uncharted territory. I was now responsible to another person and we shared our life together. We share a home, finances, goals, and a vision for our future. That vision included one day expanding our new found definition of a family to include children. In 2006, the first phase of this adventure took shape with the rounding of my mid-section. I discovered I was pregnant in October of 2006 and my projected due date was June 9, 2007. With all the glamour that typically surrounds pregnancy, the only negatives aspects that are prominently spoken of are the aches and pains associated with the third trimester. No one really talks about or prepares you for complications. Unfortunately, my pregnancy was anything but a "normal" pregnancy and there was absolutely no glamour. My pregnancy began with complications that caused the phrase "risk of miscarriage" to be spoken frequently by my doctors. For the first trimester, fear was the consuming emotion of my days. When the second trimester came, I thought the worst was finally over. However, I could not have been more wrong.

In pregnancy, the "premature rupture of membranes is the rupture of the fetal membranes before the onset of labor" (Medina 659). This rupture has been found to "complicate approximately 3 percent of pregnancies and lead to one third of preterm births (Medina 659). Nearly 50 to 75 percent of preterm ruptures result in delivery within one week of the rupture (Medina 661).

On March 11, 2007, I was at the Hoover Winter Odyssey, an indoor percussion and color guard event hosted at Hoover High School. While preparing my students to perform in the competition, an unexpected turn of events caused me to pause in the midst of the chaos and stress. Something was wrong but the specifics were unclear. A call to my doctor informed me to simply "keep an eye on this situation" and call back if anything changed. Although I took my students through the

DOI: 10.7330/9780874219821.c011

competition process, I knew something was very wrong. So, at eleven o'clock that evening, my husband took me to the hospital. In my mind, we were just going to have myself and the baby checked out to ensure there were no serious complications. So, we arrived at the hospital with nothing but each other and my purse. After 4 hours of testing and waiting, it was determined that I had experienced a preterm rupture and I would have to remain at the hospital until I delivered the baby. This period of waiting was undefined. It could be hours, days, or weeks, and the only thing for us to do was wait.

Premature births are typically caused by "spontaneous preterm labor, either by itself or following spontaneous premature rupture of the membranes" ("Premature Birth" 2). However, in most cases, the triggers for the labor are unknown. Certain external circumstances can put the mother at a higher risk, including "extremely high levels of stress" or "long working hours with long periods of standing" ("Premature Birth" 2).

I was twenty-six weeks into my pregnancy. I had only been wearing maternity clothes for 5 weeks. I was just beginning to wrap my mind around the idea of our whole life changing and what it would mean to be a parent. How could this be happening? When I think back on that week of my life, it is as if a dark cloud has settled over the memories. There were so many questions, so many frustrations, and so much was unknown. Was this my fault? Had I done something wrong? The self-deprecating feelings were overwhelming, and, despite my doctor's continued assurance that this was not a product of my own doing, the doubt still festered.

Approximately 6 percent of premature births in the United States occur prior to 28 weeks gestation and these babies will experience the greatest difficulty in their fight for survival ("Premature Birth" 2). While the survival rate for babies born after 26 weeks is 80 percent, more than 25 percent will experience long-term disabilities ("Premature Birth" 5).

The frustrations continued to mount with every question from the nurses. How was I supposed to know if I was having a contraction, when I never had a baby before? And with each visit from a doctor or neonatologist, my anxiety became almost more than I could bear. The baby would weigh between one and half pounds and two pounds if it came that week. My brain could not fathom a baby that size. And not just the size, the idea that this little being would be entering this world fighting to stay alive, and, according to my doctors, the odds were not in its favor.

In cases of preterm rupture, "expectant management of pregnancies should be undertaken in hospital because it is not possible to accurately predict which pregnancies will develop complications" (Caughey 16). Bed rest is employed to allow for "reaccumulation of amniotic fluid" and further development of the fetus (Caughey 16).

Fortunately, the odds were in our favor as a family. I was able to sustain the rupture for seven weeks without going into the labor. For seven weeks, I laid in a hospital bed at St. Vincent's Hospital. I left that bed only 6 times, but each attempt resulted in a quick reminder that the health of this baby was more important than a shower. There were many moments when the worst was expected and I became quite familiar with the term "emergency c-section." But through it all, the gentle purr of the fetal heart monitor reminded me that this baby was worth it all.

Each year, one in every eight babies born in the United States is premature ("Prematurity" 1).

My labor was finally induced on April 23, 2007 and my son was born. Although I only saw him for a moment upon delivery, he was my son. The moment he entered the world, the mental shift was immediate. This helpless little baby boy was my son. No longer was it the baby in my stomach that I was fighting to keep alive. He was my son. The reality was so quick and so strong.

Premature babies born at 34 to 36 weeks gestation will "weigh between 4 ½ and 6 pounds" and they are at an increased risk for "breathing and feeding problems, difficulties regulating body temperature, and jaundice" ("Premature Birth" 5).

The five weeks that followed my son's birth were filled with more testing, monitoring, and waiting. He weighed just over five pounds at birth and his little body was not ready for the world around him. His lungs were not fully developed, he couldn't digest properly, and his case of jaundice was significant. But the same fighter mentality he showed in the womb carried over into his fight for life after delivery.

To say that this ordeal of bringing my son into this world was life-changing would be an understatement of monumental proportions. Being a mother is an instantaneous altering of everything you have ever known. You are not just something to another person, like a wife or a daughter. You are now everything to something so small and helpless; yet something so great and full of life. The responsibility was unlike anything I had ever faced before and it was frightening and exciting all at the same time. But when I was lying in that hospital bed, these were not the same feelings that were running through my head. Instead, there were questions, fears, insecurities, and doubts.

Brayden laughed for the first time in July of 2007 and I felt sensations of joy that were so strong I thought my heart would burst.

I was numb for seven weeks. Numb to the idea that I could lose something that I never really knew but something that meant so much. Numb to the idea that this child would come into this world and could be gone in an instant. Numb to the idea that the moment I met my son I would actually know what to do, how to love, and how to be the mother he needed. But the feelings just flooded in the moment I held him for the first time. This moment would define me forever.

Brayden sat up unassisted for the first time in November of 2007.

On the surface, being in the hospital for seven weeks seems to be a horrific experience. To be confined to a bed with no opportunity to see anything other than the interstate outside your window or to breathe in fresh air seems unfathomable to most. However, it was a time that made me the mother and woman that I am today. I had seven weeks to pray, reflect, and prepare for the next chapter in my life. Seven weeks provided me with time to slow down and revel in the pregnancy while becoming more intimately connected to the child I was carrying. My life was such a crazy and hectic juggling act of family, friends, work, and teaching that I never really allowed myself time to stop and think about what being a mother would really mean. I feel that God took it upon himself to slow me down in a slightly unconventional way.

Brayden said "Mama" for the first time on a rainy day when were playing on the floor in our living room. There seemed to be nothing special about that day until he said that word. Now, I will never forget it

Change is inevitable and almost always makes you better than you were before it happened. With great confidence, I look back on the experience of bringing my son into this world with thanksgiving for how it changed me. Because of the roller coaster ride of his arrival, I am now a better wife, mother and person. The time of waiting in the hospital did so much to enrich my relationship with my husband. We were always a happy and cohesive couple, but now standing on the other side of such a life-altering situation, we have a deeper love and a stronger connection than we had prior to our son's birth. For all of the sacrifices I had to make to stay in that hospital bed, my husband sacrificed just as much. He lived at the hospital with me and slept every night on the most uncomfortable pull-out bed. He was the captain of my spirits and he kept them soaring through it all. The night prior to the induction of my labor, he had a candlelight dinner brought in for me, complete with my favorite dessert and a beautiful diamond ring that had been engraved with my son's birth date. He wanted me to remember the last night of our family of two and also have a token to signify my transition into motherhood. His commitment to me and to the expansion of our family brought us to a deeper level of understanding and readiness to be the parents God would have us to be.

Brayden's took his first steps in April of 2008. I can remember feeling so proud and so scared all at the same time. This was the beginning of his independence. This was the beginning of him no longer needing me for everything he knew. But it was also his very step towards a life that he fought so hard to live.

Being a mother involves giving over everything that you are for the benefit of your child's development and preparation for life. I struggled with feelings of inadequacy and uncertainty as I prepared to bring my son into the world. How would I know what to do? The answer to this question sat right beside me in my hospital room every day for seven weeks, for 4 weeks in the neonatal intensive care unit, and then another 3 weeks when we finally brought my son home. My mother. She came from Atlanta, leaving my dad and brother to fend for themselves, and she spent every day with me while my husband was at work. She took care of my every need to an extreme that most mother's leave behind after their child's infancy. She held my hand while I brought my son into this world and she stood by me as I watched him fight for his life in a sea of tubes, wires, and machines. I saw in her unconditional love for me the same love that I would bestow on my son. She was a friend to talk to, a shoulder to cry on, and a hand to guide me. In those three short months, she showed me what motherhood truly is.

"I love you mommy." Brayden whispered these words from his car seat in the back of my car on a normal spring day in 2008 and the tears poured from my eyes.

As I watch my son grow and develop into a little person full of personality and excitement for life, I stand in awe. I am amazed by God's divine plan. Every detail of my son's arrival into this life was specifically designed to make me the mother I am today. Because of my experience, I am a more patient, forgiving, and humble person. I am not as quick to anger. I appreciate the simple things that make up the day-to-day life between a mother and child. As a result of that faithful day in March 2007, my relationship with God, my husband, my family, and most of all, my son will never be the same.

I come home from work each day and Brayden always says "Mommy, you're here!" I look at him and smile as I think to myself, "yes baby, and thanks to God's grace, so are you."

WORKS CITED

Caughey, Aaron B., M.D., Julian N. Robinson, M.D., and Errol R. Norwitz, M.D. "Contemporary Diagnosis and Management of Preterm Premature Rupture of Membranes." *Reviews in Obstetrics & Gynecology* 1.1 (2008): 11–22. Web. 25 Feb. 2010.

Medina, Tanya M., M.D. and D. Ashley Hill, M.D. "Preterm Premature Rupture of Membranes: Diagnosis and Management." *American Family Physician* 73 (2006): 659–666. Web. 25 Feb. 2010.

"Premature Birth." *March of Dimes.* March of Dimes. January 2009. Web. 25 February 2010.

"Prematurity." *Centers for Disease Control and Prevention.* Centers for Disease Control and Prevention. 25 February 2010. Web. 25 February 2010.

REFERENCES

Abbott, Don Paul. 2007. "Kant, Theremin, and the Morality of Rhetoric." *Philosophy & Rhetoric* 40 (3): 274–92. http://dx.doi.org/10.1353/par.2007.0025.

Agnew, Lois. 1998. "Rhetorical Style and the Formation of Character: Ciceronian Ethos in Thomas Wilson's *Arte of Rhetorique.*" *Rhetoric Review* 17 (1): 93–106. http://dx.doi.org /10.1080/07350199809359233.

Aho, Tuomo, and Mikko Yrjönsuuri. 2009. "Late Medieval Logic." In *The Development of Modern Logic*, edited by Leila Haaparanta, 11–77. Oxford: Oxford University Press. http://dx.doi.org/10.1093/acprof:oso/9780195137316.003.0012.

Allen, Michael. 1986. "From Dialogue to Rhetoric: Berthoff's Double Entry Notebook with a Lanham Twist." *Writing Instructor* 5 (3): 122–31.

Anderson, Benedict. 1991. *Imagined Communities: Reflections on the Origin and Spread of Nationalism.* London: Verso.

Anderson, Floyd D., and Lawrence J. Prelli. 2001. "Pentadic Cartography: Mapping the Universe of Discourse." *Quarterly Journal of Speech* 87 (1): 73–95. http://dx.doi.org/10 .1080/00335630109384319.

Aristotle. 1984. "Topics." In *The Complete Works of Aristotle.* Vol. 1. Edited by Jonathan Barnes. Translated by W. A. Pickard-Cambridge, 167–277. Princeton, NJ: Princeton University Press.

Aristotle. 1991. *On Rhetoric: A Theory of Civic Discourse.* Translated by George A. Kennedy. New York: Oxford University Press.

Arnauld, Antoine, and Pierre Nicole. 1996. *Logic or the Art of Thinking.* Edited and translated by Jill Vance Buroker. Cambridge, UK: Cambridge University Press. http://dx.doi .org/10.1017/CBO9781139166768.

Arola, Kristin L. 2010. "The Design of Web 2.0: The Rise of the Template, the Fall of Design." *Computers and Composition* 27 (1): 4–14. http://dx.doi.org/10.1016/j.compcom .2009.11.004.

Augustine. 1948. "Divine Providence and the Problem of Evil." In *Writings of Saint Augustine.* Vol. 1. Edited by Ludwig Schopp. Translated by Robert P. Russell, 239–332. New York: Cima.

Augustine. 1985. *On Christian Doctrine.* Translated by D. W. Robertson Jr. Indianapolis, IN: Bobbs-Merrill.

Augustine. 2008. *The Confessions.* Translated by Edward Bouverie Pusey. Rockville, MD: Manor.

Aune, James Arnt. 1990. "Rhetoric after Deconstruction." In *Rhetoric and Philosophy*, edited by Richard A. Cherwitz, 253–72. Hillsdale, NJ: Erlbaum.

Aune, James Arnt. 1994. *Rhetoric and Marxism.* Boulder, CO: Westview.

Bacon, Francis. 2000. *The Advancement of Learning.* Edited by Michael Kiernan. Oxford: Clarendon.

Bacon, Francis. 2004. *The Instauratio Magna Part II: Novum Organum and Associated Texts.* Edited and translated by Graham Rees and Maria Wakely. Oxford: Clarendon.

Baehr, Craig, and Susan M. Lang. 2012. "Hypertext Theory: Rethinking and Reformulating What We Know, Web 2.0." *Journal of Technical Writing and Communication* 42 (1): 39–56. http://dx.doi.org/10.2190/TW.42.1.d.

DOI: 10.7330/9780874219821.c012

Bakhtin, M. M. 1981. *The Dialogic Imagination*. Translated by Caryl Emerson and Michael Holquist. Austin: University of Texas Press.

Ballentine, Brian D. 2009. "Hacker Ethics and Firefox Extensions: Writing and Teaching the 'Grey' Areas of Web 2.0." *Computers and Composition Online* 26 (3).

Barnett, Timothy, ed. 2001. *Teaching Argument in the Composition Course: Background Readings*. Boston: Bedford/St. Martins.

Barton, Ben F., and Marthalee S. Barton. 1993. "Ideology and the Map: Toward a Postmodern Design Practice." In *Professional Communication: The Social Perspective*, edited by Nancy Roundy Blyler and Charlotte Thralls, 49–78. Newbury Park, CA: Sage.

Baudrillard, Jean. 1995. *Simulacra and Simulations*. Translated by Sheila Faria Glaser. Ann Arbor: University of Michigan Press.

Bayer, Thora Ilin. 2009. "Hegelian Rhetoric." *Philosophy & Rhetoric* 42 (3): 203–19. http://dx.doi.org/10.1353/par.0.0036.

Bennett, Beth S. 1991. "The Rhetoric of Martianus Capella and Anselm de Besate in the Tradition of Minippean Satire." *Philosophy & Rhetoric* 24 (2): 128–42.

Berlin, James A. 1982. "Contemporary Composition: The Major Pedagogical Theories." *College English* 44 (8): 765–77. http://dx.doi.org/10.2307/377329.

Berlin, James A. 1987a. "Revisionary History: The Dialectical Method." *Pre/Text* 8 (1–2): 47–61.

Berlin, James A. 1987b. *Rhetoric and Reality: Writing Instruction in American Colleges, 1900–1985*. Carbondale: Southern Illinois University Press.

Berlin, James A. 1988. "Rhetoric and Ideology in the Writing Class." *College English* 50 (5): 477–94. http://dx.doi.org/10.2307/377477.

Berlin, James A. 1991. "Composition and Cultural Studies." In *Composition and Resistance*, edited by C. Mark Hurlbert and Michael Blitz, 47–55. Portsmouth, NH: Boynton/Cook.

Berlin, James A. 1996. *Rhetorics, Poetics, and Cultures*. Urbana, IL: National Council of Teachers of English.

Berthoff, Ann E. 1981. *The Making of Meaning: Metaphors, Models, and Maxims for Writing Teachers*. Montclair, NJ: Boynton/Cook.

Berthoff, Ann E. 1982. *Forming/Thinking/Writing: The Composing Imagination*. Montclair, NJ: Boynton/Cook.

Best, Steven, and Douglas Kellner. 1991. *Postmodern Theory: Critical Interrogations*. New York: Guilford.

Bialostosky, Don H. 1991. "Liberal Education, Writing, and the Dialogic Self." In *Contending with Words: Composition and Rhetoric in a Postmodern Age*, edited by Patricia Harkin and John Schilb, 11–22. New York: Modern Language Association.

Bitzer, Lloyd, and Edwin Black, eds. 1971. *The Prospects of Rhetoric*. Englewood Cliffs, NJ: Prentice-Hall.

Bizzaro, Patrick. 1999. "What I Learned in Grad School, or Literary Training and the Theorizing of Composition." *College Composition and Communication* 50 (4): 722–42. http://dx.doi.org/10.2307/358489.

Bizzell, Patricia. 1991. "Marxist Ideas in Composition Studies." In *Contending with Words: Composition and Rhetoric in a Postmodern Age*, edited by Patricia Harkin and John Schilb, 52–68. New York: Modern Language Association.

Blair, Hugh. 1970. *Lectures on Rhetoric and Belles Lettres*. 3 vols. New York: Garland.

Bleich, David. 1988. *The Double Perspective*. Urbana: National Council of Teachers of English.

Boethius. 2009. *De Topiciis Differentiis*. Translated by Eleonore Stump. Cornell: Cornell University Press.

Boley, Tommy J. 1979. "A Heuristic for Persuasion." *College Composition and Communication* 30 (2): 187–91. http://dx.doi.org/10.2307/356328.

Borrowman, Shane. 2008. "The Islamization of *Rhetoric*: Ibn Rushd and the Reintroduction of Aristotle into Medieval Europe." *Rhetoric Review* 27 (4): 341–60. http://dx.doi.org /10.1080/07350190802339242.

Borrowman, Shane, and Marcia Kmetz. 2011. "Divided We Stand: Beyond Burkean Identification." *Rhetoric Review* 30 (3): 275–92. http://dx.doi.org/10.1080/07350198.2011 .581942.

Bosley, Deborah S. 1992. "Gender and Visual Communication: Toward a Feminist Theory of Design." *IEEE Transactions on Professional Communication* 35 (4): 222–29. http://dx.doi .org/10.1109/47.180283.

Brereton, John C. 1995. Introduction to *The Origins of Composition Studies in the American College, 1875–1925: A Documentary History*, edited by John C. Brereton, 3–25. Pittsburgh: University of Pittsburgh Press.

Briggs, John C. 1989. *Francis Bacon and the Rhetoric of Nature*. Cambridge, MA: Harvard University Press. http://dx.doi.org/10.4159/harvard.9780674731400.

Brodkey, Linda. 1996. *Writing Permitted in Designated Places Only*. Minneapolis: University of Minnesota Press.

Brooke, Collin, and Thomas Rickert. 2011. "Being Delicious: Materialities of Research in a Web 2.0 Application." In *Beyond Postprocess*, edited by Sidney I. Dobrin, J. A. Rice, and Michael Vastola, 163–79. Logan: Utah State University Press.

Brown, Richard Harvey. 1989. *A Poetic for Sociology: Toward a Logic of Discovery for the Human Sciences*. Chicago: University of Chicago Press.

Brunschwig, Jacques. 1996. "Aristotle's Rhetoric as a 'Counterpart' to Dialectic." In *Essays on Aristotle's Rhetoric*, edited by Amélie Oksenberg Rorty, 34–55. Berkeley: University of California Press.

Burgess, Parke G. 1985. "The Dialectic of Substance: Rhetoric and Poetry." *Communication Quarterly* 33 (2): 105–12. http://dx.doi.org/10.1080/01463378509369586.

Burke, Kenneth. 1952. *A Grammar of Motives*. New York: Prentice-Hall.

Burke, Kenneth. 1954. *Permanence and Change: An Anatomy of Purpose*. Berkeley: University of California Press.

Burke, Kenneth. 1961. *Attitudes toward History*. Boston: Beacon.

Burke, Kenneth. 1966a. "Definition of Man." In *Language as Symbolic Action: Essays on Life, Literature, and Method*, 3–24. Berkeley: University of California Press.

Burke, Kenneth. 1966b. "What Are the Signs of What? (A Theory of 'Entitlement')." In *Language as Symbolic Action: Essays on Life, Literature, and Method*, 359–79. Berkeley: University of California Press.

Burke, Kenneth. 1969. *A Rhetoric of Motives*. Berkeley: University of California Press.

Burke, Kenneth. 1973. *The Philosophy of Literary Form: Studies in Symbolic Action*. 3rd ed. Berkeley: University of California Press.

Campbell, George. 1963. *The Philosophy of Rhetoric*. Edited by Lloyd F. Bitzer. Carbondale: Southern Illinois University Press.

Capella, Martianus. 1977. *The Marriage of Philology and Mercury*. Translated by William Harris Stahl and Richard Johnson. Vol. 2 of *Martianus Capella and the Seven Liberal Arts*. New York: Columbia University Press.

Capozzi, Mirella, and Gino Roncaglia. 2009. "Logic and Philosophy of Logic from Humanism to Kant." In *The Development of Modern Logic*, edited by Leila Haaparanta, 78–158. Oxford: Oxford University Press. http://dx.doi.org/10.1093/acprof:oso/9780195137 316.003.0014.

Cicero. 1970. *On Oratory and Orators* [De Oratore]. Translated by J. S. Watson. Carbondale: Southern Illinois University Press.

Clark, Gregory. 1990. *Dialogue, Dialectic, and Conversation: A Social Perspective on the Function of Writing*. Carbondale: Southern Illinois University Press.

Clark, Ruth Anne, and Jesse G. Delia. 1979. "*Topoi* and Rhetorical Competence." *Quarterly Journal of Speech* 65 (2): 187–206. http://dx.doi.org/10.1080/00335637909383470.

Connors, Robert J. 1991. "Writing the History of Our Discipline." In *An Introduction to Composition Studies*, edited by Erika Lindemann and Gary Tate, 49–71. New York: Oxford University Press.

Connors, Robert J. 1997. *Composition-Rhetoric: Backgrounds, Theory, and Pedagogy*. Pittsburgh, PA: University of Pittsburgh Press.

Connors, Robert J. 2003a. "Overwork/Underpay: Labor and the Status of Composition Teachers Since 1880." In *Selected Essays of Robert J. Connors*, edited by Lisa Ede and Andrea A. Lunsford, 181–93. Boston: Bedford/St. Martin's.

Connors, Robert J. 2003b. "The Rise and Fall of the Modes of Discourse." In *Selected Essays of Robert J. Connors*, edited by Lisa Ede and Andrea A. Lunsford, 1–12. Boston: Bedford/St. Martin's.

Connors, Robert J., Lisa S. Ede, and Andrea A. Lunsford. 1984. "The Revival of Rhetoric in America." In *Essays on Classical Rhetoric and Modern Discourse*, edited by Robert J. Connors, Lisa S. Ede, and Andrea A. Lunsford, 1–15. Carbondale: Southern Illinois University Press.

Corbett, Edward P. J. 1965. *Classical Rhetoric for the Modern Student*. New York: Oxford University Press.

Corbett, Edward P. J. 1986. "The *Topoi* Revisited." In *Rhetoric and Praxis: The Contribution of Classical Rhetoric to Practical Reasoning*, edited by Jean Dietz Moss, 43–58. Washington, DC: Catholic University of America Press.

Cox, J. Robert. 1990. "Memory, Critical Theory, and the Argument from History." *Argumentation and Advocacy* 27 (1): 1–13.

Crowley, Sharon. 1987. "Derrida, Deconstruction, and Our Scene of Teaching." *Pre/Text* 8 (3–4): 169–83.

Crowley, Sharon. 1979. "Of Gorgias and Grammatology." *College Composition and Communication* 30 (3): 279–84. http://dx.doi.org/10.2307/356396.

Crowley, Sharon. 1985. "writing and Writing." In *Reading and Writing Differently: Deconstruction and the Teaching of Composition and Literature*, edited by C. Douglas Atkins and Michael L. Johnson, 93–100. Lawrence: University Press of Kansas.

Crowley, Sharon. 1989. *A Teacher's Introduction to Deconstruction*. Urbana, IL: National Council of Teachers of English.

Crowley, Sharon. 1990. *The Methodical Memory: Invention in Current-Traditional Rhetoric*. Carbondale: Southern Illinois University Press.

Crusius, Timothy W. 1986. "A Case for Kenneth Burke's Dialectic and Rhetoric." *Philosophy & Rhetoric* 19 (1): 23–37.

Crusius, Timothy W. 1988. "Orality in Kenneth Burke's Dialectic." *Philosophy & Rhetoric* 21 (2): 116–30.

Crusius, Timothy W., and Carolyn E. Channell. 2008. *The Aims of Argument: A Text and Reader*. 6th ed. Boston: McGraw-Hill.

D'Angelo, Frank. 1984. "The Evolution of the Analytical *Topoi*: A Speculative Inquiry." In *Essays on Classical Rhetoric and Modern Discourse*, edited by Robert J. Connors, Lisa S. Ede, and Andrea A. Lunsford, 50–68. Carbondale: Southern Illinois University Press.

Dasenbrock, Reed Way. 1988. "Becoming Aware of the Myth of Presence." *JAC* 8 (1–2): 1–11.

Davis, Diane. 2010. *Inessential Solidarity: Rhetoric and Foreign Relations*. Pittsburgh, PA: University of Pittsburgh Press.

Deleuze, Gilles. 1994. *Difference and Repetition*. Translated by Paul Patton. New York: Columbia University Press.

Deleuze, Gilles, and Felix Guattari. 1987. *A Thousand Plateaus: Capitalism and Schizophrenia*. Translated by Brian Massumi. Minneapolis: University of Minnesota Press.

Derrida, Jacques. 1976. *Of Grammatology*. Translated by Gayatri Spivak. Baltimore, MD: Johns Hopkins University Press.

Derrida, Jacques. 1978. *Writing and Difference*. Translated by Alan Bass. Chicago: University of Chicago Press.

Derrida, Jacques. 1990. *Glas.* Translated by John P. Leavey Jr. and Richard Rand. Lincoln: University of Nebraska Press.

Descartes, René. 1993. *Discourse on Method and Meditations on First Philosophy* 3rd ed. Translated by Donald A. Cress. Indianapolis, IN: Hackett.

DiPardo, Anne. 1990. "Narrative Knowers, Expository Knowledge: Discourse as a Dialectic." *Written Communication* 7 (1): 59–95. http://dx.doi.org/10.1177/0741088390007001003.

Dixon, Kathleen. 1995. "Making and Taking Apart 'Culture' in the (Writing) Classroom." In *Left Margins: Cultural Studies and Composition Pedagogy*, edited by Karen Fitts and Alan W. France, 99–114. Albany: State University of New York Press.

Dostal, Robert J. 1980. "Kant and Rhetoric." *Philosophy & Rhetoric* 13 (3): 223–44.

Dumas, M. Barry. 2013. *Diving into the Bitstream: Information Technology Meets Society in a Digital World.* New York: Routledge.

Eden, Kathy. 1990. "The Rhetorical Tradition of Augustinian Hermeneutics in *De Doctrina Christiana.*" *Rhetorica* 8 (1): 45–63. http://dx.doi.org/10.1525/rh.1990.8.1.45.

Edlund, John R. 1988. "Bakhtin and the Social Reality of Language Acquisition." *Writing Instructor* 7 (2): 56–67.

Elbow, Peter. 1986. *Embracing Contraries: Explorations in Learning and Teaching.* New York: Oxford University Press.

Elbow, Peter. 1993. "The Uses of Binary Thinking." *JAC* 13 (1): 51–78.

Enos, Richard Leo. 1988. *The Literate Mode of Cicero's Legal Rhetoric.* Carbondale: Southern Illinois University Press.

Farmer, Frank. 2001. *Saying and Silence: Listening to Composition with Bakhtin.* Logan: Utah State University Press.

Farmer, Frank. 2005. "On Style and Other Unremarkable Things." *Written Communication* 22 (3): 339–47. http://dx.doi.org/10.1177/0741088305278029.

Feuerbach, Ludwig. 1983a. "Provisional Theses for the Reformation of Philosophy." Translated by Daniel Dahlstrom. In *The Young Hegelians: An Anthology*, edited by Lawrence S. Stepelevich, 156–71. Cambridge, UK: Cambridge University Press.

Feuerbach, Ludwig. 1983b. "Towards a Critique of Hegelian Philosophy." Translated by Zawar Hanfi. In *The Young Hegelians: An Anthology*, edited by Lawrence S. Stepelevich, 95–128. Cambridge, UK: Cambridge University Press.

Fleming, David. 2003. "Becoming Rhetorical: An Education in the Topics." In *The Realms of Rhetoric: The Prospects for Rhetoric Education*, edited by Joseph Petraglia and Deepika Bahri, 93–116. Albany: State University of New York Press.

Fleming, David. 2009. "Rhetoric Revival or Process Revolution? Revisiting the Emergence of Composition-Rhetoric as a Discipline." In *Renewing Rhetoric's Relation to Composition: Essays in Honor of Theresa Jarnagin Enos*, edited by Shane Borrowman, Stuart C. Brown, and Thomas P. Miller, 25–52. New York: Routledge.

Fleming, David. 2011. *From Form to Meaning: Freshman Composition and the Long Sixties, 1957–1974.* Pittsburgh, PA: University of Pittsburgh Press.

Flower, Linda. 1989. "Comment and Response." *College English* 50 (7): 765–69.

Flower, Linda. 1995. *The Construction of Negotiated Meaning: A Social Cognitive Theory of Writing.* Carbondale: Southern Illinois University Press.

Flower, Linda. 2008. *Community Literacy and the Rhetoric of Public Engagement.* Carbondale: Southern Illinois University Press.

Foreman, Joel, and David R. Shumway. 1992. "Cultural Studies: Reading Visual Texts." In *Cultural Studies in the English Classroom*, edited by James A. Berlin and Michael J. Vivion, 244–61. Portsmouth, NH: Boynton/Cook.

Foucault, Michel. 1970. *The Order of Things: An Archaeology of the Human Sciences.* New York: Vintage.

France, Alan W. 1994. *Composition as a Cultural Practice.* Westport, CT: Bergin and Garvey.

Fulkerson, Richard. 1979. "Four Philosophies of Composition." *College Composition and Communication* 30 (4): 343–48. http://dx.doi.org/10.2307/356707.

Geertz, Clifford. 1973. *The Interpretation of Cultures*. New York: Basic Books.

Gerber, John C. 1950. "The Conference on College Composition and Communication." *College Composition and Communication* 1 (1): 12.

Gigliotti, Carol. 1999. "The Ethical Life of the Digital Aesthetic." In *The Digital Dialectic: New Essays on New Media*, edited by Peter Lunenfeld, 46–66. Cambridge: MIT Press.

Goggin, Maureen Daly. 2000. *Authoring a Discipline: Scholarly Journals and the Post-World War II Emergence of Rhetoric and Composition*. Mahwah, NJ: Erlbaum.

Goleman, Judith. 1988. "Reading, Writing, and the Dialectic since Marx." In *Audits of Meaning: A Festschrift in Honor of Ann E. Berthoff*, edited by Louise Z. Smith, 107–21. Portsmouth, NH: Boynton/Cook.

Gorgias. 1972a. *Defense on Behalf of Palamedes*. Translated by George Kennedy. In *The Older Sophists*, edited by Rosamond Kent Sprague, 54–63. Columbia: University of South Carolina Press.

Gorgias. 1972b. *Encomium of Helen*. Translated by George Kennedy. In *The Older Sophists*, edited by Rosamond Kent Sprague, 50–54. Columbia: University of South Carolina Press.

Gradin, Sherrie L. 1995. *Romancing Rhetorics: Social Expressivist Perspectives on the Teaching of Writing*. Portsmouth, NH: Boynton/Cook.

"Grammar in the Freshman Composition Course." 1950. *College Composition and Communication* 1 (2): 19–21.

Grassi, Ernesto. 2001. *Rhetoric as Philosophy: The Humanist Tradition*. Translated by John Michael Krois and Azizeh Azodi. Carbondale: Southern Illinois University Press.

Green, L. D. 1990. "Aristotelian Rhetoric, Dialectic, and the Traditions of *Antistrophos*." *Rhetorica* 8 (1): 5–27. http://dx.doi.org/10.1525/rh.1990.8.1.5.

Grossberg, Lawrence. 1979. "Marxist Dialectics and Rhetorical Criticism." *Quarterly Journal of Speech* 65 (3): 235–49. http://dx.doi.org/10.1080/00335637909383476.

Habermas, Jurgen. 1984. *The Theory of Communicative Action*. 2 vols. Translated by Thomas McCarthy. Boston: Beacon.

Hairston, Maxine. 1992. "Diversity, Ideology, and Teaching Writing." *College Composition and Communication* 43 (2): 179–93. http://dx.doi.org/10.2307/357563.

Hall, Stuart. 1980. "Cultural Studies and the Centre: Some Problematics and Problems." In *Culture, Media, Language: Working Papers in Cultural Studies, 1972–79*, edited by Stuart Hall, Dorothy Hobson, Andrew Lowe, and Paul Willie, 15–47. London: Hutchinson.

Hall, Stuart. 1996. "On Postmodernism and Articulation: An Interview with Stuart Hall." Edited by Lawrence Grossberg. In *Stuart Hall: Critical Dialogues in Cultural Studies*, edited by David Moreley and Kuan-Hsing Chen, 131–50. London: Routledge.

Hawk, Bryon. 2004. "Toward a Rhetoric of Network (Media) Culture: Notes on Polarities and Potentialities." *JAC* 24 (4): 831–50.

Hawk, Byron. 2007. *A Counter-History of Composition: Toward Methodologies of Complexity*. Pittsburgh, PA: University of Pittsburgh Press.

Hegel, Georg Wilhelm Friedrich. 1975. *Logic*. Translated by William Wallace. Oxford: Clarendon.

Heifferon, Barbara, and Phyllis Mentzell Ryder. 1998. "Deconstruction." In *Theorizing Composition: A Critical Sourcebook of Theory and Scholarship in Contemporary Composition Studies*, edited by Mary Lynch Kennedy, 77–85. Westport, CT: Greenwood.

Heim, Michael. 1999. "The Cyberspace Dialectic." In *The Digital Dialectic: New Essays on New Media*, edited by Peter Lunenfeld, 24–45. Cambridge: MIT Press.

Hepp, Andreas. 2008. "Translocal Media Cultures: Networks of the Media and Globalization." In *Connectivity, Networks, and Flows: Conceptualizing Contemporary Communications*, edited by Andreas Hepp, Friedrich Krotz, Shaun Moores, and Carsten Winter, 33–58. Cresskill, NJ: Hampton.

Hill, Charles A. 2004. "Reading the Visual in College Writing Classes." In *Visual Rhetoric in a Digital World: A Critical Sourcebook*, edited by Carolyn Handa, 107–30. Boston: Bedford/St. Martin's.

Hill, Hamner H., and Michael Kagan. 1995. "Aristotelian Dialectic." *Informal Logic: Reasoning and Argumentation in Theory and Practice* 17 (1): 25–42.

Hill, Lisa L. 2000. "Stephen E. Toulmin." In *Twentieth-Century Rhetorics and Rhetoricians: Critical Studies and Sources*, edited by Michael G. Moran and Michelle Ballif, 331–35. Westport, CT: Greenwood.

Hoggart, Richart. 1957. *The Uses of Literacy.* New York: Oxford University Press.

Hohmann, Hanns. 2002. "Rhetoric and Dialectic: Some Historical and Legal Perspectives." In *Dialectic and Rhetoric: The Warp and Woof of Argumentation Analysis*, edited by Frans H. van Eemeren and Peter Houtlosser, 41–51. Dordrecht, Ger.: Kluwer. http://dx.doi.org/10.1007/978-94-015-9948-1_4.

Holmberg, Carl B. 1977. "Dialectical Rhetoric and Rhetorical Rhetoric." *Philosophy & Rhetoric* 10 (4): 232–43.

Howell, Wilbur Samuel. 1956. *Logic and Rhetoric in England, 1500–1700.* New York: Russell and Russell.

Huguelet, Theodore L. 1979. "A Silver Jubilee Lecture on Freshman Composition." *Teaching English in the Two-Year College* 6 (1): 25–28.

Hutchby, Ian. 2001. *Conversation and Technology: From the Telephone to the Internet.* Malden, MA: Polity.

Hutcheon, Linda. 1988. *A Poetics of Postmodernism: History, Theory, Fiction.* New York: Routledge. http://dx.doi.org/10.4324/9780203358856.

Jakubowski, Franz. 1976. *Ideology and Superstructure in Historical Materialism.* Translated by Anne Booth. London: Allison and Busby.

Janssens, Emile. 1968. "The Concept of Dialectic in the Ancient World." Translated by Henry W. Johnstone Jr. *Philosophy & Rhetoric* 1 (3): 174–81.

Jenkins, Henry, Sam Ford, and Joshua Green. 2013. *Spreadable Media: Creating Value and Meaning in a Networked Culture.* New York: New York University Press.

Johnson, Richard. 1987. "What Is Cultural Studies Anyway?" *Social Text* 16:38–80.

Johnson-Eilola, Johndan. 1998. "Negative Spaces: From Production to Connection in Composition." In *Literacy Theory in the Age of the Internet*, edited by Todd Taylor and Irene Ward, 17–22. New York: Columbia University Press.

Jost, Walter. 1991. "Teaching the Topics: Character, Rhetoric and Liberal Education." *Rhetoric Society Quarterly* 21 (1): 1–16. http://dx.doi.org/10.1080/02773949109390904.

Kameen, Paul J. 1980. "Rewording the Rhetoric of Composition." *Pre/Text* 1 (1): 73–93.

Kant, Immanuel. 1965. *Critique of Pure Reason.* Translated by Norman Kemp Smith. New York: St. Martin's.

Kant, Immanuel. 1987. *Critique of Judgment.* Translated by Werner S. Pluhar. Indianapolis, IN: Hacket.

Karis, Bill. 1989. "Conflict in Collaboration: A Burkean Perspective." *Rhetoric Review* 8 (1): 113–26. http://dx.doi.org/10.1080/07350198909388881.

Kaufer, David, and Gary Waller. 1985. "To Write Is to Read Is to Write, Right?" In *Reading and Writing Differently: Deconstruction and the Teaching of Composition and Literature*, edited by G. Douglas Atkins and Michael J. Johnson, 66–92. Lawrence: University Press of Kansas.

Kauffeld, Fred J. 2002. "Pivotal Issues and Norms in Rhetorical Theories of Argumentation." In *Dialectic and Rhetoric: The Warp and Woof of Argumentation Analysis*, edited by Frans H. van Eemeren and Peter Houtlosser, 97–118. Dordrecht, Ger.: Kluwer. http://dx.doi.org/10.1007/978-94-015-9948-1_8.

Keene, Michael L. 1979. "Teaching Toulmin Logic." *Teaching English in the Two-Year College* 5 (3): 193–97.

Keith, Philip M. 1977. "Burke for the Composition Class." *College Composition and Communication* 28 (4): 348–51. http://dx.doi.org/10.2307/356729.

Keith, Philip M. 1979. "Burkian Invention, from Pentad to Dialectic." *Rhetoric Society Quarterly* 9 (3): 137–41. http://dx.doi.org/10.1080/02773947909390536.

Kember, Sarah, and Joanna Zylinska. 2012. *Life after New Media: Mediation as a Vital Process.* Cambridge: MIT Press.

Kennedy, George A. 1980. *Classical Rhetoric and Its Christian and Secular Tradition from Ancient to Modern Times.* Chapel Hill: University of North Carolina Press.

Kent, Thomas. 1996. "Deconstruction." In *Encyclopedia of Rhetoric and Composition: Communication from Ancient Times to the Information Age,* edited by Theresa Enos, 164–98. New York: Garland.

Kerschbaum, Stephanie L. 2012. "Avoiding the Difference Fixation: Identity Categories, Markers of Difference, and the Teaching of Writing." *College Composition and Communication* 63 (4): 616–44.

Kinneavy, James L. 1971. *A Theory of Discourse.* Englewood Cliffs, NJ: Prentice-Hall.

Kinney, James. 1978. "Tagmemic Rhetoric: A Reconsideration." *College Composition and Communication* 29 (2): 141–45. http://dx.doi.org/10.2307/357298.

Kitzhaber, Albert R. 1955. "The University of Kansas Course in the College Teaching of English." *College Composition and Communication* 6 (4): 194–99. http://dx.doi.org/10.2307 /355533.

Kitzhaber, Albert R. 1990. *Rhetoric in American Colleges, 1850–1900.* Dallas, TX: Southern Methodist University Press.

Klancher, Jon. 1989. "Bakhtin's Rhetoric." In *Reclaiming Pedagogy: The Rhetoric of the Classroom,* edited by Patricia Donahue and Ellen Quandahl, 83–96. Carbondale: Southern Illinois University Press.

Kneale, William, and Martha Kneale. 1962. *The Development of Logic.* Oxford: Clarendon.

Kneupper, Charles. 1978. "Teaching Argument: An Introduction to the Toulmin Model." *College Composition and Communication* 29 (3): 237–41. http://dx.doi.org/10.2307/356935.

Kneupper, Charles. 1979. "Dramatistic Invention: The Pentad as Heuristic Procedure." *Rhetoric Society Quarterly* 9 (3): 130–36. http://dx.doi.org/10.1080/02773947909390535.

Kneupper, Charles. 1980. "Revising the Tagmemic Heuristic: Theoretical and Pedagogical Considerations." *College Composition and Communication* 31 (2): 160–68. http://dx.doi.org /10.2307/356370.

Knoblauch, A. Abby. 2011. "A Textbook Argument: Definitions of Argument in Leading Composition Textbooks." *College Composition and Communication* 63 (2): 244–68.

Knoper, Randall. 1989. "Deconstruction, Process, Writing." In *Reclaiming Pedagogy: The Rhetoric of the Classroom,* edited by Patricia Donahue and Ellen Quandahl, 128–43. Carbondale: Southern Illinois University Press.

Kostelnick, Charles. 1990. "The Rhetoric of Text Design in Professional Communication." *Technical Writing Teacher* 17 (3): 189–202.

Kress, Gunther. 1995. *Writing the Future: English and the Making of a Culture of Innovation.* Urbana, IL: National Council of Teachers of English.

Krotz, Friedrich. 2008. "Media Connectivity: Concepts, Conditions, and Consequences." In *Connectivity, Networks, and Flows: Conceptualizing Contemporary Communications,* edited by Andreas Hepp, Friedrich Krotz, Shaun Moores, and Carsten Winter, 13–23. Cresskill, NJ: Hampton.

Landow, George P. 1999. "Hypertext as Collage-Writing." In *The Digital Dialectic: New Essays on New Media,* edited by Peter Lunenfeld, 150–70. Cambridge: MIT Press.

Larson, Richard. 1968. "Discovery through Questioning: A Plan for Teaching Rhetorical Invention." *College English* 30 (2): 126–34. http://dx.doi.org/10.2307/374448.

Lauer, Janice M. 2004. *Invention in Rhetoric and Composition.* West Lafayette, IN: Parlor.

Leff, Michael. 2002. "The Relation between Dialectic and Rhetoric in a Classical and Modern Perspective." In *Dialectic and Rhetoric: The Warp and Woof of Argumentation Analysis,* edited by Frans H. van Eemeren and Peter Houtlosser, 53–63. Dordrecht, Ger.: Kluwer. http://dx.doi.org/10.1007/978-94-015-9948-1_5.

Leff, Michael. 2006. "Up from Theory: Or I Fought the *Topoi* and the *Topoi* Won." *Rhetoric Society Quarterly* 36 (2): 203–11. http://dx.doi.org/10.1080/02773940600605560.

Leitch, Vincent B. 1983. *Deconstructive Criticism: An Advanced Introduction.* New York: Columbia University Press.

Locke, John. 1975. *An Essay Concerning Human Understanding.* Edited by Peter H. Nidditch. Oxford: Clarendon.

Low, Andrew. 1997. "The Return of Dialectic to Its Place in Intellectual Life." *Rhetoric Review* 15 (2): 365–81. http://dx.doi.org/10.1080/07350199709359224.

Lunenfeld, Peter. 1999. "Unfinished Business." In *The Digital Dialectic: New Essays on New Media,* edited by Peter Lunenfeld, 46–66. Cambridge: MIT Press.

Lunsford, Karen J. 2002. "Contextualizing Toulmin's Model in the Writing Classroom: A Case Study." *Written Communication* 19 (1): 109–74. http://dx.doi.org/10.1177/0741088 30201900105.

Lyotard, Jean-Francois. 1989. *The Postmodern Condition: A Report on Knowledge.* Translated by Geoff Bennington and Brian Massumi. Minneapolis: University of Minnesota Press.

Mack, Peter. 1993. *Renaissance Argument: Valla and Agricola in the Traditions of Rhetoric and Dialectic.* Leiden, Neth.: Brill. http://dx.doi.org/10.1163/9789004246959.

Mahon, M. Wade. 2001. "The Rhetorical Value of Reading Aloud in Thomas Sheridan's Theory of Elocution." *Rhetoric Society Quarterly* 31 (4): 67–88. http://dx.doi.org/10.1080 /02773940109391215.

Marcus, George E., and Michael M. J. Fischer. 1986. *Anthropology as Cultural Critique: An Experimental Moment in the Human Sciences.* Chicago: University of Chicago Press.

Marcuse, Herbert. 1964. *One-Dimensional Man: Studies in the Ideology of Advanced Industrial Society.* Boston: Beacon.

Marx, Karl. 1976. "Theses on Feuerbach." Translated by Clemens Dutt, W. Lough and C. P. Magill. In *Karl Marx, Frederick Engels: Collected Works.* Vol. 5. New York: International.

Marx, Karl. (1837) 1979. "To (Father) Heinrich Marx." In *The Letters of Karl Marx,* edited and translated by Saul K. Padover, 4–12. Englewood Cliffs, NJ: Prentice-Hall.

Marx, Karl, and Frederick Engels. (1846) 1976. *The German Ideology.* Translated by Clemens Dutt, W. Lough, and C. P. Magill, 19–540. In *Karl Marx, Frederick Engels: Collected Works.* Vol. 5. New York: International.

McAdon, Brad. 2001. "Rhetoric Is a Counterpart of Dialectic." *Philosophy & Rhetoric* 34 (2): 113–50. http://dx.doi.org/10.1353/par.2001.0007.

McComiskey, Bruce. 2002a. "Ideology and Critique in Composition Studies." *JAC* 22 (1): 167–75.

McComiskey, Bruce. 2002b. "Review of *Literacy Matters: Writing and Reading the Social Self,* by Robert P. Yagelski. New York: Teachers College, 2000." *College Composition and Communication* 53 (4): 751–54. http://dx.doi.org/10.2307/1512125.

McComiskey, Bruce. 2005. Introduction to *English Studies: An Introduction to the Discipline(s),* edited by Bruce McComiskey, 1–65. Urbana, IL: National Council of Teachers of English.

McKerrow, Raymie E. 1987. "Richard Whately and the Revival of Logic in Nineteenth Century England." *Rhetorica* 5 (2): 163–85. http://dx.doi.org/10.1525/rh.1987.5.2.163.

McKerrow, Raymie E. 1989. "Critical Rhetoric: Theory and Practice." *Communication Monographs* 56 (2): 91–111. http://dx.doi.org/10.1080/03637758909390253.

McLuhan, Marshall, and Bruce R. Powers. 1989. *The Global Village: Transformations in World Life and Media in the 21st Century.* New York: Oxford University Press.

Medine, Peter E. 1994. Introduction to *The Art of Rhetoric, by Thomas Wilson,* edited by Peter E. Medine, 1–31. University Park: Pennsylvania State University Press.

Meikle, Graham, and Sherman Young. 2012. *Media Convergence: Networked Digital Media in Everyday Life.* New York: Palgrave.

Miller, Carolyn R. 2000. "The Aristotelian *Topos*: Hunting for Novelty." In *Rereading Aristotle's Rhetoric,* edited by Alan G. Gross and Arthur E. Walzerm, 130–48. Carbondale: Southern Illinois University Press.

Moffett, James. 1985. "Liberating Inner Speech." *College Composition and Communication* 36 (3): 304–8. http://dx.doi.org/10.2307/357973.

Muckelbauer, John. 2009. *The Future of Invention: Rhetoric, Postmodernism, and the Problem of Change*. Albany: State University of New York Press.

Murphy, James J. 1974. *Rhetoric in the Middle Ages: A History of Rhetorical Theory from Saint Augustine to the Renaissance*. Berkeley: University of California Press.

Neel, Jasper. 1984. "Readers, Writers, and Texts: Writing in the Abyss." *JAC* 5 (1–2): 78–106.

Neel, Jasper. 1988. *Plato, Derrida, and Writing*. Carbondale: Southern Illinois University Press.

Nelms, Gerald, and Maureen Daly Goggin. 1993. "The Revival of Classical Rhetoric for Modern Composition Studies: A Survey." *Rhetoric Society Quarterly* 23 (3–4): 11–26.

Norris, Christopher. 1982. *Deconstruction: Theory and Practice*. London: Methuen.

O'Banion, John D. 1992. *Reorienting Rhetoric: The Dialectic of List and Story*. University Park: Pennsylvania State University Press.

Ogden, C. K. 1932. *Basic English: A General Introduction with Rules and Grammar*. London: Paul, Trench, and Trubner.

Oliver, Kenneth. 1950. "The One-Legged, Wingless Bird of Freshman English." *College Composition and Communication* 1 (3): 3–6. http://dx.doi.org/10.2307/354683.

Ong, Walter J. 1974. *Ramus, Method, and the Decay of Dialogue: From the Art of Discourse to the Art of Reason*. New York: Octagon.

Organization for Economic Co-operation and Development. 2009. *Computer Viruses and Other Malicious Software: A Threat to the Internet Economy*. Paris, Fr.: OECD.

Palmer, Terri. 1998. "The Dictates of Reason: Bacon, Ramus, and the Naturalization of Invention." In *Argumentation and Rhetoric: Proceedings of the Second Conference of the Ontario Society for the Study of Argumentation, May 15–17, 1997*, edited by Hans V. Hansen, Christopher W. Tindale, and Athena V. Colman. St. Catherines, ON: OSSA.

Perelman, Chaïm, and Lucie Olbrechts-Tyteca. 1969. *The New Rhetoric: A Treatise on Argumentation*. Translated by John Wilkinson and Purcell Weaver. Notre Dame, IN: University of Notre Dame Press.

Perl, Sondra. 1975. "The New Students: A Dialectic between Language and Learning." *ADE Bulletin* 46 (September): 48–51. http://dx.doi.org/10.1632/ade.46.48.

Peters, F. E. 1968. *Aristotle and the Arabs: The Aristotelian Tradition in Islam*. New York: New York University Press.

Plato. 1961a. "Gorgias." In *The Collected Dialogues of Plato*, edited by Edith Hamilton and Huntington Cairns. Translated by W. D. Woodhead, 229–307. Princeton, NJ: Princeton University Press.

Plato. 1961b. "Phaedrus." In *The Collected Dialogues of Plato*, edited by Edith Hamilton and Huntington Cairns. Translated by R. Hackforth, 475–525. Princeton, NJ: Princeton University Press.

Plato. 1961c. "Republic." In *The Collected Dialogues of Plato*, edited by Edith Hamilton and Huntington Cairns. Translated by Paul Shorey, 575–844. Princeton, NJ: Princeton University Press.

Plutarch. 1932. *The Lives of the Noble Grecians and Romans*. Translated by John Dryden and Rev. Arthur Hugh Clough. New York: Modern Library.

Porter, James E. 2010. "Rhetoric in (as) a Digital Economy." In *Rhetorics and Technologies: New Directions in Writing and Communication*, edited by Stuart A. Selberm, 1–11. Columbia: University of South Carolina Press.

Powell, Beth, Kara Poe Alexander, and Sonya Barton. 2011. "Interaction of Author, Audience, and Purpose in Multimodal Texts: Students' Discovery of their Role as Composer." *Kairos: A Journal of Rhetoric, Technology, and Pedagogy* 15 (2)

Pratt, Mary Louise. 1991. "Arts of the Contact Zone." In *Profession 91*, edited by Phyllis Franklin, 33–40. New York: Modern Language Association.

Purdy, James P. 2010. "The Changing Space of Research: Web 2.0 and the Integration of Research and Writing Environments." *Computers and Composition* 27 (1): 48–58. http://dx.doi.org/10.1016/j.compcom.2009.12.001.

Quintilian. 1980. *Institutio Oratoria* [The Institutes of Oratory]. 4 vols. Translated by H. E. Butler. Cambridge, MA: Harvard University Press.

Raign, K. A. 1994. "Teaching Stones to Talk: Using Stasis Theory to Teach Students the Art of Dialectic." *Rhetoric Society Quarterly* 24 (3–4): 88–95. http://dx.doi.org/10.1080/027 73949409391020.

Ramage, John, Michael Callaway, Jennifer Clary-Lemon, and Zachary Waggoner. 2009. *Argument in Composition*. West Lafayette, IN: Parlor.

Ramus, Peter. 2010. *Arguments in Rhetoric against Quintilian: Translation and Text of Peter Ramus's* Rhetoricae Distinctiones in Quintilianum. Edited by James J. Murphy. Translated by Carole Newlands. Carbondale: Southern Illinois University Press.

Rawson, Elizabeth. 1975. *Cicero: A Portrait*. London: Bristol.

Reyman, Jessica. 2013. "User Data on the Social Web: Authorship, Agency, and Appropriation." *College English* 75 (5): 513–33.

Reynolds, Jean. 1999. "Deconstruction in the Composition Classroom." *Teaching English in the Two-Year College* 26 (3): 254–61.

Rice, Jeff. 2007. *The Rhetoric of Cool: Composition Studies and New Media*. Carbondale: Southern Illinois University Press.

Rice, Jeff. 2012. *Digital Detroit: Rhetoric and Space in the Age of the Network*. Carbondale: Southern Illinois University Press.

Richards, I. A. 1942. *The Republic of Plato: A New Version Founded on Basic English*. New York: Norton.

Richards, I. A. 1943. *Basic English and Its Uses*. London: Paul, Trench, and Tubner.

Rickert, Thomas, and David Blakesley. 2004. "An Interview with Mark C. Taylor." *JAC* 24 (4): 805–19.

Rogers, Everett M. 1994. *A History of Communication Study: A Biographical Approach*. New York: Free Press.

Rollins, Brooke. 2006. "Inheriting Deconstruction: Rhetoric and Composition's Missed Encounter with Jacques Derrida." *College English* 69 (1): 11–29. http://dx.doi.org/10 .2307/25472186.

Ronald, Kate. 1989. "Ann Berthoff's Dialectic: Theory and Applications." *Issues in Writing* 1 (2): 150–64.

Roskelly, Hephzibah. 1988. "The Dialogue of Chaos: An Unthinkable Order." In *Audits of Meaning: A Festschrift in Honor of Ann E. Berthoff*, edited by Louise Z. Smith, 96–106. Portsmouth, NH: Boynton/Cook.

Rubenstein, Richard E. 2003. *Aristotle's Children: How Christians, Muslims, and Jews Rediscovered Ancient Wisdom and Illuminated the Dark Ages*. Orlando, FL: Harcourt.

Rubinelli, Sara. 2006. "The Ancient Argumentative Game: ὅπω and *loci* in Action." *Argumentation* 20 (3): 253–72. http://dx.doi.org/10.1007/s10503-006-9010-2.

Said, Edward. 1983. *The World, the Text, and the Critic*. Cambridge, MA: Harvard University Press.

Sanchez, Raul. 2001. "Composition's Ideology Apparatus: A Critique." *JAC* 21 (4): 741–59.

Sanchez, Raul. 2005. *The Function of Theory in Composition Studies*. Albany: State University of New York Press.

Schilb, John. 1989. "Deconstructing Didion: Poststructuralist Rhetorical Theory in the Composition Class." In *Literary Nonfiction: Theory, Criticism, Pedagogy*, edited by Chris Anderson, 262–86. Carbondale: Southern Illinois University Press.

Schroeder, Christopher. 1997. "Knowledge and Power, Logic and Rhetoric, and Other Reflections in the Toulmin Mirror: A Critical Consideration of Stephen Toulmin's Contributions to Composition." *JAC* 17 (1): 95–107.

Schuster, Charles I. 1985. "Mikhail Bakhtin as Rhetorical Theorist." *College English* 47 (6): 594–607. http://dx.doi.org/10.2307/377158.

Schwartz, Joseph. 1955. "One Method of Training the Composition Teacher." *College Composition and Communication* 6 (4): 200–4. http://dx.doi.org/10.2307/355534.

Selber, Stuart A. 2010. Introduction to *Rhetorics and Technologies: New Directions in Writing and Communication*, edited by Stuart A. Selber, 1–11. Columbia: University of South Carolina Press.

Sheridan, Thomas. (1780). 1984a. *A Complete Dictionary of the English Language*. London: Dodsley, Dilly, and Wilke. *Research Publications: The Eighteenth Century*, microform, reel 2909, no. 3.

Sheridan, Thomas. (1762). 1984b. *Course of Lectures on Elocution*. London: Strahan. *Research Publications: The Eighteenth Century*, microform, reel 2436, no. 3.

Sheridan, Thomas. (1775). 1991. *Lectures on the Art of Reading*. London: Dodsley, Wilke, Dilly, and Davies. *Research Publications: The Eighteenth Century*, microform, reel 4851, no. 8.

Snow, Malinda. 1977. "The Writer-Audience Dialectic in the Comp. Class." *FERN: Freshman English Resource Notes* 3 (1): 6–7.

Sorapure, Madeleine. 2010. "Information Visualization, Web 2.0, and the Teaching of Writing." *Computers and Composition* 27 (1): 59–70. http://dx.doi.org/10.1016/j.compcom.2009.12.003.

Spellmeyer, Kurt. 1993. *Common Ground: Dialogue, Understanding, and the Teaching of Composition*. Englewood Cliffs, NJ: Prentice Hall.

Sprague, Rosamond Kent. 1972. "Dissoi Logoi." In *The Older Sophists*, edited by Rosamond Kent Sprague, 279–93. Columbia: University of South Carolina Press.

Stump, Eleonore. 1983. "Dialectic." In *The Seven Liberal Arts in the Middle Ages*, edited by David L. Wagner, 125–46. Bloomington: Indiana University Press.

Stump, Eleonore. 1989. *Dialectic and Its Place in the Development of Medieval Logic*. Ithaca, NY: Cornell University Press.

Surber, Jere Paul. 1998. *Culture and Critique: An Introduction to the Critical Discourses of Cultural Studies*. Boulder, CO: Westview.

Swift, Christopher. 2010. "Herbert Marcuse on the New Left: Dialectic and Rhetoric." *Rhetoric Society Quarterly* 40 (2): 146–71. http://dx.doi.org/10.1080/02773941003614472.

Taylor, Mark C. 2001. *The Moment of Complexity: Emerging Network Culture*. Chicago: University of Chicago Press.

Taylor, Warner. 1929. *A National Survey of Conditions in Freshman English*. University of Wisconsin Bureau of Education and Research, Bulletin no. 11, May 1929.

Teston, Christa. 2009. "A Grounded Investigation of Genred Guidelines in Cancer Care Deliberations." *Written Communication* 26 (3): 320–48. http://dx.doi.org/10.1177/0741088309336937.

Timmerman, David M. 1993. "Ancient Greek Origins of Argumentation Theory: Plato's Transformation of 'Dialegesthai' to Dialectic." *Argumentation and Advocacy* 29 (1): 116–23.

Toulmin, Stephen Edelston. 1958. *The Uses of Argument*. Cambridge, UK: Cambridge University Press.

Trimbur, John. 1987. "Beyond Cognition: The Voices of Inner Speech." *Rhetoric Review* 5 (2): 211–21. http://dx.doi.org/10.1080/07350198709359146.

Ulmer, Gregory L. 1994. *Heuretics: The Logic of Invention*. Baltimore, MD: Johns Hopkins University Press.

Ulmer, Gregory L. 2005. *Electronic Monuments*. Minneapolis: University of Minnesota Press.

Vancil, David L. 1979. "Historical Barriers to a Modern System of *Topoi*." *Western Journal of Speech Communication* 43 (1): 26–37. http://dx.doi.org/10.1080/10570317909373951.

Vandenberg, Peter. 1996. "Deconstruction." In *Keywords in Composition Studies*, edited by Paul Heilker and Peter Vandenberg, 58–61. Portsmouth, NH: Boynton/Cook Heinemann.

van Dijck, José. 2013. *The Culture of Connectivity: A Critical History of Social Media*. New York: Oxford University Press. http://dx.doi.org/10.1093/acprof:oso/9780199970773.001.0001.

van Eemeren, Frans H., and Peter Houtlosser. 2002. "And Always the Twain Shall Meet." In *Dialectic and Rhetoric: The Warp and Woof of Argumentation Analysis*, edited by Frans H. Van Eemeren and Peter Houtlosser, 3–12. Dordrecht, Ger.: Kluwer. http://dx.doi.org/10.1007/978-94-015-9948-1_1.

van Eemeren, Frans H., and Rob Grootendorst. 2004. *A Systematic Theory of Argumentation: The Pragma-Dialectical Approach*. Cambridge, UK: Cambridge University Press.

Vesterman, William. 2005. *Reading and Writing Short Arguments*. 5th ed. Mountain View, CA: Mayfield.

Vickers, Brian. 1988. *In Defense of Rhetoric*. Oxford: Clarendon.

Vickers, Brian. 1996. "Bacon and Rhetoric." In *The Cambridge Companion to Bacon*, edited by Markku Peltonen, 200–31. Cambridge, UK: Cambridge University Press. http://dx.doi.org/10.1017/CCOL052143498X.009.

Vitanza, Victor J. 1979. "A Tagmemic Heuristic for the Whole Composition." *College Composition and Communication* 30 (3): 270–74. http://dx.doi.org/10.2307/356393.

Vitanza, Victor J. 1997. *Negation, Subjectivity, and the History of Rhetoric*. Albany: State University of New York Press.

Wagner, David L. 1983. "The Seven Liberal Arts and Classical Scholarship." In *The Seven Liberal Arts in the Middle Ages*, edited by David L. Wagner, 1–31. Bloomington: Indiana University Press.

Wallace, Karl R. 1972. "*Topoi* and the Problem of Invention." *Quarterly Journal of Speech* 58 (4): 387–95. http://dx.doi.org/10.1080/00335637209383137.

Walzer, Arthur E. 2000. "Aristotle on Speaking 'Outside the Subject': The Special Topics and Rhetorical Forums." In *Rereading Aristotle's Rhetoric*, edited by Alan G. Gross and Arthur E. Walzer, 38–56. Carbondale: Southern Illinois University Press.

Walzer, Arthur E. 2003. *George Campbell: Rhetoric in the Age of Enlightenment*. Albany: State University of New York Press.

Warnick, Barbara. 2000. "Two Systems of Invention: The Topics in the *Rhetoric* and *The New Rhetoric*." In *Rereading Aristotle's Rhetoric*, edited by Alan G. Gross and Arthur E. Walzer, 107–29. Carbondale: Southern Illinois University Press.

Weaver, Richard. 1953. *The Ethics of Rhetoric*. Chicago: Regnery.

Weiser, M. Elizabeth. 2009. "'As Usual I Fell on the Bias': Kenneth Burke's Situated Dialectic." *Philosophy & Rhetoric* 42 (2): 134–53. http://dx.doi.org/10.1353/par.0.0033.

Welch, Kathleen E. 1993. "Dialectic/Rhetoric/Writing." In *Learning from the Histories of Rhetoric: Essays in Honor of Winnifred Bryan Horner*, edited by Theresa Enos, 133–43. Edwardsville: Southern Illinois University Press.

Whately, Richard. 1963. *Elements of Rhetoric*, edited by Douglas Ehninger. Carbondale: Southern Illinois University Press.

Whately, Richard. 2008. *Elements of Logic*. 8th ed. Amsterdam: International Debate Education Association.

Williams, Raymond. 1961. *The Long Revolution*. New York: Harper and Row.

Williams, Raymond. 1993. "Culture Is Ordinary." In *Studying Culture: An Introductory Reader*, edited by Ann Gray and Jim McGuigan, 5–14. London: Edward Arnold.

Willis, Paul. 1980. "Notes on Method." In *Culture, Media, Language: Working Papers in Cultural Studies, 1972–79*, edited by Stuart Hall, Dorothy Hobson, Andrew Lowe, and Paul Willie, 88–95. London: Hutchinson.

Wilson, Thomas. 1972. *The Rule of Reason Conteinyng the Arte of Logique*, edited by Richard S. Sprague. Northridge, CA: San Fernando Valley State College Press.

Wilson, Thomas. 1994. *The Art of Rhetoric*, edited by Peter E. Medine. University Park: Pennsylvania State University Press.

Winterowd, W. Ross. 1973. "'Topics' and Levels in the Composing Process." *College English* 34 (5): 701–9. http://dx.doi.org/10.2307/375337.

Woods, William F. 1981. "Composition Textbooks and Pedagogical Theory 1960–1980." *College English* 43 (4): 393–409. http://dx.doi.org/10.2307/377128.

Yarbrough, Stephen R. 2004. "Passing Theories through Topical Heuristics: Donald Davidson, Aristotle, and the Conditions of Discursive Competence." *Philosophy & Rhetoric* 37 (1): 72–91. http://dx.doi.org/10.1353/par.2004.0013.

Yelin, Louise. 1978. "Deciphering the Academic Hieroglyph: Marxist Literary Theory and the Practice of Basic Writing." *Journal of Basic Writing* 2 (1): 13–29.

Zappen, James P.. 2009. "Kenneth Burke on Dialectical-Rhetorical Transcendence." *Philosophy & Rhetoric* 42 (3): 279–301. http://dx.doi.org/10.1353/par.0.0039.

Zompetti, J. P. 2006. "The Value of *Topoi*." *Argumentation* 20 (1): 15–28. http://dx.doi.org/10.1007/s10503-005-1458-y.

ABOUT THE AUTHOR

BRUCE McCOMISKEY is professor of English and director of professional writing at the University of Alabama at Birmingham, where he teaches a variety of courses in rhetoric and composition, discourse analysis, and literary theory. His publications include *Teaching Composition as a Social Process* (Utah State UP, 2000), *Gorgias and the New Sophistic Rhetoric* (Southern Illinois UP, 2002), and two edited collections, *City Comp: Identities, Spaces, Practices* (SUNY P, 2003, coedited with Cynthia Ryan) and *English Studies: An Introduction to the Discipline(s)* (NCTE, 2006). Other publications have appeared in *College English, College Composition and Communication, JAC, Rhetoric Review, Rhetorica, Philosophy and Rhetoric, Rhetoric Society Quarterly, Composition Forum, Teaching English in the Two-Year College,* and the *Journal of Interdisciplinary Humanities.* A past recipient of the James L. Kinneavy Award, McComiskey's current research focuses on rhetoric in the Dead Sea Scrolls and microhistories of composition.

INDEX